THE CONFEDERATION AND THE CONSTITUTION

The Critical Issues

Gordon S. Wood

UNIVERSITY
PRESS OF
AMERICA

LANHAM • NEW YORK • LONDON

124404

Copyright © 1979 by

Gordon S. Wood

University Press of America,™ Inc.

4720 Boston Way
Lanham, MD 20706

3 Henrietta Street
London WC2E 8LU England

ISBN: 0-8191-0821-9

Originally published by Little, Brown and Company in 1973

All University Press of America books are produced on acid-free
paper which exceeds the minimum standards set by the National
Historical Publications and Records Commission.

Library of Congress Catalog Card Number: 79-66423

CONTENTS

iii

WHAT WAS THE RELATION OF
THE CONSTITUTION TO DEMOCRACY?

INTRODUCTION

In the nineteenth century, William Gladstone called the American Constitution "the most wonderful work ever struck off at a given time by the brain and purpose of man." It was an exaggerated and very unhistorical statement, but one that epitomized nineteenth-century American thinking about the origins of the Constitution. Even today, as Peter Gay has reminded us, the Constitution still seems to be the climax of the Enlightenment, the fulfillment of the hopes of philosophes everywhere that the eighteenth-century's science of freedom could finally be put into practice. Yet we must remember that the formation of the Constitution was very much a historical event and like all great events a product not as much of reasoned purpose as of complicated historical circumstances and clashing views and interests. The Constitution was in fact born in controversy. Because the Constitution has endured so long, it is difficult to appreciate the problematic character of the experiment the Founding Fathers were attempting. Never in modern times had men, emulating Lycurgus, created such a sprawling republican government covering half a continent. Since the undertaking was unprecedented and precarious, it was inevitable that Americans in 1787-88, as unsure then as we are now of the future, should have disagreed over the formation of the Constitution. That disagreement raised the issues debated ever since by historians.

What was the character of the Confederation period? What were the origins of the movement for the Constitutional Convention? Was the Constitution a proper and proportionate remedy for the difficulties of the Confederation period? What was the nature and source of the division between the Federalists and Antifederalists? And what was the relation of the new federal Constitution to popular government or democracy? Each of these questions which so intrigue present historians can be traced back to the disputes of the 1780's.

It is understandable that the Federalist viewpoint should have dominated our thinking about the origins of the Constitution throughout much of our history. Not only were the Federalists the victors in the controversy, at least to the extent of establishing in 1787-88 a stronger national government pretty much to their liking, but among them were nearly all the noted men of the Revolutionary era — Washington, Franklin, Madison, John Adams — the very men whose writings would be preserved and glorified in subsequent generations. Almost overnight the Constitution lost its contentiousness; in fact, it soon gained such veneration among Americans that critical investigation of its origins became virtually impossible. It had become the inevitable expression of the American people's providential progression toward democracy, an act of salvation by a group of demigods, the Founding Fathers, who had rescued the nation from the confusion and anarchy into which the Revolution was drifting in the 1780's. This Federalist interpretation of the era found classic expression in John Fiske's *The Critical Period of American History* (1888) which fixed in the popular mind the designation with which the 1780's have been subsequently discussed.

Even when Fiske's book was published, however, forces were at work in American political and intellectual life that would fundamentally challenge this Federalist viewpoint. During the last three decades of the nineteenth century the Supreme Court declared unconstitutional a number of state laws attempting economic and social reforms. These decisions, which seemed to be frustrating the will of the people to carry out their wishes, provoked a far reaching debate over judicial review, the nature of the Constitution, and its relation to democracy. By the early twentieth century, the controversy had generated a large polemical literature among publicists and lawyers into which historians were inevitably drawn. While this controversy was provoking a new and more realistic conception of law, historians were beginning their own "revolt against formalism" that was eventually to reshape American historical thinking. Absorbing the diffused ideas of Marx and later of Freud and the new assumptions of behaviorist psychology, historians sought to probe beneath the surface of events, to understand judicial decisions, laws, constitutions, and other political acts not, like Gladstone, as produced by abstract reasoning, but rather as created by the political process and interacting economic and social interests. These polemical and historiographic developments generated more books and documents on the formation of the Constitution than any other time in our history. Beginning with the centennial celebration of the Constitution and extending into the early decades of the twentieth century a remarkable series of works appeared: classic articles on the origins of judicial review by scholars like J. B. Thayer and Edward S. Corwin, culminating in Charles G. Haine's *The American Doctrine of Judicial Supremacy* (1914); studies on the ratification of the Constitution in the several states; O. G. Libby's pathbreaking statistical investigation of voting behavior, *The Geographical Distribution of the Vote of the Thirteen States on the Federal Constitution* (1894); some important articles on constitutionalism and federalism by Andrew C. McLaughlin;

editions of contemporary essays and pamphlets on the Constitution by Paul
L. Ford; the mammoth *Documentary History of the Constitution of the
United States of America 1786–1870*, 5 vols. (1894–1905); and Max Farrand's
Records of the Federal Convention of 1787, 3 vols. (1911), which led to his
important survey, *The Framing of the Constitution of the United States*
(1913), summing up a generation of thought by emphasizing that the Constitution was not a timeless and rational document but "a bundle of compromises" designed to meet very specific needs and defects of the Articles of
Confederation.

These documentary collections and pragmatic and experimental
studies of the origins of the Constitution helped to free writing about the
Constitution from its nineteenth-century formalistic and theoretical bonds
and to lay the basis for a more realistic interpretation of its formation. Yet
the same late nineteenth-century forces that had led to this new realism had
also pictured the Constitution as an undemocratic bulwark against majoritarian reform and had thus prepared the way for an iconoclastic interpretation that went well beyond seeing it simply as the pragmatic adjustment to
particular problems of the Confederation. J. Allen Smith in his *Spirit of
American Government, A Study of the Constitution: Its Origin, Influence
and Relation to Democracy* (1907) was the first to give historical legitimacy
to the emerging view that the Constitution, far from being a natural expression of American democracy, was in fact an aristocratic, reactionary document
designed by its checks and balances, difficulty of amendment, and judicial
review, to thwart the popular will and the democratic tendencies of the
Revolution. With Smith's book and the writings of others making a similar
point about the undemocratic character of the Constitution, the atmosphere
was ready for the historiographic explosion Charles Beard would make with
An Economic Interpretation of the Constitution of the United States (1913).

An Economic Interpretation was the most influential history book
ever written in America. It came to represent and dominate an entire generation's thinking about history and particularly the origins of the Constitution; and even today, despite severe denigration, it casts a long shadow over
much of the writing on the Constitution. Beard saw the struggle over the
Constitution as "a deep-seated conflict between a popular party based on
paper money and agrarian interests and a conservative party centered in the
towns and resting on financial, mercantile, and personal property interests generally." His underlying assumption shared by others writing during the Progressive period was that men's consciousness and ultimately their behavior
were the products of their social and economic situation. Whatever the merits
of Beard's study, this assumption is crucial to all modern history writing, and
for historians of America it is still the great legacy of the Progressive generation of historians. Yet Beard was not satisfied simply to state his convic-

tion that economic and social interests determined behavior and ideas; he sought to prove it in the case of the Constitution by emphasizing the personalty holdings of the Founding Fathers, in particular those in public securities, and by insinuating that their interest in the Constitution was stimulated by their expectation that these securities would increase in value under a stronger national government. It was this crude attempt at "scientific" proof that ultimately discredited Beard's book, for not only did Beard rest his case on a very limited conception of motivation but he left his evidence open to challenge on its own terms, as both Robert E. Brown and Forrest McDonald showed a generation or so later. It seems clear that Beard's interpretation of the origins of the Constitution in a narrow sense — that the Founding Fathers' holdings of securities dictated their beliefs and actions — is dead, and no further time should be spent on it. Yet Beard's interpretation in a larger sense, in the sense represented by Smith and other Progressive historians — that the Constitution was in some way a reaction by well-to-do elite elements of American society to popular agrarian interests riding the democratic impulse of the Revolution — still seems very much alive.

Indeed, because the Progressive interpretation still seems to be the only one that can encompass the entire Revolutionary era, it continues to fascinate many historians who have long concluded that Beard's particular conception of the origins of the Constitution was wrong. Ironically, the historian who seems most influenced by Beard, that is, most absorbed in the strictly economic and selfish backroom determinants of politics, is Beard's foremost critic, Forrest McDonald. After demonstrating in his *We The People: The Economic Origins of the Constitution* (1958) by an elaborate analysis of the economic interests of the delegates to the federal and state conventions in 1787–88 that Beard's interpretation of a polar economic alignment over the Constitution did not work, McDonald went on to describe in *E Pluribus Unum: The Formation of the American Republic 1776–1790* (1965) such a scramble among such a vast number of parochial competing economic interests that the emergence of the Constitution could be explained only as "the miracle of the age." Such a blatantly and narrowly economic description of the period, however much it owed to Beard, did not satisfy other historians who were attempting at the same time to modernize and extend the general Progressive interpretation of the Revolutionary period.

In his *Articles of Confederation* (1940) and *The New Nation* (1950), Merrill Jensen, the generally accepted heir of the Progressive viewpoint, carried into the middle of the century the Progressive conception of early American politics as a persistent duality rooted in a fundamental socioeconomic division. On one side Jensen ranged the aristocratic and commercial classes, the "nationalists," who continually sought to promote their creditor and mercantile interests by strengthening the central government at the expense of the democratic agrarian majorities in the independent states. On the other side Jensen placed the true "federalists," the local democrats, who feared central power and clung to state sovereignty in defense of the rural and debtor interests of the bulk of the population. The dialectic between these two groups over three turbulent decades, said Jensen, explained the history of the Revolutionary era. In the 1760's and early 70's popular radicals had led the struggle against Great Britain and entrenched colonial aristocracies in order to realize local self-governments responsive to their interests, and they had then created the decentralized Articles of Confederation as the perfect embodiment of their agrarian democratic ideas. By the early 1780's, however, these local democrats had lost interest in maintaining the organizations they had built to bring about the Revolution, and their apathy enabled enterprising creditor and commercial aristocrats who had been displaced by the Revolutionary movement to move back into political power and engineer a "conservative counter-revolution" by overthrowing the Articles of Confederation and creating a strong national government designed to protect their aristocratic and mercantile interests.

With the outlines of the scheme nicely laid, it remained for others, including Jensen's students, E. James Ferguson and Jackson Turner Main, to fill in and refine it. While Ferguson, in his *Power of the Purse: A History of American Public Finance 1776–1790* (1961), explored the nationalist movement of the 1780's, clarifying the ways in which creditor, army, and commercial groups fed into the demand for a stronger continental government, Main in a series of articles and books rounded out and developed the basic Progressive dichotomy of politics in the 1780's. He concluded that the struggle over the Constitution was essentially a continuation of a conflict between two fairly consistent socioeconomic "parties" in each state during the 1780's: commercial-urban combinations led by cosmopolitan notables against agrarian groups led by new men with local connections and outlooks. New York state in particular was the focus of several studies during the 1960's by George Dangerfield, Staughton Lynd, and Alfred Young which emphasized the social and economic elements that lay behind the struggle over the Constitution. All these works appeared to be pointing away from the restrictive economic interpretation of Beard and, as Lee Benson in *Turner and Beard: American Historical Writing Reconsidered* (1960) suggested, toward a broad social interpretation in which the conflict over the Constitution is viewed as the consequence of opposing ideologies rooted in differing social circumstances — an interpretation that examination of the debates over the Constitution seemed to confirm.

Since World War II, however, these neo-Progressive studies have been running against a contrary tide of historical interpretation aptly summed up in the title of Benjamin Wright's book about the Revolutionary era, *Consensus and Continuity 1776–1787* (1958). The Constitution may have been the result of a bundle of compromises, said Wright, but what was most impressive about its formation were "the major assumptions upon which there was no need for compromise," including such things as representative government, periodic elections, the legal supremacy of a written constitution, the amendment process, separation of powers and checks and balances, and a separate court system. "The nature and extent of this basic agreement throws far more light upon the political and constitutional thought of Americans in 1787 than do the disputes over questions which were nearly always matters of detail, or which were based largely upon sectional disagreement, or upon the size of the several states." Indeed, argued Wright, in a larger context, the American achievement becomes obvious. Americans in 1787 simply did not have to confront such issues as monarchy, hereditary privilege, feudalism, or the conflicting claims of church and state ‍that so bedeviled European state-making in the same period.

Such a comparative perspective, also presented with a somewhat more radical emphasis on the American achievement in the magisterial volumes of Robert R. Palmer's *The Age of the Democratic Revolution* (1959, 1964), had been foreshadowed by the writing of the previous decade. During the 1950's, historians like Daniel Boorstin and Louis Hartz repeatedly emphasized the uniqueness of American culture in comparison with Europe. Americans lacked a feudal heritage, rigid class distinctions, and deep ideological divisions; they had never really had a democratic revolution in a European sense, and consequently they could never have had any sort of aristocratic Thermidorian reaction to it. Because the Americans had been Lockeans from the very beginning of their history, their Revolutionary period was notable for its relative lack of social conflict and for its general continuity of leaders and goals. Within the Western context the American Revolution was scaled down to its proper size, making the Progressive interpretation of an internal social conflict overthrowing an American ancient regime seem an anachronism.

By the late 1950's and early 1960's, the reinterpretation of American history in terms of its consensus and continuity was in full swing. Robert E. Brown, the most doctrinaire of these consensus historians fiercely attacked the views and scholarship of the twin pillars of the Progressive school of historians, Beard and Carl Becker, and relentlessly sought to bring down the whole Progressive structure. Brown used detailed studies of both eighteenth-century Massachusetts and Virginia to demonstrate that colonial America was essentially a middle-class democracy with a broad suffrage and without any of the ingredients for a class conflict between radicals and conservatives. In his *Reinterpretation of the Formation of the American Constitution* (1963), Brown concluded that the middle-class property-owning nature of American society and the conservatism of the American Revolution made it impossible any longer to believe that the Constitution was put over undemocratically in an undemocratic society by a small group of personalty property holders looking after their own interests. Thus, for the consensus historian the Constitution became a democratic adjustment to practical problems that arose in the 1780's and consequently a fulfillment rather than a repudiation of the Revolution. It was an interpretation that looked back to Farrand's *Framing of the Constitution of the United States* as much as the neo-Progressive interpretation looked back to Beard's book published in the same year.

Yet the historical debate in the 1950's and 1960's over the nature of the Revolutionary era was leading in directions that few anticipated. By emphasizing that the Revolution was a rationally conservative movement having little to do with a deep-seated conflict in American society, and involving mainly a constitutional argument with Britain over principles and rights, the consensus historians transformed the Revolution into a supremely intellectual affair and thereby provoked a renewed interest in the ideas of the period. Since most historians in the first half of the twentieth century had been absorbed in a scientific and behaviorist approach to the Revolution, much of the best work in Revolutionary and constitutional thought had been carried on in the meantime by nonbehaviorists in government departments and others with an old-fashioned interest in political theory — scholars like Andrew C. McLaughlin, Edward S. Corwin, Charles McIlwain, William S. Carpenter, Charles Warren, and Benjamin Wright. These writers kept alive the late nineteenth-century interest in constitutional ideas such as separation of powers, federalism, sovereignty and judicial review, but they did not for the most part deal with ideas as determinants of historical events. But beginning in the early 1950's with the work of Edmund S. Morgan on the Stamp Act and climaxing in the late 1960's with Bernard Bailyn's study of the ideological origins of the Revolution, historians expanded the traditional interest in the ideas of the Revolutionary era and began to put together a late eighteenth-century intellectual world that they had scarcely known of, a world of republican ideology obsessed with virtue and luxury that owed far more to Machiavelli than it did to Locke. As part of the general reaction to the earlier Progressive interpretation, ideas took on a more important and more deterministic role in the explanation of events in the Revolutionary era. It now seemed that political issues and economic interests could no longer be comprehended apart from the larger intellectual and cultural world in which they operated.

Although Douglass Adair had long stressed the importance of this intellectual world to the Founding Fathers, it was not until the appearance of Cecelia Kenyon's "Men of Little Faith: The Anti-Federalists on the

Nature of Representative Government," *William and Mary Quarterly*, 3d Ser., 12 (1955), based on the explicit assumption "that the ideological context of the Constitution was as important in determining its form as were the economic interests and motivations of its framers," that serious attention was focused on the peculiar ideology of the 1780's and specifically on the thought of the Antifederalists, an attention that was expressed by a spate of documentary collections of Antifederalist thinking in the 1960's. Yet this attempt to redress the partiality of the Progressive interpretation and to reinforce the consensus view by examining the ideas of the Antifederalists inevitably began to turn against itself, for the interpretation of the Constitution's formation as it was originally expressed by the Antifederalists in the 1780's — that the Constitution was an aristocratic document foisted on the people in violation of the spirit of '76 — was remarkably similar to that of the Progressive historians which those consensus historians interested in ideas had originally sought to repudiate.

Thus, the consensus historians' interest in the ideas of the Antifederalists, particularly their dread of aristocracy, has ironically strengthened the neo-Progressive view of the origins of the Constitution. There was an intellectual disagreement with social overtones in 1787–88 that those who emphasized the consensus and continuity of the period could not easily explain. Yet at the same time those historians who stressed the deep-seated socioeconomic conflict that presumably lay behind the dispute over the Constitution could not readily account for the rapid acceptance, indeed, glorification, of the Constitution by the whole of American society once ratification was accomplished. In a recent study of New York ratification, Linda De Pauw has gone so far as to deny any sort of socioeconomic division within the state over the Constitution and even to view ratification as some sort of triumph for the Antifederalists. Although the rhetoric of the ratification debates over the Constitution may have split along an aristocratic-democratic seam, American society in 1787–88 does not appear to have been sharply or deeply divided into two coherent classes corresponding to the Federalists and Antifederalists. Although the talk prevalent in 1787 of aristocracy versus democracy cannot perhaps be taken literally, it does seem to reflect a feeling of social distinction between the Federalist and Antifederalist spokesmen that has to be accounted for. The problem may not be one of class warfare but one of social and political antagonism between elites or would-be elites often representing similar but differently established interests competing for the support of what was often called "the weight of the community."

Despite differences of interpretation, both groups of historians — those attempting to refurbish the old Progressive interpretation and those denying conflict and emphasizing the consensus and continuity of the period — have reached toward agreement, leaving some difficult problems unresolved. Both appear to accept the findings of Jensen and others about the achievements of the Confederation and the uncriticalness of the 1780's, which has highlighted the dynamic and revolutionary character of the movement for the Constitution and by implication has turned it into something of a conspiracy by a small, vigorous group with a positive program. For if the 1780's were not truly critical and the problems could have been remedied by a strengthening of the Articles of Confederation as proposed in the New Jersey plan, then some such conspiratorial explanation seems to be needed to account for the extraordinary radical nature of the Federalist-proposed Virginia plan that formed the basis of the Constitution. Hence, recent historians like Forrest McDonald, John P. Roche, Robert A. Rutland, Stanley Elkins, and Eric McKitrick have all contrasted the youthful energy, farsightedness, and political effectiveness of the Federalists with the inertia, particularism, and political inferiority of the Antifederalists. Indeed, the Federalists' élan and dash has reached such adulation — McDonald, for example, called them "giants on the earth" — that we may be on the verge of returning to the nineteenth-century image of the Founding Fathers as demigods. Although the Constitution was formed by a dynamic minority, it was, it seems, a minority whose effort demonstrated, in Roche's words, "a classic example of the potentialities of a democratic elite."

That the Federalists represented an elite, democratic or not, however, was precisely the point of the Antifederalists' objection and one the Federalists were most eager to minimize and obscure. Because of the Antifederalist obsession with aristocracy, the Federalists in the ratification debates were forced to emphasize over and over, as Martin Diamond has indicated in his analysis of *The Federalist* papers, the Constitution's thoroughly popular and republican character. Whether an elite that uses democratic rhetoric to clothe its aims is any less of an elite is an issue that has troubled American democratic politics since the eighteenth century. And whether this elite was seeking to promote substantial economic and social interests that ran counter to the popular will is the central question around which the historical debate over the origins of the Constitution will continue to revolve.

For these reasons alone the Constitution's formation will always fascinate those interested in the political problems of a democratic society. But because the Constitution is at the heart of American political life, controversy over its origins and historical writing about it can never cease. Its creation is one of those great recurring events in American history that will continue to be probed and interpreted in accord with the ever changing perspectives of the present.

THE CONFEDERATION
AND THE CONSTITUTION
The Critical Issues

WHAT WERE THE SOURCES OF THE CONSTITUTIONAL CONVENTION?

The Nationalists of 1781–1783 and the Economic Interpretation of the Constitution

E. James Ferguson

It was John Fiske who made the phrase "the critical period" famous in American history. "It is not too much to say," he wrote in his classic study published in 1888, "that the period of five years following the peace of 1783 was the most critical moment in all the history of the American people." His book nicely summarized the Federalist view of the origins of the Constitution that dominated nineteenth-century thinking: the 1780's were a time of near chaos in which the confederation government, such as it was, was falling apart and the several states, beset by debtor and paper money advocates who were pressing creditor and commercial interests to the wall, were flying off in separate directions — creating a desperate situation retrieved only at the last moment by the high-minded intervention of the Founding Fathers. It seemed in retrospect as if it could not have happened in any other way. The formation of the Constitution thus became, as George Bancroft put it, "the movement of the divine power which gives unity to the universe, and order and connection to events."

It was against this sort of nineteenth-century interpretation that Charles Beard wrote his An Economic Interpretation of the Constitution, *published in 1913. Actually, nothing in John Fiske's book, or in Bancroft's work for that matter, precluded an economic interpretation of the Constitution. Both had talked of debts, paper*

1

money, and the problems of commerce in the 1780's, yet neither made any serious effort to connect these economic problems to the way men thought about constitutional issues. Some men simply were narrow-minded while others were nationally minded, and there seemed to be no need to explain why. What bothered Beard and the Progressive generation of historians about their predecessors' interpretation of the Constitution was not their total ignoring of economic problems but their superficial and abstract conception of the historical process, their one-dimensional sense of the way things happened, and their lack of any explanatory analysis of men's motives and interests. Beard thus sought, as he said later, to bring into the forefront of historical consideration "those realistic features of economic conflict, stress, and strain" which presumably lay beneath the high-sounding language of the participants' public statements and declarations.

This desire to break through the crust of events and to discover the hidden interests shaping the opinions and behavior of the participants lies behind all the writing of the Progressive generation of historians, including those like Merrill Jensen who have carried that tradition into the present. In The New Nation *published in 1950, Jensen directly confronted Fiske's picture of the 1780's and for the first time in American history treated the Confederation period in its own right as a period deserving a careful and balanced assessment apart from its role in explaining the origins of the Constitution. He found that the so-called "critical period" was not so critical after all, and that in fact the collapse of the Confederation was not the necessary consequence of its weakness or incompetence. Much had already been done by both the states and the Confederation government to stabilize the finances and economy of the country. Despite a temporary depression in the middle 80's, the commercial outlook was not bleak, and indeed the decade was marked by extraordinary economic and demographic growth. If the states could have been brought to accept a national tariff and the national regulation of commerce, Jensen concluded, the Confederation would have been fully capable of surviving and functioning as a federal government.*

Curiously, most present scholars, even those who dispute the Progressive tradition out of which Jensen wrote, generally accept his assessment of the Confederation period. However, once these findings of Jensen and his followers about the positive achievements of both the Confederation and the states and the absence of severely depressed economic conditions in the 1780's are accepted, then explaining the subsequent formation of the Constitution becomes something of a problem. Most often it has been solved by suggesting, as Jensen did, that the Constitution was the work of a small but tightly organized minority of continental-

minded men with a large vision of what the United States should be, a dynamic minority who overpowered a disorganized, ineffectual, and particularist-minded majority. The historian most assiduous in following out and refining this conception of the Constitution is Professor E. James Ferguson of Queens College, whose essential argument is here summarized. Although Ferguson has disavowed any attempt to refurbish Beard's economic interpretation of the Constitution, he can easily be located within the Progressive tradition of scholarship in that he clearly believes that economic and social interests are the principal determinants of behavior. There may have been no crisis such as that described by Fiske, but, Ferguson argues, there was certainly an elitist conglomeration of propertied and mercantile interests, expressed as early as 1781–83, which sought throughout the period to strengthen the national government. By avoiding the crude and restricted conceptualizations of motivation used by Beard, Ferguson has succeeded in presenting the most sophisticated economic interpretation of the Constitution yet attempted.

In spite of such leaders as George Washington, Alexander Hamilton, James Madison, Robert Morris, and others who were later enrolled among the Founding Fathers, the Nationalist movement of 1781–1783 has not made a distinct impression on historical interpretations of the early national period. Surprisingly, it is seldom brought into disputes over the economic background of the Constitution — a matter to which it is precisely relevant.[1]*

It should make a difference to historians that constitutional revision and Hamiltonian funding were first linked together not in 1787, not in 1790, but in the closing years of the Revolution. The movement to reorganize the central government was started by the Nationalists of 1781–1783. They coupled economic with political objectives, formulated a program, and lined up a body of actual and potential supporters for whom such a program had a special appeal. The merger of political and economic goals was organic, and the essential elements of Hamiltonian funding were adopted with the Constitution.

The effort to strengthen Congress began in 1780, in many ways the most discouraging year of the war, when military defeats and the depreciation of paper money seriously undermined patriot morale. Congress, con-

From E. James Ferguson, "The Nationalists of 1781–1783 and the Economic Interpretation of the Constitution," *The Journal of American History*, 56 (1969), 241–245, 259–261. Reprinted by permission.
* [See pp. 157–160 for notes to this article. — Ed.]

vinced that any further output of Continental currency would destroy what little value it still had, ended emissions late in 1779 — a courageous act, but one that left it without funds. As long as Continental currency had value, Congress enjoyed a freedom of action incommensurate with its constitutional powers under the still unratified Articles of Confederation. The stoppage of emissions disclosed its weakness.[2]

Any political change appealed to some persons more than to others and could be expected to have differential effects upon various groups of the population. In principle, central government was antithetical to liberty, which most Americans associated with local self-rule. Since the war had begun, however, there had been second thoughts on this matter. To the extent that state governments had fallen under "popular" influence, people who had opposed democratic tendencies favored a stronger central authority as the only available check upon abuses of local majorities. This sentiment was most articulated at the time by elite groups in the middle states, but it was a predisposing influence everywhere and certainly an element in the support for political reform.[3]

The drive for political reform was associated with changes in economic policies. By 1780, the war was supported by massive confiscations; state and federal officers seized what they needed. The people at large were surprisingly patient under these impositions, yet there was widespread resentment against arbitrary acts of government.[4] Other irritants were legal tender laws and economic controls. Such regulations were a general nuisance.[5] Merchants, especially, felt victimized by economic legislation. It could be and was argued that regulations were hopeless, that the answer to high prices and the scarcity of goods was to abolish restraints on trade, and that the solution to governmental fiscal problems was deep taxation and the abandonment of paper money. Such proposals were impractical under the circumstances, but existing policy was so clearly bankrupt that a case could be made for moving in another direction. Although merchants and other businessmen made profits amidst inflation and in the teeth of economic controls, sound money and free trade were better suited to their ethics and presumably to their interests.[6]

A different group of recruits to the cause of stronger government was the officer corps of the Continental army from Washington down. After the capture of General John Burgoyne and the formation of the French alliance, military victory seemed within sight; yet, at this very point, the American war effort faltered. In the winter of 1779–1780, the Continental army suffered as much as at Valley Forge. "We begin to hate the country for its neglect of us," warned Hamilton in 1780.[7] The officers wanted a government that could raise, pay, clothe, feed, and arm enough troops to win the war.

A more direct interest in stronger central government was that of the public creditors. As Congress fell into insolvency, it ceased paying interest on the public debt. The creditors, who emerged as a political force in 1780, had reason to urge the establishment of a government capable of paying its debts.[8]

The converging influence of these groups began to affect state and federal policy and to create a disposition toward stronger central government, more "authority," less "liberty" in the conduct of public affairs, and, in the economic sphere, sound money and the abandonment of restraints on trade.[9] The formula appealed primarily to the elite, especially in the middle states, to merchants in general, and to special interest groups such as the army officers and the public creditors. It would be a distortion, however, to attribute the Nationalist impulse wholly to the interest or influence of particular groups. The controlling factor was a national emergency which called for new measures. The degree of support, which the proposal to confer additional powers on Congress eventually received in all the states, shows that leaders at every level were alarmed by the critical state of the war and persuaded that something drastic had to be done about it.

The man who more than anyone else worked out the Nationalist program and gave the movement some degree of organization was Morris. Congress, impressed by the urgent need for reform, appointed him superintendent of finance in 1781. A wealthy Philadelphia merchant, a leader of the conservative anti-constitutionalist party in Pennsylvania, and a security holder, he combined in his own person most of the elements of the Nationalist movement. From long and outstanding service in Congress he had gained an unequalled mastery of congressional administrative and business affairs. He was widely respected, also widely hated, but such duties and powers were soon conferred upon him that he became a virtual prime minister — the real director of congressional policy from the time he took office in the spring of 1781 until the close of the war. Morris proved to be a superb administrator. He was also a statesman, the first in the line of the nation's early financial ministers who tried to steer its institutional development from the treasury.[10]

Associated with Morris were some of the outstanding leaders of the later movement for the Constitution. Madison, who attended Congress from 1780 to 1783, was a strong Nationalist; and he backed Morris' program. In 1782, Hamilton served as Morris' tax receiver, a kind of personal representative, in New York, before moving on to Congress to become one of the most uncompromising advocates of a national system. In the army the foremost influence for Nationalist reform was Washington. Although his military position kept him out of civil administration, he continually urged Congress and the country to give more power to the central government.

The Union was a league of states rather than a national system because Congress lacked the power of taxation. This was not an oversight. In drafting the Articles of Confederation, Americans registered their hatred of centralized European systems and their high regard for liberty — which they associated with the supremacy of local government — by denying Congress the power to tax. As Congress needed money to execute its functions, it was in principle dependent on the states at every turn. In practice, it had some leeway, for it could issue paper money and contract loans at home and abroad. By 1780, however, its leeway was pretty well used up. Paper money was failing fast, and neither foreign nor domestic loans were ever large enough to sustain more than a fraction of the expense of fighting the war.[11]

Early in 1781, after a last futile effort to revive Continental currency, Congress struck at the heart of its problem by requesting the states to grant a permanent 5 percent duty on imports to be collected by federal officers and placed at Congress' disposal. As an amendment to the Articles of Confederation, the impost resolution had to be ratified by every state legislature. Congress at first brought it forward as a war measure, a way of securing an income wholly under federal control and, therefore, acceptable to European nations as security for additional loans then being sought. Within a few months, however, the capture of Cornwallis and signs that Britain was ready to make peace altered its significance. The impost, and whatever federal taxes might later be added to it, were to be a fund for discharging the entire Revolutionary debt.[12]

The impost breached the primary restriction upon congressional authority and was the essential first step in building an effective central government. Of equal importance was federal control of the Revolutionary debt itself. That a federal debt existed at all was inconsistent with the structure of the Union. Congress, it is true, had authority to contract loans, but, since it lacked the taxing power, it could not guarantee repayment. Under the Articles of Confederation, Congress was supposed to get money from requisitions on the states. This system never worked, not entirely because the states were negligent, but because their fiscal systems were geared to local priorities and the use of state currency. With the best of motives, the states could often meet Continental requisitions only with great difficulty, if at all. In a country in which the operative fiscal systems were those of thirteen local and diverse entities, a federal debt was an anomaly.[13]

More compatible with the structure of the Union was the procedure outlined by the Articles of Confederation for dealing with the expenses of the Revolution. Each state was to be assessed according to the value of its landed property. When requisitions proved to be ineffectual, the logical solution — one in harmony with the political system — was to give each state its share of the debt and let each state pay in its own way. In fact, something like this began to happen during the last years of the war. Various states began to settle accounts for debts owed to citizens and soldiers. They absorbed all kinds of claims — not only claims against the state governments but also claims against Congress. There was a good chance that the entire mass of unsettled debts would slip into state possession.[14]

Loss of the debt portended disaster to the Nationalist movement. Without a debt there would be little reason to ask for the taxing power, since, when the war was over, paying the debt was about the only thing that Congress would need much money for. Led by Morris, the Nationalists rejected the idea that the states should take over any part of the federal debt. "There is in it," wrote Morris, "a principle of disunion implied which must be ruinous." The debt belonged wholly to Congress. "The creditors trust the Union, and there can be no right to alter the pledge which they have accepted for any other, even for a better one, without their free consent." [15] The obligation to the creditors could be honored only if Congress itself possessed the means of payment. Even if requisitions worked, which they obviously did not, they would not do. Nothing would avail but the impost and other federal taxes. In short, Morris and the Nationalists made payment of the debt contingent upon a revision of the Articles of Confederation to give Congress the taxing power. "The political existence of America," Morris declared, "depends on the accomplishment of this plan." [16]

Morris tried to make sure that unsettled claims against Congress would remain a federal obligation, and at his suggestion Congress resolved in 1782 to send commissioners to all parts of the country to register federal debts due to civilians.[17] The next year Congress declared the large sums owed to the Continental army to be a federal responsibility and refused to allow the states to assume payment of them.[18] Under Morris' guidance the Nationalist Congress clung to the federal debt and enlarged it. At the close of the war, the debt consisted of about $11,000,000 in loan office certificates — the government bonds of the Revolution. By 1786, when the bulk of the unsettled accounts had been examined and new securities issued in recognition of claims against Congress, the debt had risen to more than $28,000,000.[19]

A debt this large was justification enough for the impost, indeed for a whole battery of federal taxes. It was a "bond of union" in the sense of creating a need to confer additional powers upon Congress. It was a bond of union in still another way. The fact was well understood that funding the English national debt had consolidated the Revolution of 1689 by creating a vested interest in the new regime. Irrespective of historical examples, however, the primacy of economic self-interest was a maxim seldom challenged in the eighteenth century. If the federal debt could be funded — that is, the interest regularly paid by means of the import and other federal taxes — security holders throughout the nation could be expected to give their loyalty to the central government. Economic self-interest was that "active principle of the human mind" the Nationalists sought in order to weaken the identification of Americans with their states and generate allegiance to the Union.[20] As Morris phrased it in a report to Congress: a peculiar advantage of domestic loans was that "they give stability to Government by combining together the interests of moneyed men for its support, and consequently in this Country a domestic debt, would greatly contribute to that Union, which seems not to have been sufficiently attended to, or provided for, in forming the national compact." [21]

Up to this point Nationalist objectives were political — to secure federal taxes and to bond the Union with the cement of self-interest. It was the economic program associated with constitutional revision, however, that gave the movement its particular character. The pursuit of political ends by economic means was certain to have economic consequences, some of them integral to and inseperable from the political changes being sought, and others not necessary, perhaps, but closely related to them.

One necessary result was an increase in business capital. That Congress, if fortified by taxation, would fund the debt was certain; otherwise, its improved status could not be actualized, and it must remain a shadow, its powers unexerted. And funding was certain to create domestic capital. After interest payments on the debt ceased in the closing years of the war, the $11,000,000 in loan office certificates, which then comprised the federal debt, had depreciated in market value. If the securities were funded, if regular taxes like the impost were devoted to paying the interest, their market value could be expected to rise, increasing the wealth of the holders.

Morris in 1782 submitted a funding program to Congress remarkably similar to Hamilton's plan in 1790. He recommended a new loan in which old securities would be received at face value in exchange for new securities. After considering a discrimination between original and present holders, he rejected it as detrimental to the public interest. In outlining his plan, he proposed that only the interest be provided for, that payment of the principal be deferred to the indefinite future, and that, in the meantime, a sinking fund be employed to purchase and retire outstanding securities. Funding on this basis, he argued, would immediately benefit the nation. Since interest on invested capital in the United States was higher than the interest payments required to support the debt, the new capital created by funding, if properly invested, would bring a net increase in national income. Moreover, since the securities were held by propertied men, the gains from an increase in security values would go to persons in a position to use them not for consumption but for investment. As Morris phrased it, funding would distribute property "into those hands which would render it most productive." He also expected that it would encourage foreign investment in federal securities. He considered the inflow of money a clear gain to the country, since Americans could employ money at rates of return higher than the interest paid to foreign investors. In short, a national debt was an economic as well as a political blessing.[22]

An increase in domestic capital implied, if it did not entail, the founding of commercial banks. Despite a growing need for banks, none had existed in colonial times, and American businessmen had been forced to rely very largely on credit extended by British merchants. But as was demonstrated by the establishment of banks in Philadelphia, New York, and Boston during and after the Revolution, American businessmen were ready to start banking enterprises with money they had made in the war. Funding the debt would provide more capital for such projects. Banking operations, in turn, would multiply the effect of the capital generated by funding, for, as was well understood, banks could expand loans to several times the reserves actually on hand.[23]

Note issues by banks were a prospective substitute for state paper money. In trying to cope with the shortage of coin and dearth of credit facilities — perennial problems of America's economy — colonial governments had employed paper currency, issuing it in public expenditures and in making loans to farmers. It was fiat money, not redeemable in gold or silver, based instead on anticipation of tax receipts and the repayment of loans. In colonial times the paper money system had worked pretty well. Businessmen in most colonies, if not always enthusiastic, were reconciled to it as the only thing possible under the circumstances. What confidence they had in it was destroyed, however, by the depreciation that occurred during the Revolution.[24] In a more democratic age, propertied men had lost faith in the integrity of legislative bodies; they were afraid that popularly controlled legislatures would deliberately undermine the currency in order to wipe out private and public debts. They wanted to end the paper money system. Because it was unlikely that the country could acquire enough coin or bullion to afford a metallic circulating medium, the only alternative was banks of issue whose notes would serve as a medium of exchange. Funding the Revolutionary debt was a way of solving this problem. The capital created by funding, placed in banks, would provide backing for bank note emissions, which, if on a sufficient scale, would afford a stable currency beyond reach of popular legislatures. The paper money era might well be brought to an end if state governments could be induced to give up paper emissions altogether and conduct their finances by borrowing from banks.[25]

During his term of office, Morris organized the nation's first bank, the Bank of North America, which began operations in 1782.[26] Its capital was only $400,000, not considered a large sum (Morris was able to raise this amount only by buying $254,000 in shares for the government), and it was

entirely specie. Morris was aware that he might have employed public securities as part of the bank's capital if the value of securities had been supported by regular interest payments. But, since no interest was being paid,
he dared not include them in his venture.[27] In other respects, however, his
plans demonstrated how well he had defined his goals and the means to
reach them. He hoped to expand the bank's capital to the point where it
would be "a principal pillar of American credit." He intended, as soon as
possible, to bring about a retirement of federal and state paper money and
to replace it with bank notes. In fact, he made a start in this direction by
floating a mercantile currency consisting of Bank of North America notes
and his personal notes. In 1782 and 1783, he had about $1,000,000 of this
paper outstanding. It passed at par, or nearly so, in all parts of the country.
It was readily accepted by merchants and received as legal tender by most of
the states.[28] Morris' larger plans for the bank were too optimistic; certainly
they were unrealized. Yet they failed of at least partial accomplishment
mainly because they were predicated upon political reforms which did not
come to pass.

Owing in no small degree to Morris' leadership, what one might call
a mercantile capitalist reorganization of the country's economic institution
had become integrated with constitutional revision. Between 1781 and 1783,
Morris, as virtual director of congressional policy, set forth a system that
fully anticipated the later Federalist program: a government invigorated
by taxation; a funded debt whose increase in market value would augment
business capital; a national bank that would enhance the effect of capital
accumulation, afford commercial credit, and provide a nongovernmental
circulating medium beyond reach of state legislatures. Morris in 1783 even
proposed the federal assumption of state debts.[29] The measures that constituted this system, and to a large extent the rationale behind them, were
communicated to Congress. To what extent they were known to the country
at large, or their implications grasped by persons unversed in economic reasoning, can only be conjectured; but the system and the logical relationship
of its parts were plainly visible to anyone who was informed about congressional affairs.

The Nationalist movement declined rapidly at the end of the war.
Although ratified by all but one state, the impost amendment of 1781 failed;
hence, the debt was not funded and the economic reforms contingent upon
funding did not materialize. The Bank of North America severed its connection with the government and never became a national institution. Morris lost influence over congressional policy and retired from office with his
major goals unaccomplished. Yet the elements which the Nationalists had
put together survived and perpetuated a need to execute their program.
They had, in effect, created a national debt, vested title to it in Congress,

and aroused a general expectation that the debt would be paid by means of federal taxes. In 1783, Congress submitted another request for the impost grant to the states, and for several years there was a reasonable chance of its adoption.[30]

In 1786 a new crisis reinvigorated the movement for constitutional reform. Shays' Rebellion, the paper money scandal in Rhode Island, and lesser disturbances in other parts of the country rekindled conservative fear of "unchecked democracy." Perhaps the lowest common denominator of the motives of the Founding Fathers was the desire to impose restraints upon majority rule in order to preserve a republican form of government. But sentiments like this were hardly new in 1786. What gave them peculiar urgency at this time was not entirely the disorders caused by the postwar economic depression; it was the fact that the movement to strengthen the central government had come to a dead end.

After the war, Congress and the states contested for possession of the Revolutionary debt and the consequent exercise of taxing power.[31] As the all-but-unanimous agreement upon the impost amendment showed, there was a general consensus that the Union needed to be "patched together," that Congress should be allowed to fund the debt, and that, for this reason, it should be given a limited power of taxation. Yet, the impost was not unanimously ratified; and, as requisitions on the states did not raise much money, Congress lacked funds to discharge interest on the debt. Congress was in the anomalous position of asserting ownership of the debt, but not being able to pay it.

The states claimed the debt. Responding to appeals from their own citizens who were federal creditors, the states paid interest on the debt with certificates and paper money. States redeemed federal securities by accepting them for taxes and in the sale of land. Some states went further. By 1786, Maryland, Pennsylvania, and New York had carried out a transaction by which they gave their citizens state securities in exchange for federal securities. In this and other ways, various states absorbed more than $8,000,000 in securities — a sum approaching one third of the principal of the federal debt. As other states planned similar action, there was a distinct possibility that most of the debt would soon be absorbed by the states or converted into state debts.

As this unhappy prospect materialized, the impost ran into fatal difficulties. The only state that had not ratified it in one form or another by 1786 was New York. The legislature then approved it, but with stipulations that Congress would not accept. To make matters worse, Congress discovered that the earlier ratifications of Pennsylvania and Delaware were, for quite different reasons, also unacceptable. The Pennsylvania legislature refused to reconsider its position.[32]

That seemed to be just about the end of the impost amendment. In despair, Congress entertained the idea of distributing the debt among the states. The procedure proposed was simple: give each state its share of the total debt and allow it to pay its share in any way it pleased. Such a step was practical and in accord with the political realities of the Confederation.[33] It signified, however, the complete abandonment of the plan for strengthening the central government. Furthermore, a distribution of the debt was certain to promote disintegrative tendencies in the Union. When the states permanently committed their taxes to the justifiable purpose of paying Congress' creditors, it was not hard to foresee that Congress would be left with attenuated functions, little revenue, and no excuse to ask for more. Self-interest would no longer cement the Union; it would bind the creditors to their states.

The failure of the impost amendment in 1786 had a note of finality, for the absorption of the federal debt by the states destroyed any real hope of securing unanimous ratification in the future. Constitutional revision as heretofore projected had failed; some other way had to be found to achieve it. The Philadelphia Convention took place in this context. The Founders met not only to protect government from the mob but also to save the nation from disunion. It should be added that the crisis was a prospective, not an existent, one. By 1787 the country was recovering from economic depression, and it had no overwhelming problems. The real crisis involved the future of the Union.

The Philadelphia Convention of May 1787 exploited a general consensus favorable to reform and the force of economic interests in stronger central government which had arisen since the war, particularly in the matter of federal regulation of trade.[34] Throwing out the Articles of Confederation altogether, the Convention drafted a plan for a national government with powers exceeding anything the Nationalists of 1781–1783 had dared to imagine. All the delicate questions of state interest upon which the impost foundered were swept aside by the grant of unlimited power of taxation to Congress,[35] a power which George Mason observed "clearly discovers that it is a national government and no longer a Confederation. . . ." [36] Another Nationalist objective was nailed down by prohibiting the states from issuing paper money. So deep was the aversion of the Convention to fiat money that it considered denying the power to issue it even to Congress, but decided in the end to preserve this last resource for emergencies. . . .

What bearing does the Nationalist movement of 1781–1783 have upon the interpretation of the Constitution? First, the economic content of the earlier movement does not necessarily imply that economic motives were primary in the actual process by which the Constitution was drafted and adopted. It does not discount the range of the Constitution's appeal to many elements of the population: to gentlemen fearful of disorder, to frontiersmen desirous of military protection, to merchants and mechanics interested in federal trade regulation, and to all kinds of people who were disgusted by the erratic government of the Confederation or alarmed by the threat of disunion. Such considerations cut across economic, class, and sectional lines; and, in 1787, they fairly well united the country's elite behind the Constitution. For this reason, it is impossible to sustain Charles A. Beard's distinction between realty and personalty interests among the gentlemen at the Convention, who, if they were so divided, were doubly united in the determination to erect barriers against popular misrule.

Second, a review of Nationalist antecedents does not tend to maximize the role of crass economic interest in the adoption of the Constitution. Certainly, there were a good many individuals who held stakes in the new government too great to be gainsaid. In 1790, the 280 largest security holders had $7,880,000, nearly two thirds of the federal securities for which ownership can be exactly established from the records. The top 100 holders had $5,000,000.[37] Beneath them was a segment of the propertied class whose holdings were large enough to imply crass economic motive. Yet, if security holders were an influential group, they were only a small fraction of the population; and their motives have to be regarded as mixed. Superimposed upon what might be interpreted as a crass interest was the general allegiance of merchants and businessmen to institutional reforms long sponsored by the Nationalists, a group value system that elevated their endorsement of the Constitution and the Hamiltonian financial program to the level of moral principle.

What can be said with certainty is that the Constitution does have an economic interpretation,[38] one that does not have to be elucidated by doubtful attempts to construct the inner motives of the Founders or depend upon a Beardian or anti-Beardian assessment of the role of security holders. The relationship of economic goals to constitutional revision was neither fabricated nor foisted on the country by interested men; it was organic. If the government was to be strengthened, it had to exercise the taxing power and pay the debt. The profits of speculators were incidental — the price that had to be paid for any degree of centralized authority, even for what most of the Antifederalist leaders were ready to accept in 1787. It is hard to find a prominent man who did not admit the necessity of paying the debt and who, thereby, acquiesced in speculative gains and the advantages to be conferred on the North as opposed to the South.[39] Other Nationalist objectives, such as currency reform and the promotion of banks, were not essential to constitutional reform, yet they were inherent in the funding of the debt and made almost mandatory by the constitutional prohibition of paper money. If the nation wanted a stronger government, it had to accept part or all of the mercantile capitalist formula of economic change.

Thus, an historical necessity existed, which would continue as long as payment of the federal debt impinged upon political reform. If the establishment of a new frame of government had been delayed until circumstances changed — until the debt had disappeared and the nation faced the international crises of the French Revolution — it might well have come in a different guise. In the period immediately after the War of Independence, however, constitutional revision entailed the realization of a mercantile capitalist economic program. The Nationalists of 1781–1783 composed the formula, kept it current after the war by preserving the federal debt, and in some measure committed the nation to an acceptance of at least their basic goals.[40] In 1787 the desire to form a more adequate government had many sources, but in certain fundamental ways the Nationalists had determined under whose auspices and to what ends the reorganization of the Union would take place.

The Progress of Constitutional Theory Between the Declaration of Independence and the Meeting of the Philadelphia Convention

EDWARD S. CORWIN

In order to understand fully the criticalness of conditions in the 1780's, one must separate the difficulties flowing from the inadequacies of the Confederation from those flowing from the deficiencies of the several states. The Confederation government may not have been a failure in what it was designed to do, yet the 1780's may still be considered a crucial period because of problems in the constitutions of the separate states. It was essentially this point that Edward S. Corwin, one of the great constitutional scholars of American history, focused on in his discussion of American political thinking in the 1780's.

Despite the criticism of the Confederation by those who despaired of its ability to solve specific problems of finance, commerce, or foreign policy, the desire to reform the Articles of Confederation gained its greatest strength from the evils experienced within the states, particularly from the abuses of state legislative power. The economic and social instability engendered

*by the Revolution found political expression in the state leg-
islatures at the very time when they were larger, more representative, and more powerful than ever before in American
history. Rapidly shifting legislatures were continually passing,
repealing, suspending, and altering their laws, filling their legislative books, as Madison charged, with more acts in the decade
following independence than in the previous century. And even
more alarming, this fluctuating legislation seemed repeatedly unjust. Paper money acts, stay laws, and other debtor relief legislation seemed to creditors and other established groups to be
making law contemptible. The state legislatures had replaced the
royal governors as the power to be feared, swallowing up both
the executive and judicial functions into themselves. Within a
decade after the Declaration of Independence, Corwin argued,
many Americans had become disillusioned with their early experience in state constitution-making and were looking to the
central government to provide some sort of remedy.*

*In the end it was not pressure from above, from the manifest
debility of the Confederation, that provided the main impulse
for the Federalist movement of 1787; rather, it was pressure from
below, from the problems of politics within the states, that
eventually made constitutional reform of the central government
possible. It was the vices coming out of the state governments,
Madison told Jefferson in 1787, "so frequent and so flagrant as
to alarm the most steadfast friends of Republicanism" that "contributed more to that uneasiness which produced the Convention,
and prepared the public mind for a general reform, than those
which accrued to our national character and interest from the
inadequacy of the Confederation to its immediate objects." Once
the issues were perceived in this way, the movement for constitutional reform achieved an impetus it had not had earlier in the
1780's. It was no longer simply a matter of cementing the union
or satisfying the demands of creditor, mercantile or army interests.
It now seemed to be a matter involving the fate of republican
government itself.*

Critics of Gladstone's famous aphorism on the Constitution seem
often to assume that he supposed the members of the Philadelphia Conven-

Reprinted with permission from Edward S. Corwin, "The Progress of
Constitutional Theory Between the Declaration of Independence and
the Meeting of the Philadelphia Convention," *American Historical Review,* 30 (1925), 511–536.

tion to have emptied their minds of all experience upon their arrival in the convention city.[1]* The assumption is an entirely gratuitous one. Unquestionably the problems before the Convention were suggested by the experience of its members and were not posed *ex thesi*. But the fact remains, nevertheless, that the solutions which the Convention supplied to those problems no infrequently owed far more to the theoretical prepossessions of its members than they did to tested institutions.

For Americans hardly less than for Frenchmen the period of the Constitution was "an age of rationalism," whereby is intended not a blind ignoring of the lessons of experience, but confidence in the ability of reason, working in the light of experience, to divert the unreflective course of events into beneficial channels; and in no respect was man more the master of his destiny than in that of statecraft. Surely if any man of the time may be regarded as representative of the sober, unimaginative intelligence of America, it was Washington, in whose "Circular Letter addressed to the Governors," of June 8, 1783, occurs the following passage:

> The foundation of our empire was not laid in the gloomy age of ignorance and superstition; but at an epoch when the rights of mankind were better understood and more clearly defined, than at any other period. The researches of the human mind after social happiness have been carried to a great extent; the treasures of knowledge acquired by the labors of philosophers, sages, and legislators, through a long succession of years, are laid open for our use, and their collected wisdom may be happily applied in the establishment of our forms of government. . . . At this auspicious period, the United States came into existence as a nation; and, if their citizens should not be completely free and happy, the fault will be entirely their own.[2]

The same sense of command over the resources of political wisdom appears again and again in the debates of the Convention, in the pages of the *Federalist,* and in writings of contemporaries.[3]

Nor does the economic interpretation of history, of which one has heard much in late years, detract greatly from the significance of such facts. No one denies that the concern felt by the Fathers for the rights of property and contract contributed immensely to impart to American constitutional law its strong bias in favor of these rights from the outset, but the concession only serves to throw certain still unanswered questions into a higher relief. For, what warrant had these men for translating any of their interests as *rights;* and why did they adopt the precise means which they did to advance their interests or secure their rights — in other words, why did they

* [See pp. 160-162 for notes to this article. — Ed.]

choose the precise system set up by the Constitution to do the work which they put upon it? Questions of this nature are altogether incapable of answer by any theory of human motive standing by itself. As Sir Henry Maine has phrased it: "Nothing in law springs entirely from a sense of convenience. There are always certain ideas existing antecedently on which the sense of convenience works, and of which it can do no more than form some new combination; and to find these ideas," he adds, "is exactly the problem." [4]

A colloquy which occurred between Madison and Sherman of Connecticut in the early days of the Philadelphia Convention as to its purposes affords an excellent preface to the more particular intention of this paper. "The objects of the Union," Sherman had declared, "were few," defense, domestic good order, treaties, the regulation of foreign commerce, revenue. Though a conspicuous omission from this enumeration is of any mention of commerce among the states and its regulation, it was not this omission which drew Madison's fire:

> He differed from the member from Connecticut in thinking the objects mentioned to be all the principal ones that required a National Government. Those were certainly important and necessary objects; but he combined with them the necessity, of providing more effectually for the security of private rights, and the steady dispensation of Justice. Interferences with these were evils which had more perhaps than any thing else, produced this convention. Was it to be supposed that republican liberty could long exist under the abuses of it practiced in some of the States? [5]

These views were heartily chorused by other members: the faulty organization of government within the states, threatening as it did, not alone the Union, but republican government itself, furnished the Convention with a problem of transcendent, even world-wide importance.[6]

In short, the task before the Convention arose by no means exclusively from the inadequacies of the Articles of Confederation for "the exigencies of the Union"; of at least equal urgency were the questions which were thrust upon its attention by the shortcomings of the state governments for their purposes. Indeed, from the point of view of this particular study the latter phase of the Convention's task is, if anything, the more significant one, both because it brings us into contact at the outset with the most persistent problem of American constitutional law — that which has arisen from the existence of a multiplicity of local legislatures with indefinite powers; and also because it was to the solution of this phase of its problem that the Convention brought its "political science" most immediately to bear.

The singular juxtaposition in the Revolutionary state constitutions of legislative supremacy and the doctrine of natural rights need not detain us here.[7] In the words of a contemporary critic of those constitutions: Although their authors "understood perfectly the principles of liberty," yet most of them "were ignorant of the forms and combinations of power in republics."[8] Madison's protest, on the other hand, against "interferences with the steady dispensation of justice" had reference to something more subtle — to what, in fact, was far less a structural than a functional defect in these early instruments of government. That the majority of the Revolutionary constitutions recorded recognition of the principle of the separation of powers is, of course, well known.[9] What is not so generally understood is that the recognition was verbal merely, for the reason that the material terms in which it was couched still remained undefined; and that this was true in particular of "legislative power" in relation to "judicial power."

It is pertinent in this connection to compare the statement by a modern authority of what is law to-day with actual practice contemporaneous with the framing of the Constitution of the United States. "The legislature," writes Sutherland in his work on *Statutory Construction,*

> may prescribe rules of decision which will govern future cases. . . . But it has no power to administer judicial relief — it can not decide cases nor direct how existing cases or controversies shall be decided by the courts; it can not interfere by subsequent acts with final judgments of the courts. It can not set aside, annul, or modify such judgments, nor grant or order new trials, nor direct what judgment shall be entered or relief given. No declaratory act, that is, one professing to enact what the law now is or was at any past time, can affect any existing rights or controversies.[10]

Turn now to the operation of the principle of the separation of powers in a typical instance in 1787. The New Hampshire constitution of 1784 contained the declaration that "in the government of this State, the three essential powers thereof, to wit, the legislative, executive and judicial, ought to be kept as separate and independent of each other as the nature of a free government will admit or as is consistent with the chain of connection that binds the whole fabric of the constitution in one indissoluble bond of union or amity." Notwithstanding which the laws of New Hampshire for the years 1784–1792 are replete with entries showing that throughout this period the state legislature freely vacated judicial proceedings, suspended judicial actions, annulled or modified judgments, cancelled executions, reopened controversies, authorized appeals, granted exemptions from the standing law, expounded the law for pending cases, and even determined the merits of disputes.[11] Nor do such practices seem to have been more aggravated in New Hampshire than in several other states. Certainly they were widespread, and they were evidently possible in any of the states under the views then obtaining of "legislative power."[12]

Neither is the explanation of such views far to seek. Coke's fusion

of what we should to-day distinguish as "legislative" and "judicial" powers
in the case of the "High Court of Parliament" represented the teaching of
the highest of all legal authorities before Blackstone appeared on the scene.[13]
What is equally important, the Cokian doctrine corresponded exactly to the
contemporary necessities of many of the colonies in the earlier days of their
existence.[14] Thus, owing to the dearth not only of courts and lawyers, but
even of a recognized code of law, bodies like the Massachusetts General
Court had thrust upon them at first a far greater bulk of judicial and administrative work, in to-day's sense of these terms, than of lawmaking proper,
while conversely such judges as existed in these early days performed administrative as well as judicial functions, very much as had been the case with
the earliest itinerant judges in England. By the middle of the eighteenth
century, it is true, a distinct improvement had taken place in these regards.
Regularly organized systems of courts now existed in all the colonies. A bar
trained in the common law was rapidly arising. Royal governors sometimes
disallowed enactments interfering with the usual course of justice in the
ordinary courts, on grounds anticipatory of modern doctrine.[15] Then, however, came the outbreak of the Revolution, and with it a reversion to more
primitive practices and ideas, traceable in the first instance to the collapse
of the royal judicial establishment, but later to the desire to take a short
course with enemies of the new régime, against whom, first and last, every
state in the Union appears to have enacted bills of pains and penalties of
greater or less severity.[16] Furthermore, it should be observed that, owing to
a popular prejudice, certain of the states — notably New York and Massachusetts — at first withheld equity powers from their courts altogether, while
several others granted them but sparingly.[17] The result was fairly to compel
the legislature to intervene in many instances with "special legislation,"
disallowing fraudulent transactions, curing defective titles, authorizing urgent sales of property, and the like.[18] Between legislation of this species and
outright interferences with the remedial law itself there was often little to
distinguish.

That, therefore, the vague doctrine of the separation of powers
should at first have been interpreted and applied in the light of this history
is not astonishing. This, as we have seen, left legislative power without definition on its side toward judicial power, except as the power of the supreme
organ of the state, which meant, however, the withholding from judicial
power of that which, to the modern way of thinking, is its highest attribute
— to wit, power of deciding with finality. Nothing could be more instructive
in this connection than some sentences from Jefferson's *Notes on Virginia*,
dating from about 1781. Pointing out that the Virginia constitution of 1776
incorporated the principle of the separation of powers, Jefferson proceeds
to expound this principle in a way which leaves it meaning little more than

a caution against plurality of offices. "No person shall exercise the powers of more than one of them [the three departments] at the same time," are his words. But even more significant is the following passage:

> If, [it runs] the legislature assumes executive and judiciary powers, no opposition is likely to be made; nor, if made, can it be effectual; because in that case they may put their proceedings into the form of an act of assembly, which will render them obligatory on the other branches. They have, accordingly, in many instances, decided rights which should have been left to judiciary controversy; and the direction of the executive, during the whole time of their session, is becoming habitual and familiar.[19]

The concept of legislative power here expressed is obviously a purely formal one: "legislative power" is any power which the legislative organ may choose to exercise by resort to the ordinary parliamentary processes.

And not less striking is the recital which Hamilton gives in *Federalist,* number 81, of certain objections by opponents of the Constitution to the powers of the Supreme Court:

> The authority of the Supreme Court of the United States, which is to be a separate and independent body, will be superior to that of the legislature. The power of construing the laws according to the *spirit* of the Constitution will enable that court to mould them into whatever shape it may think proper; especially as its decisions will not be in any manner subject to the revision or correction of the legislative body. This is as unprecedented as it is dangerous. . . . The Parliament of Great Britain, and the legislatures of the several States, can at any time rectify, by law, the exceptionable decisions of their respective courts. But the errors and usurpations of the Supreme Court of the United States will be uncontrollable and remediless.

Hamilton's answer to all this was simply that "the theory neither of the British, nor the State constitutions, authorizes the revisal of a judicial sentence by a legislative act," that "the impropriety of the thing" even in the case of the United States Constitution rested not on any distinctive provision thereof, but "on the general principles of law and reason"; that a legislature could not, "without exceeding its province . . . reverse a determination once made in a particular case," though it might "prescribe a new rule for future cases"; and that this principle applied "in all its consequences, exactly in the same manner and extent, to the State governments as to the national government." [20] This answer, for which is cited only the authority of Montesquieu, is conclusive from the standpoint of modern constitutional doctrine; but its contradiction of the views and practices which were prevalent in 1787 is manifest.

Finally, the structural and functional shortcomings of the early state constitutions played directly into the hands of both popular and doctrinal tendencies which distinctly menaced what Madison called "the security of private rights." Throughout the Revolution the Blackstonian doctrine of "legislative omnipotence" was in the ascendant. Marshall read Blackstone and so did Iredell — to what effect later developments were to make clear.[21] And even more radical doctrine was abroad. One Benjamin Hichborn's assertion, in a speech delivered in Boston in 1777, that civil liberty was "not a government by laws," but "a power existing in the people at large" "to alter or annihilate both the mode and essence of any former government" "for any cause or for no cause at all, but their own sovereign pleasure"[22] voiced an extension to the right of revolution hitherto unheard of outside the pages of Rousseau; and even so good a republican as John Adams was disturbed at manifestations of social ferment which he traced to a new spirit of equality.[23]

The sharp edge of "legislative omnipotence" did not pause with the Tories who, as enemies of the state, were perhaps beyond the pale of the Constitution. Everywhere legislative assemblies, energized by the reforming impulse of the period, were led to attempt results which, even when they lay within the proper field of lawmaking, we should to-day regard as requiring constitutional amendments to effect them. Virginia, as Bancroft writes, used her "right of original and complete legislation to abolish the privileges of primogeniture, cut off entails, forbid the slave-trade, and establish the principle of freedom in religion as the inherent and inalienable possession of spiritual beings";[24] while elsewhere the liberal forces of the hour assailed the vested interest of negro slavery more directly. Vermont, Massachusetts, and New Hampshire ridded themselves of slavery by constitutional amendment or in consequence of judicial construction of the Constitution.[25] In Pennsylvania, Rhode Island, and Connecticut, on the other hand, gradual emancipation was brought about by ordinary legislative enactment.[26] Yet the cause of reform did not have it all its own way. When a similar measure was proposed in New Jersey, it drew forth a protest on constitutional grounds which is remarkable in its anticipation of later doctrines.[27]

But it was not reform, nor even special legislation, which early affixed to the state legislature a stigma of which as an institution it has never even yet quite ridded itself.[28] The legislation just reviewed belonged for the most part to the period of the war and was the work of a society which, the Tory element apart, was politically unified and acknowledged an easily ascertainable leadership. Once, however, hostilities were past and the pressure alike of a common peril and a common enthusiasm removed, the republican lute began to show rifts. The most evident line of cleavage at first was that between seaboard and back country; but this presently became coincident to a large extent with a much more ominous division into creditors and debtors. That class of farmer-debtors which now began to align itself with the demagogues in the state legislatures, in opposition to the mercantile-creditor class, was experiencing the usual grievance of agriculturists after a war, that of shouldering the burden of the return to normalcy. But the point of view of the creditor class may not be justly ignored either. By their provincial policies with respect to commerce the state legislatures had already seriously impaired legitimate interests of this class,[29] and they now proceeded to attack what under the standing law were its unchallengeable rights. In each of the thirteen states a "rag money" party appeared, which in seven states triumphed outright, while in several others it came near doing so. Nor was payment even in paper currency always the creditor's lot, for besides rag-money measures and tender laws, or in lieu of them, statutes suspending all actions upon debts were enacted, payment of debts in kind was authorized, and even payment in land.[30]

It is a frequent maxim of policy that things must be permitted to grow worse before their betterment can be attempted to advantage. The paper-money craze at least proved serviceable in invigorating the criticism which had begun even earlier of the existing state governments. One such critic was Jefferson, who in his *Notes on Virginia* bitterly assailed the Virginia constitution of 1776 for having produced a concentration of power in the legislative assembly which answered to "precisely the definition of despotic government." Nor did it make any difference, he continued, that such powers were vested in a numerous body "chosen by ourselves"; "one hundred and seventy-three despots" were "as oppressive as one"; and "an elective despotism was not the government we fought for, but one which should not only be founded on free principles, but in which the powers of government should be so divided and balanced among several bodies of magistracy, as that no one could transcend their legal limits, without being effectually checked and restrained by the others." [31]

And this was also the point of view of the Pennsylvania Council of Censors, in their celebrated report of 1784.[32] Extending through some thirty finely printed pages, this document listed many examples, "selected," we are told, "from a multitude," of legislative violations of the state constitution and bill of rights. Several of the measures so stigmatized were of a general nature, but those for which the censors reserved their severest strictures were acts involving the rights of named parties. Thus fines had been remitted, judicially established claims disallowed, verdicts of juries set aside, the property of one given to another, defective titles secured, marriages dissolved, particular persons held in execution of debt released — and all by a species of legislative activity which had been explicitly condemned both by "the illustrious Montesquieu" and "the great Locke."

Two years later came the early volumes of John Adams's *Defence of the Constitutions,* in answer to M. Turgot's criticism that the American constitutions represented "an unreasonable imitation of the usages of England." In reality the work was much less a "defence" than an exhortation to constitutional reform in other states along the lines which Massachusetts had already taken under Adams's own guidance. A new and significant note, however, appears in this work. In his earlier writings Adams had assumed with Montesquieu that the great source of danger to liberty lay in the selfishness and ambition of the governors themselves. But with the lesson of the paper-money agitation before him, he now gives warning of the danger to which republics, when they have become populous and overcrowded and the inevitable doom of poverty has appeared in their midst, are peculiarly exposed from the rise of parties. "Misarrangements now made," he writes, "will have great, extensive, and distant consequences; and we are now employed, how little soever we may think of it, in making establishments which will affect the happiness of a hundred millions of inhabitants at a time, in a period not very distant." [33]

Copies of the *Defence* reached the United States early in 1787, and were circulated among the members of the Philadelphia Convention, reviving and freshening belief in "political science" and particularly in the teachings of Montesquieu. Yet in one respect at least the idea of reform for which Adams's work stood and that which the Convention represented were poles apart. For while the former still illustrated the opinion that constitutional reform was a purely local problem, the Convention represented the triumph of the idea that reform to be effective must be national in scope and must embrace the entire American constitutional system in a single coherent programme. That such a programme could have been elaborated without the signal contribution to it of the effort for local reform is, on the other hand, altogether improbable.

It was Walter Bagehot's opinion that Americans were prone to give credit to the Constitution which was more justly due themselves. "The men of Massachusetts," he declared, "could work *any* constitution." [34] What had evidently impressed him was the American habit of supplying shortcomings in the Constitution by construction rather than outright amendment. Yet for construction to do really effective work, it must have elbow-room and a handle to take hold of; and at least the merit of having afforded these can not be denied the Constitution.

Nor were the early state constitutions entirely lacking in invitation to this American aptitude for documentary exegesis, which had its origin, one suspects, in an earlier taste for theological disquisition. The executive veto, which was the practical nub of all Adams's preachments, was brought about, to be sure, through specific provision being made for it in the written constitution, and to so good purpose that it is to be found to-day in nearly every constitution in the country.[35] The other suggested remedy of critics of "the legislative vortex," on the contrary, was introduced solely by the processes of interpretation and without the slightest textual alteration being made in the constitutions involved. This was judicial review. Thus while the executive veto and judicial review have a common explanation in the political necessity which they were devised to meet, the manner in which they were respectively articulated to the American constitutional system was widely and for us most significantly divergent. The executive veto was and remains mere matter of fact without the slightest further interest for us; judicial review is both a practice and a *doctrine,* and in the latter aspect especially is of immediate interest.

As a practice judicial review made its initial appearance in independent America in 1780, in the case of Holmes *v.* Walton,[36] in which the supreme court of New Jersey refused to carry out an act of the legislature providing for the trial of a designated class of offenders by a jury of six, whereas, the court held, the state constitution contemplated the common-law jury of twelve. Although the opinion of the court apparently was never published, the force of the example may have been considerable. From this time on the notion crops up sporadically in other jurisdictions, at intervals of about two years, in a series of dicta and rulings which — thanks in no small part to popular misapprehension as to their precise bearing — brought the idea before the Philadelphia Convention.[37] And meantime the main premises of the *doctrine* of judicial review — the principles whereby it came to be annexed to the written constitution — had been worked out.

First and last, many and various arguments have been offered to prove that judicial review is implied in the very nature of a written constitution, some of them manifestly insufficient for the purpose; though that is not to say that they may not have assisted in securing general acceptance of the institution. "Superstitions believed are, in their effect, truths"; and it has accordingly happened more than once that the actual influence of an idea has been out of all proportion to its logical or scientific merits. These more or less spurious proofs of judicial review, however, we here pass by without further consideration, in order to come at once to what, on both historical and logical grounds, may be termed the true doctrine of judicial review. This embraces three propositions: First, that the Constitution is supreme; second, that it is law, in the sense of a rule enforceable by courts; and third, that judicial interpretations of the standing law are final, at least for the cases in the decision of which they are pronounced. Let us consider the two latter propositions somewhat further.

The claim of the Constitution to be considered *law* may rest on either one of two grounds, depending on whether "law" be regarded as an unfolding of the divine order of things or as an expression of human will — as an act of knowledge (or revelation) or an act of power.[38] Considered from the former point of view — which is that of Locke and other exponents of the law of nature — the claim of the Constitution to be obeyed is due simply to its content, to the principles which it incorporates because of their intrinsic sanctity; considered from the latter point of view — that of Hobbes and the "positive school of jurisprudence" — its claim to obedience is due to its source in a sovereign will — that of the people. Actually both views have been taken at different times, but that judicial review originally owed more to the former than to the latter conception seems fairly clear.

Of all the so-called "precedents" for judicial review antecedent to the Convention of 1787, the one which called forth the most elaborate argument on theoretical grounds and which produced the most evident impression on the membership of the Convention, was the Rhode Island case of Trevett *v.* Weeden,[39] which was decided early in 1786. The feature of the case which is of immediate pertinence is the argument which it evoked against the act on the part of the attorney for defendant, James Varnum. In developing the theory of a law superior to legislative enactments, Varnum appealed indifferently to the Rhode Island charter, "general principles," "invariable custom," "Magna Carta," "fundamental law," "the law of nature," "the law of God"; asserting with reference to the last, that "all men, judges included," were bound by it "in preference to any human laws." In short, Varnum, going directly back to the Cokian tradition, built his argument for judicial review on the loose connotation of the word "law" still obtaining in the eighteenth century, especially among American readers of Coke and Locke — to say nothing of the host of writers on the Law of Nations. Nor is the conduciveness of such an argument to judicial review open to conjecture. In the first place, it kept alive, even after the fires of revolution had cooled, the notion that the claim of law to obedience consists in its intrinsic excellence rather than its origin. Again, it made rational the notion of a hierarchy of laws in which the will of merely human legislators might on occasion be required to assume a subordinate place. Lastly, by the same token, it made rational the notion of judges pitting knowledge against sheer legislative self-assertion.

Contrariwise, the Blackstonian concept of legislative sovereignty was calculated to frustrate judicial review not only by attributing to the legislature an uncontrollable authority, but also by pressing forward the so-called "positive" conception of law and the differentiation of legal from moral obligation which this impels. Fortunately, in the notion of popular sovereignty the means of checkmating the notion of legislative sovereignty was available. For, once it became possible to attribute to the people at large a lawmaking, rather than a merely constituent, capacity, the Constitution exchanged its primary character as a statement of sacrosanct principles for that of the expressed will of the highest lawmaking power on earth.[40]

But to produce judicial review, the notion of the Constitution as law must be accompanied by the principle of the finality of judicial constructions of the law, which obviously rests upon a definition of the respective roles of "legislative" and "judicial" power in relation to the standing law. In other words, judicial review raised from the other side of the line the same problem as did "legislative interferences with the dispensation of justice"; and, in fact, it can be shown that the solution of the two problems proceeded in many jurisdictions *pari passu*.[41] The whole subject is one which demands rather ample consideration.

Although the functional differentiation of the three powers of government, first hinted in Aristotle's *Politics*,[42] necessarily preceded their organic distribution to some extent, it is not essential for our purposes to trace either process further back than to Coke's repeated insistence in his *Institutes* that "the King hath wholly left matters of Judicature according to his laws to his Judges." [43] In these words, it is not too much to say, the royal prerogative, which had long lain fallow in this respect, was thrust forever from the province of the courts. One of these same courts, on the other hand, was "the High Court of Parliament"; and Coke nowhere suggests that "the power of judicature" which he attributes to Parliament is to be distinguished from the power which Parliament ordinarily exercised in "proceeding by bill." [44] Far different is the case of Locke. His declaration that "the legislative or supreme authority cannot assume to itself a power to rule by extemporary arbitrary decrees, but is bound to dispense justice and decide the rights of the subject by promulgated standing laws and known authorized judges" represents progress towards a "material" as against a merely "formal" definition of legislative power, both in the total exclusion which it effects of the legislative body from the business of judging and also in the ideal which it lays down of statute law.[45] Noteworthy, too, from the same point of view is Montesquieu's characterization of the judges as "but the mouthpieces of the law," accompanied, as it is, by the assertion that the mergence of "the judiciary power" with "the legislative" would render the judge "a legislator" vested with arbitrary power over the life and liberty of the subject.[46]

As usual, Blackstone's contribution is somewhat more difficult to assess. He adopts without qualification the views just quoted from Locke and Montesquieu, and he urges that "all laws should be made to commence *in futuro*." Yet the very illustration he furnishes of his definition of "municipal law" as "a rule . . . permanent, uniform, and universal" violates this precept radically, since it shows that in his estimation the *ex post facto* operation of a rule, however undesirable in itself, does not affect its title to be regarded as "law." Nor, in fact, does it occur to him, in assigning to Parliament power to "expound" the law, to distinguish those instances in which the exercise of this power would mark an intrusion upon judicial freedom of decision, while his sweeping attribution to Parliament of jurisdiction over "all mischiefs and grievances, operations and remedies that transcend the ordinary course of the laws" — a matter evidently to be judged of by Parliament itself — lands us again in the Cokian log from which we set out.[47]

The differentiation of legislative and judicial power, upon which judicial review pivots, appears to have been immediately due, not to any definition of legislative *power,* but to a definition of judicial *duty* in relation to the standing law and especially to the law of decided cases. In the opening sentence of Bacon's Essay on Judicature one reads: "Judges out to remember that their office is *'jus dicere'* and not *'jus dare'*; to interpret law, and not to make or give law" — words which have been reiterated many times as embodying the doctrine of *stare decisis.*[48] Coke employs different language, but his thought is not essentially different: "judges discern by law what is just"; the law is "the golden metwand whereby all men's causes are justly and evenly measured." He also notes the artificiality of the law's "reason and judgment," and pays full tribute to the burden of study and experience "before that a man can attain to the cognizance of it." [49] Judicial duty is thus matched with judicial aptitude — the judges are the experts of the law — or, in the words of Blackstone, its "living oracles," sworn to determine, not according to their own private judgment, "but according to the known laws and customs of the land; not delegated to pronounce a new law, but to maintain and expound the old one." [50]

In brief, it is the duty of judges to conserve the law, not to change it, a task for which their learning pre-eminently fits them. Yet a mystery remains to clear up; for how came this *duty* of subordination to the law to be transmuted into a claim of exclusive *power* in relation to it — the power of interpreting it with final force and effect? By the doctrine of the separation of powers, the outstanding prerogatives of each department are no doubt its peculiar possession; but still that does not explain why in the final apportionment of territory between the legislative and judicial departments in the United States, the function of law-interpretation fell to the latter. The fact is that we here confront *the* act of creation — or perhaps it would be better to say, act of prestidigitation — attending the elaboration of the doctrine of judicial review; and what is more, we know the authors of it — or some of them.

In his argument in the case of Trevett *v.* Weeden, Varnum put the question: "Have the judges a power to repeal, to amend, to alter, or to make new laws?" and then proceeded to answer it thus: "God forbid! In that case they would be legislators. . . . But the judiciary have the sole power of judging of laws . . . and can not admit any act of the legislatures as law against the Constitution." And to the same effect is the defense which James Iredell penned of the North Carolina supreme court's decision in Bayard *v.* Singleton,[51] while Davie, his associate in the case, was in attendance upon the Convention at Philadelphia.

> The duty of that [the judicial] department [he wrote] I conceive in all cases is to decide according to the laws of the State. It will not be denied, I suppose, that the constitution is a law of the State, as well as an act of Assembly, with this difference only, that it is the *fundamental* law, and unalterable by the legislature, which derives all its power from it. . . . The judges, therefore, must take care at their peril, that every act of Assembly they presume to enforce is warranted by the constitution, since if it is not, they act without lawful authority.

Nor is this a power which may be exercised by ministerial officers, "for if the power of judging rests with the courts their decision is final." [52]

Here are all the premises of the doctrine of judicial review either explicitly stated or clearly implied: the superiority of the Constitution to statute law — the case of the common law had still to be dealt with; its quality as law knowable by judges in their official capacity and applicable by them to cases; the exclusion of "legislative power" from the ancient field of parliamentary power in law-interpretation, except in circumstances in which the law is subject to legislative amendment. The classical version of the doctrine of judicial review in *Federalist,* number 78, improves upon the statement of these premises but adds nothing essential to them.

We turn now to that phrase of the problem which confronted the Philadelphia Convention in consequence of the insufficiences of the government established by the Articles of Confederation. And at the outset let it be remarked that with all their defects, and serious as these were, the Articles none the less performed two services of great moment: they kept the idea of union vital during the period when the feeling of national unity was at its lowest ebb; and they accorded formal recognition that the great powers of war and foreign relations were intrinsically national in character. Those two most dramatic and interesting functions belonged to the general government from the first and became the central magnet to which other powers necessarily gravitated.

The essential defect of the Articles of Confederation, as has been so often pointed out,[53] consisted in the fact that the government established by them operated not upon the individual citizens of the United States but upon the states in their corporate capacity — that, in brief, it was not a government at all, but rather the central agency of an alliance. As a consequence, on the one hand, even the powers theoretically belonging to the Congress of the Confederation were practically unenforceable; while, on the other hand, the theoretical scope of its authority was unduly narrow. Inasmuch as taxes are collectible from individuals, Congress could not levy them; inasmuch as commerce is an affair of individuals, Congress could not regulate it; and its treaties had not at first the force of laws, since to have given them that operation would again have been to impinge upon individuals directly and not through the mediation of the state legislatures. Furthermore, the powers withheld from Congress remained with the states — which is to say, *with their legislatures.* The evil thence resulting was thus a double one. Not only was a common policy impracticable in fields where it was most evidently necessary, but also the local legislatures had it in their power to embroil both the country as a whole with foreign nations and its constituent parts with each other. So the weakness of the Confederation played directly into the hands of the chief defect of government within the states themselves — in excessive concentration of power in the hands of the legislative department.

The endeavors which were made to render the Articles of Confederation a workable instrument of government proceeded, naturally, along the two lines of amendment and construction. In theory the Articles were amendable; but owing to the requirement that amendments had to be ratified by all the states, in practice they were not so.[54] Recourse, therefore, had early to be had to the other method, and eventually with fruitful results.

Yet the possibilities of constitutional construction, too, were at the outset seriously curtailed by the transmutation of the Blackstonian teaching into the dogma of state sovereignty.[55] Fortunately, the notion of American nationality, which the early fervors of the Revolution had evoked into something like articulate expression, did not altogether lack a supporting interest. This consisted in the determination of the states with definite western boundaries to convert the territory between the Alleghenies and the Mississippi into a national domain. Their spokesman accordingly advanced the argument that the royal title to this region had devolved, in consequence of the Revolution, not upon the states with "sea-to-sea" charters, but upon the American people as a whole [56] — a premise of infinite possibilities, as soon appeared.

On the very last day of 1781 Congress passed the act incorporating the Bank of North America. Not only was there no clause of the Articles which authorized Congress to create corporations, but the second article specifically stipulated that "each State retains its sovereignty, freedom, and independence, and every power, jurisdiction, and right which is not by the

Confederation expressly delegated to the United States in Congress assembled." Quite naturally, the validity of the charter was challenged, whereupon its defense was undertaken by James Wilson. The article just quoted Wilson swept aside at the outset as entirely irrelevant to the question. Inasmuch, said he, as no state could claim or exercise "any power or act of sovereignty extending over all the other States or any of them," it followed that the power to "incorporate a bank commensurate to the United States" was "not an act of sovereignty or a power . . . which by the second Article . . . must be expressly delegated to Congress in order to be possessed by that body." Congress's power, in fact, rested on other premises.

> To many purposes [he continued] the United States are to be considered as one undivided nation; and as possessed of all the rights and powers, and properties by the law of nations incident to such. Whenever an object occurs to the direction of which no particular state is competent, the management of it must of necessity belong to the United States in Congress assembled.[57]

In short, from the very fact of its exercise on a national scale a power ceased to be one claimable by a state. The reflection is suggested that if the Articles of Confederation had continued subject to this canon of construction, they might easily have come to support an even greater structure of derived powers that the Constitution of the United States does at this moment.

The question, however, upon which the permanently fruitful efforts of constitutional construction were at this time brought to bear was that of treaty enforcement; and while the story is not a new one, its full significance seems not to have been altogether appreciated. The starting-point is furnished by the complaints which the British government began lodging with Congress very shortly after the making of the peace treaty that the state legislatures were putting impediments in the way of British creditors and were renewing confiscations of Loyalist property contrary to Articles IV and VI, respectively, of the treaty.[58]

Now it should be observed that the immediate beneficiaries of these articles were certain classes of *private persons*, whose claims, moreover, were such as would ordinarily have to be asserted against other individuals *in court*. If, therefore, it could only be assured that the state courts would accord such claims proper recognition and enforcement, the obligation of the United States as a government, under the treaty, would be performed and the complaints of the other party to the treaty must thereupon cease. But how could this be assured? The answer was suggested by the current vague connotation of the word "law" and the current endeavor to find in "judicial power" a check upon legislative power in the states.

Nor can there be any doubt as to who first formulated this solution. It was Alexander Hamilton in his argument before a municipal court in New York City in the case of Rutgers v. Waddington in 1784, practically contemporaneously with British protests above referred to.[59] The case involved a recent enactment of the state legislature creating a right of action for trespass against Tory occupants of premises in favor of owners who had fled the city during the British possession. In his capacity as Waddington's attorney, Hamilton assailed the act as contrary to principles of the law of nations, to the treaty of peace, which he asserted implied an amnesty, and the Articles of Confederation, and as, therefore, void. Only the manuscript notes of his argument are extant, but these sufficiently indicate its bearing for our purpose:

> Congress have made a treaty [they read in part]. A breach of that would be a breach of their constitutional authority. . . . as well a County may alter the laws of the State as the State those of the Confederation. . . . While Confed. exists its cons. Autho. paramount. But how are Judges to decide? Ans.: Cons. giving Jud. Power only in prize causes in all others Judges of each State must of necessity be judges of United States. And the law of each State must adopt the laws of Congress. Though in relation to its own Citizens local laws might govern, yet in relation to foreigners those of United States must prevail. It must be conceded Lèg. of one State cannot repeal law of United States. All must be construed to Stand together.[60]

There is a striking parallel between the cases of Rutgers v. Waddington and Trevett v. Weeden, and especially between the subsequent fate of Hamilton's argument in the one and Varnum's in the other. In each case the court concerned decided adversely to the party relying upon the statute before it, but did so on grounds which avoided its committing itself on the issue of judicial review. In each case, nevertheless, the exponents of Blackstonian absolutism raised loud protests in behalf of the threatened legislative authority, with the result of spreading the impression that the judges had met the issue squarely. Yet since what the judges had said hardly bore out this impression, interested attention was naturally directed in turn to the franker and more extensive claims of counsel; and while Varnum was spreading his argument broadcast as a pamphlet, Hamilton was reiterating his views in his "Letters from Phocion." [61]

Of the various repercussions from Hamilton's argument in Rutgers v. Waddington the most important is the report which John Jay — a fellow New Yorker — rendered to Congress as secretary for foreign affairs, in October, 1786, on the subject of state violations of treaties. The salient passage of this document reads as follows:

> Your secretary considers the thirteen independent sovereign states as having, by express delegation of power, formed and vested in Congress a perfect though limited sovereignty for the general and national purposes specified in the confederation. In this sovereignty they cannot severally participate (except by their delegates) or have concurrent jurisdiction. . . . When therefore a treaty is constitutionally made, ratified and published by Congress, it immediately becomes binding on the whole nation, and super-added to the laws of the land, without the intervention, consent or fiat of state legislatures.

It was therefore, Jay argued, the duty of the state judiciaries in cases between private individuals "respecting the meaning of a treaty," to give it full enforcement in harmony with "the rules and maxims established by the laws of nations for the interpretation of treaties." He accordingly recommended that Congress formally deny the right of the state legislatures to enact laws construing "a national treaty" or impeding its operation "in any manner," that it avow its opinion that all acts on the statute books repugnant to the treaty of peace should be at once repealed, and that it urged the repeal to be in general terms which would leave it with the local judiciaries to decide all cases arising under the treaty according to the intent thereof "anything in the said acts . . . to the contrary notwithstanding." [62]

The following March Congress adopted the resolutions which Jay had proposed, without a dissenting vote, and in April, within a month of the date set for the assembling of the Philadelphia Convention, transmitted them to the legislatures, by the majority of which they were promptly complied with.[63] Nor is the theory on which such repeals were based doubtful. We find it stated in the declaration of the North Carolina supreme court in the above-mentioned case of Bayard v. Singleton, which was decided the very month that the Convention came together, that "the Articles of Confederation are a part of the law of the land unrepealable by any act of the general assembly."

From all this to Article VI of the Constitution is manifestly only a step, though an important one. The supremacy which Jay's plan assured the national treaties is in Article VI but part and parcel of national supremacy in all its phases; but this broader supremacy is still guaranteed by being brought to bear upon individuals, in contrast to states, through the intervention in the first instance often of the state courts. Thus the solution provided of the question of treaty enforcement, whereby the cause of national supremacy was linked with that of judicial review, clearly foreshadowed the ultimate character of the national government as a government acting upon individuals in the main rather than upon the states. Logically, national power operative through courts is a deduction from a government over individuals; chronologically, the order of ideas was the reverse.

The theory that the Articles of Confederation were for some purposes law, directly cognizable by courts, entirely transformed the character of the Confederation so far forth, and must sooner or later have suggested the idea of its entire transformation into a real government. Nor was judicial review the only possible source of such a suggestion. As Madison points out in the *Federalist,* "in cases of capture; of piracy; of the post-office; of coins, weights, and measures; of trade with the Indians; of claims under grants of land by different States; and, above all, in the case of trials by courts-martial in the army and navy," the government of the Confederation acted immediately on individuals from the first.[64] Again, proposals which were laid at various times before the states for conferring a customs revenue on Congress, though none was ever finally ratified, served to bring the same idea before the people, as also did the proposals which never reached the states from Congress to endow the latter with "the sole and exclusive" power over foreign and interstate trade.[65]

But even earlier the suggestion of a "continental conference" for the purpose of framing a "Continental Charter" akin to Magna Carta had been propounded in that famous issue of *Common Sense* in which the signal was given for independence itself. It would be the task of such a body, wrote Paine, to fix "the number and manner of choosing members of Congress and members of assembly," and to draw "the line of business and jurisdiction between them (always remembering that our strength is continental and not provincial)." Such a charter would also secure "freedom and property to all men," and indeed, would fill the place of monarchy itself in the new state. "That we may not appear to be defective even in earthly honors, let a day be solemnly set apart for proclaiming the charter; let it be brought forth placed on the divine law, the word of God; let a crown be placed thereon, by which the world may know that so far we approve monarchy that in America the law is King." [66]

In this singular mixture of sense and fantasy, so characteristic of its author, are adumbrated a national constitutional convention, the dual plan of our federal system, a national bill of rights, and "worship of the Constitution"; and this was some months before the earliest state constitution and nearly four years before Hamilton's proposal, in his letter to Duane of September 3, 1780, of "a solid, coercive Union." [67]

But the great essential precursor to the success of all such proposals was the consolidation of a sufficient interest transcending state lines, and this was slow in forming. It was eventually brought about in three ways: first, through the abuse by the states of their powers over commerce; secondly, through the rise of the question — in which Washington was especially interested — of opening up communications with the West; thirdly, on account of the sharp fear which was aroused among property owners everywhere by the Shays Rebellion. The last was the really decisive factor. The call for a constitutional convention which had emanated from Annapolis in the autumn of 1786 was heeded by only three states, Virginia, New Jersey, Pennsylvania, and was ignored by Congress; but the call which Congress itself issued in the following February under the stimulus imparted by the uprising in Massachusetts was responded to by nine states in due course — New Hampshire being the last on account of the late date of the assembling of its legislature.[68] Testimony from private sources is to the same effect; it shows how the Massachusetts uprising completed the work of the paper-money craze in convincing men that constitutional reform had ceased to be a merely local problem.[69]

In this connection a paper prepared by Madison in April, 1787, and entitled "Vices of the Political System of the United States,"[70] becomes of great interest both for its content and because of the leading part later taken by its author in the work of the Convention. The title itself is significant: "the Political System of the United States" is *one,* and therefore the problem of its reform in all its branches is a single problem; and the argument itself bears out this prognosis. The defects of the Confederation are first considered: the failure of the states to comply with the requisitions of Congress, their encroachments on the central authority, their violations of the treaties of the United States and the Law of Nations, their trespasses on the rights of each other, their want of concert in matters of common interest, the lack of a coercive power in the government of the Confederation, the lack of a popular ratification of the Articles — all these are noted. Then in the midst of this catalogue appears a hitherto unheard-of specification: "want of guaranty to the States of their constitutions and laws against internal violence" — an obvious deduction from the Shays Rebellion.

It is, however, for the legislative evils which he finds within the states individually that Madison reserves his strongest words of condemnation. "As far as laws are necessary," he writes, "to mark with precision the duties of those who are to obey them, and to take from those who are to administer them a discretion which might be abused, their number is the price of liberty. As far as laws exceed this limit, they are a nuisance; a nuisance of the most pestilent kind." Yet "try the Codes of the several States by this test, and what a luxuriancy of legislation do they present. The short period of independency has filled as many pages as the century which preceded it." Nor was this multiplicity of laws the greatest evil — worse was their mutability, a clear mark "of vicious legislation"; and worst of all their injustice, which brought "into question the fundamental principle of republican Government, that the majority who rule in such governments are the safest Guardians both of public Good and private rights."

Indeed Madison proceeded to argue, in effect, that majority rule was more or less of a superstition. No doubt the evils just recounted were traceable in part to the individual selfishness of the representatives of the people; but their chief cause lay in a much more stubborn fact — the natural arrangement of society.

> All civilized societies [he wrote] are divided into different interests and factions, as they happen to be creditors or debtors — rich or poor — husbandmen, merchants or manufacturers — members of different religious sects — followers of different political leaders — inhabitants of different districts — owners of different kinds of property, etc., etc. In republican Government the majority however composed, ultimately give the law. Whenever therefore an apparent interest or common passion unites a majority what is to restrain them from unjust violations of the rights and interests of the majority, or of individuals?

Merely moral or persuasive remedies Madison found to be useless when addressed to political selfishness — which itself never lacks a moral excuse — nor does he once refer to the teachings of Montesquieu, for the reason, it may be surmised, that the model constitution of the Union by this test had broken down at the very moment of crisis. One device, nevertheless, remained untried: the enlargement of the geographical sphere of government. For the advantage of a large republic over a small one, Madison insisted, was this: owing, on the one hand, to the greater variety of interests scattered through it, and, on the other, to the natural barrier of distance, a dangerous coalescence of factions became much more difficult. "As a limited monarchy tempers the evils of an absolute one; so an extensive Republic meliorates the administration of a small Republic."

And how precisely was this remedy to be applied in the case of the United States? In the paper before us, Madison seems to imply the belief that the states ought to surrender all their powers to the national government, but his letters make it plain that this was not his programme. Rather, the powers of the central government should be greatly enlarged, and it should be converted into a real government, operative upon individuals and vested with all the coercive powers of government; then this enlarged and strengthened government, which on account of the territorial extent of its constituency would with difficulty fall a prey to faction, should be set as a check upon the exercise by the state governments of the considerable powers which must still remain with them. "The national government" must "have a negative in all cases whatsoever on the legislative acts of the states," he wrote, like that of the King in colonial days. This was "the least possible abridgment of the State sovereignties." "The happy effect" of such an arrangement would be "its control on the internal vicissitudes of State policy and the aggressions of interested majorities on the rights of minorities and individuals." Thus was the Balance of Power, which Montesquieu had borrowed from the stock teachings of the eighteenth-century diplomacy, to transform it into a maxim of free constitutions, projected into the midway field of federal government.

Every constitutional system gives rise, in relation to the interests of the people whom it is designed to serve, to certain characteristic and persistent problems. The most persistent problem of the American constitutional system arises from the fact that a multitude of state legislatures are assigned many of the most important powers of government over the individual. Originally, indeed, the bias in favor of local autonomy so overweighted the American constitutional system in that direction that it broke down entirely, both within the states, where the basic rights of property and contract were seriously infringed, and throughout the nation at large, because from the central government essential powers had been withheld.

In the solution of the problems thence resulting, four important constructive ideas were successively brought forward in the years immediately preceding the Philadelphia Convention, all of them reflecting the doctrine of the separation of powers or the attendant notion of a check and balance in government. The abuses resulting from the hitherto undifferentiated character of "legislative power" were met by the idea that it was something intrinsically distinct from "judicial power," and that therefore it was exceeded when it interfered with the dispensation of justice through the ordinary courts. Then building upon this result, the finality of judicial determinations was represented as extending to the interpretation of the standing law, a proposition which, when brought into association with the notion of a higher law, yielded the initial form of the doctrine of judicial review. Meantime, the idea was being advanced that the Articles of Confederation were, in relation to acts of the local legislatures, just such a higher law, thus suggesting a sanction for the acts of the Confederation which in principle entirely transformed its character. Finally, from Madison, who from the first interested himself in every phase of the rising movement for constitutional reform both in his own state and the country at large, came the idea that the problem of providing adequate safeguards for private rights and adequate powers for a national government was one and the same problem, inasmuch as a strengthened national government could be made a make-weight against the swollen prerogatives of the state legislatures. It remained for the Constitutional Convention, however, while it accepted Madison's main idea, to apply it through the agency of judicial review. Nor can it be doubted that this determination was assisted by a growing comprehension in the Convention of the *doctrine* of judicial review.[71]

WHAT WAS THE FEDERALIST-ANTIFEDERALIST DEBATE ABOUT?

The Constitutional Convention

ALPHEUS THOMAS MASON

*By 1787, as Alpheus Thomas Mason, McCormick Professor of Juris-
prudence at Princeton University, points out, everyone agreed that
some reform of the Articles of Confederation was necessary. Yet
not everyone was prepared for the proposals being formulated by
James Madison and others that resulted in the Constitution emerging from the Philadelphia Convention in the fall of 1787. Madison's plans for reform, suggested by him in a series of letters to
friends in the spring of 1787 and later embodied in the Virginia
plan that formed the basis for the new federal Constitution, were,
as he said, no mere expedients, but struck at the heart of the state
sovereignty underlying the Articles of Confederation and promised
a systematic change of government.*

*Although the Antifederalists were sorely under-represented in
the Constitutional Convention, if indeed they were represented at
all, it was there in Philadelphia that the crucial issue between the
Federalists and Antifederalists was decided. Although the Anti-
federalists, or more correctly, the anti-nationalists in the Convention won several important battles — with the elimination of the
congressional veto of state legislation and the abandonment of
proportional representation in both houses of the legislature —
they had in substance lost the war even before the ratification
debates began. Once the New Jersey plan, embodying the essentials of the Articles of Confederation, was rejected in favor of a
semblance of the Virginia plan, a national republic stemming
mostly from and operating on individuals, the Antifederalists in
the ratifying conventions were compelled to argue their case on
Federalist terms. Many who had wanted changes in the structure*

*of the central government now found themselves forced, as
Richard Henry Lee complained, to accept "this or nothing." Even
the strongest of the Antifederalist arguments, the Constitution's
lack of a bill of rights, represented a concession to the Federalist
position, because, as Antifederalist Luther Martin of Maryland
said, "Had the government been formed on principles truly federal . . . legislating over and acting upon the states only in their
collective or political capacity, and not on individuals, there would
have been no need of a bill of rights, as far as related to the rights
of individuals, but only as to the rights of states."*

*Mason ably describes the opposing arguments in the Convention
over the two plans and captures the "ambiguous interplay" among
the contestants out of which emerged a document no one clearly
anticipated or was satisfied with. In retrospect, it is particularly
intriguing to note the profound disappointment of Madison and
other nationalists with the results of the Convention, a disappointment which measures the extent of radical reform they intended
and raises the question of precisely what problems they hoped the
Constitution would solve.*

The hard facts of the critical period had undermined the premises
on which the Articles of Confederation had been built. Some revision was
necessary. No one denied that the central government must have more
power. The crucial question was what kind and how much.

Even the Articles conferred on Congress undisputed power to de-
clare war, make peace, and to deal with foreign relations. Its basic infirmity
lay in the fact that ultimate sovereignty, the source of Congress' limited
authority, rested with the states. Article II, the heart of the Articles, explicitly reserved to each state not only "its sovereignty, freedom and independence," but also "every power, jurisdiction and right" not "expressly
delegated" to the Congress.

Obvious inadequacies made it clear that the power distribution
would have to be altered in favor of the central authority. This concession
emphatically did not imply the scrapping of the Articles or repudiation of
the Confederation's cornerstone — state sovereignty. Thus, while the states
might revise the Articles, perhaps even approximate a viable federal system,
they would retain ultimate sovereignty. In the exercise of powers not delegated to Congress, the states would remain supreme. In effect, a sharp line

would separate the two spheres. As long as sovereignty remained with the states, they could grant or withdraw power at their pleasure.

This seems to have been the solution hoped for by opponents of radical overhaul prior to the Convention. In light of the inexorable demands of the critical period, the states were prepared to make concessions.

Antifederalists favored yielding to the center, but always with due restrictions, never going so far as to advocate relinquishing state sovereignty. The Philadelphia newspaper correspondent "Legion" said that the powers of Congress ought to be increased, but only with "great caution and circumspection. . . . Perhaps it would be best to grant the additional powers to Congress for a certain limited time, until it could be observed how they operated and answered the purpose. If they did, continue them — if not sufficient, enlarge them, until found adequate to the government of a great commercial people." [1]* "Amicus Patriae" of Boston wrote in the same vein, emphasizing that there was no need to alter the fundamental structure. The situation required only that Congress be given the power to regulate trade and collect duties. No other powers were needed. The new ones could be tried for a few years and repealed if they proved dangerous to liberty.[2]

It is therefore understandable that the resolution adopted at Annapolis in 1786, calling for the Philadelphia Convention, suggested no radical departure from the existing system. The Convention was to ". . . take into consideration the situation of the United States to devise such further provisions as shall appear . . . necessary to render the Constitution of the Federal Government adequate to the exigencies of the Union. . . ." Revisions were to be reported to Congress and would become effective only when agreed to by Congress and by every state legislature.[3] When Congress, the only body authorized under the Articles to propose amendments, finally legitimized the Annapolis resolution, it restricted the forthcoming Convention to "the sole and express purpose of revising the Articles of Confederation. . . ." Six states had already commissioned delegates before Congress acted. None of their mandates exceeded the bounds authorized at Annapolis. Delaware, in fact, specifically forbade any alteration of Article V, which guaranteed each state one vote in Congress. Rhode Island refused to send any delegates. Three states — New York, Connecticut, and Massachusetts — adopted the restrictive provision of Congress' declaration, expressly barring more than revision of the Articles. South Carolina, Maryland, and New Hampshire empowered their delegates in language resembling that of the Annapolis resolution. . . .

None of the delegates had been empowered to strike at the core of state supremacy. "Revise and amend" was the order of the day. Grant Con-

* [See p. 163 for notes to this article. — Ed.]

gress more power, limited and restricted; and, even more significantly, let the states grant it, let the Congress under the Articles approve it, and let the states — all of them — ratify it. Uproot state sovereignty? No! Only a few, notably Alexander Hamilton and George Read of Delaware, would have preferred completely to wipe out the states.[4] But, just as adherents of state sovereignty had bowed to the overwhelming need to strengthen the central government, thereby arriving at what they considered "middle ground," so also had the nationalists modified their more extreme goals. Six weeks before the delegates assembled, Madison had written Edmund Randolph that, whereas his preference might have led him to advocate a "consolidation of the states," his view had been tempered by a recognition of the possible. "In truth," he had confessed, "my ideas of reform strike so deeply at the old Confederation, and lead to such a systematic change, that they scarcely admit of the expedient."

> I hold it for a fundamental point, that an individual independence of the States is utterly irreconcilable with the idea of an aggregate sovereignty. I think, at the same time, that a consolidation of the States into one simple republic is not less unattainable than it would be inexpedient. Let it be tried, then, whether any middle ground can be taken, which will at once support a due supremacy of the national authority, and leave in force the local authorities so far as they can be subordinately useful.[5]

In the end considerations of principle and expediency conspired to produce Madison's "middle ground."

The Madison-Randolph plan, while rejecting the idea of "consolidation," was calculated to undercut both cornerstones of state supremacy. Distribution of power between the national and state governments was heavily weighted in favor of the former. As Madison proposed to Randolph: "Let it [the national government] have a negative, in all cases whatsoever, on the Legislative acts of the States, as the King of Great Britain heretofore had." [6] This negative was considered "essential, . . . the least possible abridgement of the State sovereignties." Without it "every positive power that can be given on paper" to the national government would be "unavailing." There would clearly be no line circumscribing national power. More than that, the other cornerstone of state supremacy would be destroyed: state sovereignty as the legitimate source of power would bow to popular sovereignty. "To give the new system its proper energy," Madison declared, "it will be desirable to have it ratified by the authority of the people, and not merely by that of the Legislatures." [7]

Even before the Convention, one notes a lurking suspicion that the states might lose their pre-eminence. Nor were these fears unfounded. For although Madison's plan would have preserved the states so far as they could be "subordinately useful," its nationalizing features contained the potential for effective "consolidation," an implication which did not escape notice at the Convention — or later. But having gone on record in favor of some change, it seemed inconsistent to oppose the elevated objectives of the Convention. Whether more than "revision" could be achieved was at best problematical. The authorization at Annapolis did not extend beyond these bounds. Furthermore, the Convention proposals would have to be submitted to Congress and transmitted to the states. It seemed extremely unlikely that Congress and the states would sign their own death warrants. For revision of the Articles, unanimous approval by the thirteen states was required, and Rhode Island had already expressed its unequivocal disapproval by refusing to send delegates. Thus, strident nationalists would have to run a barrier-studded gauntlet to uproot the existing system. . . .

Though slightly outnumbered, delegates enamored of Antifederalism promptly made their presence felt. Hardly had the Virginia Plan, embodying the proposals Madison submitted to Randolph, been presented that state sovereignties were stirred. Charles Pinckney immediately asked whether Randolph "meant to abolish the State Governts. altogether." [8] Randolph explained that he "only meant to give the national government a power to defend and protect itself." His plan would take from the states "no more sovereignty than is competent to this end." [9] On May 30, 1787, the day after the Virginia Plan had been proposed, Gouverneur Morris "explained the distinction between a *federal* and *national* supreme Govt," making it clear that he considered Randolph's answer evasive. Morris thought the Virginia Plan would alter — indeed displace — the basic structure of the Articles of Confederation. The Articles were a "federal" government, whereas Randolph's proposals would establish a "national, supreme" government, resting on the principle that "in all communities there must be one supreme power, and one only." [10] Elbridge Gerry, replying to Morris, quickly challenged the authority of the Convention to effect a revolution:

> A distinction has been made between a *federal* and *national* government. We ought not to determine that there is this distinction for if we do, it is questionable not only whether this convention can propose a government totally different or whether Congress itself would have a right to pass such a resolution as that before the house. . . . If we have a right to pass this resolution we have a right to annihilate the confederation. . . .[11]

Authorization or no authorization, the Convention proceeded to debate the Virginia Plan on its merits. If its nationalizing implications were not made clear by the questions Gerry . . . raised, they ought to have been. Indeed, as early as May 20, four days before the delegates assembled, George Mason had written his son: "The most prevalent idea in the principal States seems to be a total alteration of the present federal system. . . .[12] The next day he expressed the same opinion to Arthur Lee.[13] Writing to James Monroe on May 29, William Grayson declared that the delegates from the East were advocating "a very strong government, & wish to prostrate all ye. state legislature, & form a general system out of ye. whole. . . ." The Virginia Plan, Grayson noted, involved uprooting state sovereignty through the mechanism of popular ratification. Said he: "The people of America don't appear to me to be ripe for any great innovations & it seems they are ultimately to ratify or reject. . . ." [14]

Discussion of the Virginia Plan brought more and more into focus the threats it embodied to the continued existence of the states. Two features in particular raised valid questions as to the survival of the states as viable units in the proposed scheme of government. Dickinson, among others, had chided Wilson for failure of the Virginia Plan to provide for state representation. The legislative negative on state laws also came under attack. Persistent requests for a precise definition of national power under the Virginia Plan were met by dogged refusals to be committed. On June 8, Madison "could not but regard an indefinite power to negative legislative acts of the States as absolutely necessary to a perfect system." "Experience," he argued, "had envinced [sic] a constant tendency in the States to encroach on the federal authority; to violate national Treaties, to infringe the rights & interests of each other; to oppress the weaker party within their respective jurisdictions." National power to negative all state laws deemed improper was "the mildest expedient that could be devised for preventing these mischiefs." "Appeal to coercion" would be the only alternative. Thus, a national negative, extending to "all cases," would "render the use of force unnecessary." [15]

Madison's unequivocal stand for "indefinite" national power did not go unchallenged. Hugh Williamson of North Carolina objected that the effect might be to "restrain the States from regulating their internal" affairs.[16] Gerry feared that such power would "enslave the States." [17] Roger Sherman of Connecticut "thought the cases in which the negative ought to be exercised, might be defined. . . ." [18]

Opposition to "indefinite" national power erupted again in the discussion of the provision for proportional representation. Paterson's elaborate argument of June 9 reflected the fear of small states that they would be dominated by the superior voting power of the larger states. Proportional representation would strike "at the existence of the lesser States." Paterson argued for a guarantee to each state of an equal vote in the new Congress, premising his reasoning on the absence of the Convention's authority to alter the basic structure of the Articles of Confederation. "We ought to keep within its limits," he warned, "or we should be charged by our constituents with usurpation." More than that, the commissions of the delegates were not only the measure of their power; "they denoted also the sentiments of the States on the subject of our deliberation."

> The idea of a national Govt. as contradistinguished from a federal one, never entered into the mind of any of them, and to the public mind we must accommodate ourselves. We have no power to go beyond the federal scheme, and if we had the people are not ripe for any other. We must follow the people; the people will not follow us. *The proposition* [proportional representation] could not be maintained whether considered in reference to us as a nation, or as a confederacy. A confederacy supposes sovereignty in the members composing it & sovereignty supposes equality. If we are to be considered as a nation, all State distinctions must be abolished, the whole must be thrown into hotchpot, and when an equal division is made, then there may be fairly an equality of representation. . . .

Paterson vowed that New Jersey would "never confederate on the plan" proposed; the state "would be swallowed up." He would not only "oppose the plan here but, on his return home, do everything in his power to defeat it there." [19] At this juncture, Wilson sharply challenged: "If N.J. will not part with her Sovereignty it is in vain to talk of Govt." [20]

The impending impasse came to a head on June 15, when Paterson brought forward a plan founded on principles diametrically opposed to those on which the Virginia Plan rested. Alluding to his alternative on June 9, he confessed strong attachment "to the plan of the existing confederacy." "No other amendments were wanting," he had declared, "than to mark the orbits of the States with due precision, and provide for the use of coercion. . . ." [21] In short, the Articles of Confederation would be the foundation of the New Jersey Plan.

Both the Virginia and New Jersey Plans presumed to alter the Articles of Confederation so as to render it "adequate to the exigencies" of the union.[22] There the similarity ends. The chasm dividing the advocates of a strong national government and their opponents before the Convention now reappeared in stark clarity. That the New Jersey Plan reflected much more than fear for the future position of the *small* states is evidenced by the differences between Paterson's proposals and those of Randolph on issues other than representation.

Under the Virginia Plan[23] the national legislature would have been empowered "to legislate in all cases to which the separate States are incompetent, or in which the harmony of the United States may be interrupted by the exercise of individual Legislation"; it would negate any state law deemed contrary to the national constitution. By implication, the national legislature itself would decide the cases "to which the separate States are incompetent." The Virginia Plan also called for a national executive and a national judiciary whose execution and enforcement of national laws would have been brought directly to bear on individuals. No longer could the states, through failure to heed the laws of Congress and the authority of their courts, shield individuals from the coercive power of the national government. Finally, the Virginia Plan contemplated popular ratification, a device calculated to destroy state sovereignty and enthrone national supremacy.

The New Jersey Plan,[24] on the other hand, would have perpetuated the twin keystones of state supremacy: state power and state sovereignty. Throughout, it sought to protect the states as the dominant centers of authority. Although additional legislative powers were to be vested in the national Congress, all violations were first to be "adjudged by the Common law Judiciarys" of the several states. It not only declared that "none of the [legislative] powers . . . vested in the United States in Congress shall be exercised without the consent" of an unspecified number of states, but also provided that the national executive should be removable by Congress on the application of a majority of the state governors. Representation in Congress would, of course, have remained the same. Article XIII, requiring unanimous approval of amendments by the thirteen states, would also remain unaltered. . . .

The New Jersey Plan, then, was much more than an expression of the small states' desire to maintain equal footing with the larger states in the national legislature. Paterson's resolutions were grounded in mixed principles and inspired by mixed motives. Said Madison:

> This plan had been concerted among the deputations or members thereof, from Cont. N.Y. N.J. and perhaps Mr. Martin from Maryd. who made with them a common cause on different principles. Cont. and N.Y. were agst. a departure from the principle of the Confederation, wishing rather to add a few new powers to Congs. than to substitute, a National Govt. The States of N.J. and Del. were opposed to a National Govt. because its patrons considered a proportional representation of the States as the basis of it. The eagourness displayed by the Members opposed to a National Govt. from these different [motives] began now to produce serious anxiety for the result of the Convention — Mr. Dickinson said to Mr. Madison you see the consequence of pushing things too far. . . .[25]

Mixed motives did not, however, blunt the sure sense of direction that welded the plan into a consistent whole. Madison was also acutely aware that prior accord on the representation issue would greatly facilitate settlement of the dispute over allocation of power between the national and state governments. Elbridge Gerry later suggested that before proceeding to the question of representation the delegates should settle the issue of the nature and scope of national power. Madison objected, insisting that representation be first considered.

> It wd. be impossible to say what powers could be safely & properly vested in the Govt. before it was known, in what manner the States were to be represented in it. He was apprehensive that if a just representation were not the basis of the Govt. it would happen, as it did when the Articles of Confederation were depending, that every effectual prerogative would be withdrawn or withheld, and the New Govt. wd. be rendered as impotent and as short lived as the old.[26]

"The great difficulty lies in the affair of Representation; and if this could be adjusted, all others would be surmountable," Madison had remarked.[27] The logic of Madison's insight would be borne out, but not before deadlock over representation almost stalemated the Convention.

For a whole month, from June 15 when Paterson proposed the New Jersey Plan until July 16 when the Connecticut Compromise was consummated, the issue of representation dominated the discussion. Both sides, it should be emphasized, tightly bound the question of state equality in the national legislature to the related issues of national power and state sovereignty. Paterson virtually equated state sovereignty with equal state representation. "If the sovereignty of the States is to be maintained," he contended in his speech of June 16, "the Representatives must be drawn immediately from the States, not from the people: and we have no power to vary the idea of equal sovereignty." [28] The Convention was powerless, he maintained, to alter Article V of the Confederation. By giving each state an equal vote, it had provided the "basis" of the Confederation: "equal Sovereignty." Article XIII, moreover, required the unanimous consent of the thirteen equal states to alter the Confederation. "If the confederacy was radically wrong, let us return to our States, and obtain larger powers, not assume them of ourselves. What is unanimously done, must be unanimously undone." [29] Paterson strongly implied that any other procedure would be revolutionary. . . .

Still to be faced in connection with the representation issue were the questions of whether the national legislature ought to consist of two branches and, if so, whether the first branch ought to be elected by the people instead of the states. Opposing popular election, Luther Martin elaborated the significance of state representation. He agreed that the legislative branch ought to be bicameral. This would be an effective means of checking the "dangerous" potentialities of concentrated power. Martin also confessed that "when the confederation was made, congress ought to have been invested with more extensive powers. . . ." "The time is now come," he conceded, "that we can grant them not only new powers, but to modify their government, so that the state governments are not endangered." To be acceptable, however, changes must be consistent with the basic character of the Articles. Thus, Martin concluded: "But whatever we have now in our power to grant, the grant is a state grant, and therefore it must be so organized that the state governments are interested in supporting the union." [30]

Popular election of the first branch, a condition which James Wilson regarded "not only [as] the cornerstone, but as the foundation of the fabric," [31] was agreed to on June 21. On June 27, the Convention voted unanimously to proceed to "the most fundamental points; the rules of suffrage in the two branches. . . ." [32] Martin spoke for three hours "with much diffuseness and considerable vehemence" [33] in defense of the smaller states against the large, and in defense of all the states against the proposed national government. "[T]he Genl. Govt. ought to be formed for the States, not for individuals," he contended. "[I]f the States were to have votes in proportion to their numbers of people, it would be the same thing whether their representatives were chosen by the Legislatures or the people. . . ." [34] Equal state representation must be preserved in both branches, this being prerequisite to the maintenance of state sovereignty.

Martin and his supporters lost this battle. The next day the Convention decided "that the right of suffrage in the first branch . . . ought not to be according to the rule established in the articles of confederation but according to some equitable ratio of representation." [35] Then came the matter of the upper house; it took the form of a motion to give each state an equal vote. The germ of compromise was planted the same day, when Doctor Johnson of Connecticut suggested:

> . . . On the whole he thought that as in some respects the States are to be considered in their political capacity, and in others as districts of individual citizens, the two ideas embraced on different sides, instead of being opposed to each other, ought to be combined; that in *one* branch the *people*, ought to be represented; in the *other*, the *States*.[36]

The seeds planted on June 29 bore fruit after more than two weeks of bitter debate. Madison agreed with Dr. Johnson that "the mixed nature of the Govt. ought to be kept in view," but he "thought too much stress was laid on the rank of the States as political societies."[37] Madison saw the issue of proportional versus equal representation in the second branch more in terms of the position of the states in the union than as a meaningful struggle between large and small states. He therefore entreated the small states "to renounce a principle wch. was confessedly unjust, which could never be admitted, & if admitted must infuse mortality into a Constitution which we wished to last forever. . . ."[38]

So vital did Madison, Wilson, and Hamilton consider representation in the upper house that it could not be divorced from the related questions of power and sovereignty. Equal state representation would embrace
a principle inconsistent with the underlying theory of the new government.
"I would always exclude inconsistent principles in framing a system of government," Madison emphasized. "I would compromise on this question, if
I could do it on correct principles, but otherwise not — if the old fabric of
the confederation must be the ground-work of the new, we must fail." [39]
His meaning could hardly be clearer.

"Can we forget for whom we are forming a Government?" Wilson
pleaded. "Is it for *men,* or for the imaginary beings called States? Will our
honest constituents be satisfied with metaphysical distinctions?" Echoing
Madison's warning, Wilson insisted that inconsistent principles would crum-
ble the whole structure. "The rule of suffrage ought on every principle to
be the same in the 2d. as in the 1st. branch. If the Government be not laid
on this foundation, it can neither be solid nor lasting, any other principle
will be local, confined & temporary. . . . We talk of States, till we forget what
they are composed of. . . ." [40]

The Convention seemed hopelessly deadlocked. Stalemate was formally confirmed on July 2, when the Convention divided 5–5–1 on the resolution to accord each state an equal vote in the upper house. General C. C.
Pinckney now proposed that a committee be formed to attempt a compromise. On July 5, the committee presented its report; two proposals, embodying the "partly national, partly federal" principle, were recommended, "on
condition that both shall be generally adopted." [41] The first branch of the
legislature would be popularly elected and based on proportional representation. It would also have the exclusive power of originating money bills.
In the second branch each state would have an equal vote.

The committee's proposals — except for the one according the first
branch exclusive authority for originating money bills — embraced no new
middle ground. Nationalists had already rejected the very notion of state
equality in the second branch as destructive of effective government. Understandably, they continued to oppose this presumably vital concession to
the advocates of state sovereignty. Deeply incensed, Madison was "not only
fixed in his opposition to the Report of the Comme. but was prepared for
any want that might follow a negative of it." [42] He "could not regard the
exclusive privilege of originating money bills as any concession," since it
"left in force all the objections which had prevailed agst. allowing each
State an equal voice." [43] Gouverneur Morris was no less emphatic. "He conceived the whole aspect of it to be wrong. . . . State attachments, and State
importance have been the bane of this Country," he exclaimed. "We cannot
annihilate; but we may perhaps take out the teeth of the serpents. . . . This

Country must be united," Morris entreated. "If persuasion does not unite it, the sword will," [44] he warned ominously. . . .

Wilson's suggestion that the report be reconsidered was "tacitly agreed to." As the nationalists prepared to take their last stand, Charles Pinckney, attempting to salvage a measure of proportional representation in the second branch, moved that:

> . . . instead of an equality of votes the States should be represented in the 2d. branch as follows: N.H. by 2 members. Mas 4. R.I. 1. Cont. 3. N.Y. 3. N.J. 2. Pa. 4. Del. 1. Md. 3. Virga. 5. N.C. 3. S.C. 3. Geo. 2. making in the whole 36.[45]

Wilson seconded the motion, and Madison "concurred" in it "as a reasonable compromise." [46] But Jonathan Dayton and Roger Sherman lodged protests which effectively pinpointed the dual motives driving the promoters of equal state representation. "The smaller States," Dayton insisted, "can never give up their equality." He would "in no event yield that security for their rights." Sherman favored "the equality of votes not so much as a security for the small States; as for the State Govts. which could not be preserved unless they were represented & had a negative in the Genl. Government." [47]

King, Madison, and Wilson made final pleas in favor of Pinckney's "compromise" motion. Their speeches read like the grim protests of men forced to swallow a bitter pill. King "was sure that no Govt. could last that was not founded on just principles." The delegate from Maryland "preferred the doing of nothing, to an allowance of an equal vote to all the States." "It would be better," he thought, "to submit to a little more confusion & convulsion, than to submit to such an evil." [48] Madison, no less apprehensive for the future of the new government, reminded the Convention of "the consequences of laying the existing confederation on improper principles." "If the proper foundation of Government was destroyed," he warned, "by substituting an equality in place of a proportional Representation, no proper superstructure would be raised. . . ."

To the speeches of King and Madison, James Wilson "would add a few words only." State equality in the second branch was "a fundamental and perpetual error" which "ought by all means to be avoided." In response to the argument that "an equal vote in one branch of the Legislature is essential to their [the states'] preservation," Wilson admitted that the states "ought to be preserved." "But does it follow that an equality of votes is necessary for the purpose?" [49] In the minds of a bare majority of the Convention, the answer, apparently, was affirmative. For Pinckney's motion, which aimed at persuading the Convention to accept what Madison had called "a reasonable compromise," failed to pass, confirming Elbridge Gerry's prediction that it had "no hope of success." [50] The next day, July 16, the

Convention approved "the whole of the report from the grand Committee" by a vote of 5–4–1. The so-called Connecticut Compromise had been accepted, but not before the die-hard nationalists tried unsuccessfully to undo it. . . .

Enemies of a strong national government, as well as friends of the small states, had good reason to hail the Connecticut Compromise as a victory. The term "compromise" is a misnomer. Notwithstanding the implications of Luther Martin's remarks of July 10 — that adherents of equal state representation, having lost their battle in the first branch of the legislature, were entitled to equal representation in the second branch — the Connecticut Compromise bears no earmarks of compromise. Proportional representation in the first branch had been determined prior to the struggle over representation in the second, prior to the "partly national, partly federal" formula suggested by Dr. Johnson, formalized by Ellsworth's motion, and acted on by the committee. Strong national government men had lost a battle, but not the war.

For over a month supporters of the Virginia Plan, embodying the essence of Madison's "middle ground," had fought to stave off what they thought would vitiate the nationalizing features of the new system. Repeatedly the nationalists had insisted that equal state representation would infect the new government with the same disease that plagued the Articles. National supremacy would be undermined in two ways: (1) equal representation would make the states a constituent part of the national government, thereby creating the likelihood that the states would defeat the exercise of national power; and (2) state representation — instead of popular representation — in the second branch would taint the principle of popular sovereignty, denying the people proper representation in their government. Thus, state supremacy, state power, and state sovereignty — the very infirmity which the new system was designed to correct — would permeate the new government.

It is understandable that opponents of the Virginia Plan were inflexible on the issue of state representation. No less understandable is the desperate struggle of those who, fearful that even their "middle ground" would be seriously undermined, refused to accept the finality of that fateful vote on July 16, until convinced that hopeless stalemate would otherwise result.

When the Convention met on July 17, Gouverneur Morris still entertained hope that the representation issue might be reopened. His motion to reconsider the Connecticut Compromise, however, was not even seconded.[51] Instead, the Convention proceeded to reject the provision in the Virginia Plan calling for a legislative negative on state laws which, in the opinion of the national legislature, contravened the new constitution.

On May 31, the nationalists had won an easy victory on this issue.[52] They had failed on June 8 to strengthen the negative by endowing the legislature with a veto over state laws deemed merely "improper." [53] Now it was urgent that the original resolution be retained. Madison had written Randolph before the Convention assembled that he conceived a national veto power the least possible abridgement of the State sovereignties.[54] On June 8, he still believed ". . . indefinite power to negative legislative acts of the States absolutely necessary to a perfect system." [55] During the debate on July 17, he reiterated his conviction that "nothing short of a negative" would control "the propensity of the States to pursue their particular interests in opposition to the general interest." To the very end Madison continued to support the negative as "the most mild & certain means of preserving the harmony of the system. . . ." [56]

Thus, only a day after the nationalists had suffered a major defeat, making all the more necessary the preservation and strengthening, if possible, of the legislative negative, the Convention voted against Madison's "mildest expedient." Madison's "middle ground," that solid foundation on which an effective national government was supposed to rest, was beginning to resemble quicksand into which the underpinnings of national supremacy were rapidly sinking.

But appearances are often deceptive. Immediately following rejection of the legislative negative, the Convention unanimously adopted the substance of the supremacy clause.[57] The version, adopted as Article VI, paragraph 2, initially written into the New Jersey Plan, was virtually the same as that Luther Martin presented to the Convention on July 17. Rejection of the legislative negative in favor of the supremacy clause closely parallels Jefferson's approach to ways of controlling unbridled state legislative power. Writing Madison from Paris, June 20, 1787, he queried the wisdom of so drastic a check as the legislative negative:

> The negative proposed to be given them [Congress] on all the acts of the several legislatures is now for the first time suggested to my mind. Prima facie, I do not like it. It fails in an essential character that the hole and the patch should be commensurate. But this proposes to mend a small hole by covering the whole garment. Not more than one out of one hundred state-acts concern the confederacy. This proposition, then, in order to give them one degree of power, which they [Congress] ought to have, gives them ninety-nine more, which they ought not to have, upon the presumption that they will not exercise the ninety-nine.

Jefferson went on to suggest judicial review as the proper remedy, a function plainly implied in the supremacy clause. "Would not appeal," he asked, "from the state judicature to a federal court, in all cases where the act of

Confederation controuled the question, be as effectual a remedy, and exactly commensurate to the defect?"[58] Gouverneur Morris and Roger Sherman used much the same reasoning. On July 17, they agreed that judicial review, operating under the supremacy clause, was an effective substitute for the onerous legislative negative.[59]

The nationalists had won an unwitting victory. At the time, however, it seemed like another defeat. In the minds of nationalists, judicial review did not compensate for the loss of a legislative negative. . . . To the very end, Madison lamented the Convention's failure. Asked how a certain commercial problem would be handled, Madison replied on September 12:

> There will be the same security as in other cases. The jurisdiction of the supreme Court must be the source of redress. So far only had provision been made in the plan against injurious acts of the States. His own opinion was, that this was insufficient, — A negative on the State laws alone could meet all the shapes which these could assume. But this had been overruled.[60]

Madison's and Wilson's relentless protests clearly imply that the opposition had, in their judgment, once again undercut the foundations of Madison's "middle ground." Neither side anticipated that judicial review, operating through the supremacy clause and controlling state laws contravening the Constitution, might become a formidable check on any state action threatening national supremacy.

Unwittingly, the nationalists had partially recovered the losses they had incurred by the Connecticut Compromise. . . . National power and its supremacy — ingredients which both nationalists and their opponents thought had been undermined by the Connecticut Compromise — were restored by the combined operation of the supremacy clause, the necessary-and-proper clause, and judicial review. Both sides, still influenced by the implications of the Connecticut Compromise, seemed generally unaware of the restoration of national supremacy which took place after July 16. The necessary-and-proper clause passed unanimously, without debate. Despite the necessary-and-proper clause, Mason and Ellsworth believed, the Constitution drew a line between national and state power. "The United States will have a qualified sovereignty only," Mason declared. "The individual States will retain a part of the Sovereignty."[61] Ellsworth was even more specific: "The U.S. are sovereign on one side of the line dividing the jurisdictions — the States on the other — each ought to have power to defend their respective Sovereignties."[62]

Notwithstanding these apparent disclaimers, the Convention had provided for national supremacy. It remained to undercut the other denationalizing effect of the Connecticut Compromise: the claim of state sovereignty based on representation in the Senate. The question of whether ultimate sovereignty — the legitimate *source* of power allocated in the Constitution — would rest with the states or with the people came before the delegates for final decision on July 23. Resolution 15 of the Virginia Plan, providing for popular rather than state ratification of the proposed constitution, after only brief debate had been approved on June 12.[63] At that time, Madison and Wilson favored popular ratification on principle. Madison called the provision "essential." It was "indispensable that the new Constitution should be ratified in the most unexceptionable form and by the supreme authority of the people themselves." Sherman and Gerry, sensing the revolutionary implications, favored ratification by the state legislatures. The Articles of Confederation, Sherman pointed out, prescribed the proper method of ratification.[64]

It was now nearly two months since the Convention had begun. Passage of the Connecticut Compromise had rendered the issue of ratification more crucial than ever. Debate revealed the nationalists' sense of urgency. Ellsworth's motion, seconded by Paterson, took the form of reversing the prior decision. The New Jersey delegate moved that the proposed Constitution be referred to the state legislatures for ratification. . . .

Reverting to the fundamentals of 1776, Gouverneur Morris pointed out: "The amendmt. moved by Mr. Ellsworth erroneously supposes that we are proceeding on the basis of the Confederation. This Convention is unknown to the Confederation." Recognizing the revolutionary nature of popular ratification, Morris explained:

> . . . If the Confederation is to be pursued no alteration can be made without the unanimous consent of the Legislatures: Legislative alterations not conformable to the federal compact, would clearly not be valid. The Judges would consider them as null & void. Whereas in case of an appeal to the people of the U.S., the supreme authority, the federal compact may be altered by a *majority of them;* in like manner as the Constitution of a particular State may be altered by a majority of the people of the State. . . .[65]

After Morris' bold assertion of the *right* of peaceful revolution — the right of the people to alter or abolish an existing government and establish a new one — Madison spelled out the case for popular sovereignty. Involved was the distinction between a mere confederation and a constitution. He considered "the difference between a system founded on the Legislatures only, and one founded on the people, to be the true difference between a *league* or *treaty,* and a Constitution." [66]

Surprisingly — or perhaps understandably, in light of what advocates of state sovereignty thought they had won in the Connecticut Compromise — the sentiment in favor of popular ratification was much greater on this July 23 than it had been on July 12, when the provision was originally

approved. Then the vote had been 6–3–2.[67] Now the delegates turned down
Ellsworth's motion for state ratification by a vote of 7–3. By the overwhelming margin of 9–1 it was agreed to "refer the Const. after the approbation
of Congs. to assemblies chosen by the people." [68] Nationalists had won a
great victory. Notwithstanding equal state representation in one branch of
the national legislature, ultimate sovereignty by virtue of popular ratification would rest with the people.

Advocates of state ratification made a last attempt to recover. In the
discussion concerning the number of affirmative votes necessary to ratify the
Constitution, Luther Martin "insisted on a reference to the State Legislatures," and warned of "the danger of commotions from a resort to the people
& to first principles in which the Governments might be on one side & the
people on the other. . . ."[69] Madison brushed the Marylander's objections
lightly aside: "The people were in fact, the fountain of all power, and by
resorting to them, all difficulties were got over." The people ". . . could
alter constitutions as they pleased. It was a principle in the Bills of Rights,
that first principles might be resorted to." [70]

The Convention's decision to resort to "first principles" helped to
neutralize the disabling effects of the Connecticut Compromise. States had
not been abolished, but their role as constituent parts of the national government was reduced. National power had been strengthened and national
supremacy provided for in the supremacy clause, judicial review, and the
necessary-and-proper clause. Representation by states tainted the principle
of popular representation, but ratification by the people firmly imbued the
government with popular sovereignty. The dual foundations of state supremacy under the Articles — state power and state sovereignty — had been
considerably shaken. In their place the Constitution set the twin cornerstones
of national supremacy — indefinite national power and popular sovereignty.
Absence of any precise line circumscribing national power created the possibility that national supremacy *could* lead to an effectively "consolidated"
system. With the notable exception of Yates and Lansing who left Philadelphia on July 10, Antifederalists were slow to realize these ominous possibilities, nor were the nationalists more than dimly aware of them.

That neither side was completely satisfied with the finished document is quite understandable. Starting from positions poles apart, both sides
seemed blind to the significance of the Convention's actions following the
July 16 decision to endorse the Connecticut Compromise. Alert to the denationalizing effects of equal state representation, nationalists had opposed
it. And, ironically, their strenuous effort to safeguard national power by the
legislative veto met with ignominious defeat the day after the Connecticut
Compromise was adopted. If July 16, a Monday, seemed like "Black Monday," the next day must have appeared even gloomier. Madison, Hamilton,

Wilson, *et al.* had already tempered their more extreme desires. Now even Madison's "middle ground" seemed in jeopardy. A vital principle had, apparently, been vitiated. The nationalists never recovered from the shocks of July 16 and 17. The remainder of the Convention abounds with sentiments of their despair. The supremacy clause and judicial review, as a kind of substitute for the legislative negative, left much to be desired. Gloom pervades the letter Madison wrote to Jefferson on September 6, 1787:

> . . . The extent of them [the resolutions comprising the new Constitution] may perhaps surprise you. I hazard an opinion nevertheless that the *plan, should* it *be adopted,* will neither effectually *answer* its *national object,* not [nor] prevent the local *mischiefs* which everywhere *excite disgusts* agst. the *State Governments.* . . .[71]

Madison was not the only pessimist. Others looked hopefully to a second Convention to undo the Connecticut Compromise and reinstate the legislative negative. Charles Pinckney, who had earlier failed in his attempt to build up Randolph's original version of the negative, tried on August 23 to restore it. Failing, he also favored a second Convention.[72] On August 31, Gouverneur Morris and Edmund Randolph voiced similar hopes. Morris was "ready for a postponement. He had long wished for another Convention, that will have the firmness to provide a vigorous Government, which we are afraid to do." Randolph agreed.[73] Morris was simply reiterating his candid judgment of August 17, when he declared: "We are acting a very strange part. We first form a strong man to protect us, and at the same time wish to tie his hands behind him." [74] On the last day of the Convention, Hamilton confessed that:

> . . . No man's ideas were more remote from the plan than his own were known to be; but is it possible to deliberate between anarchy and Convulsion on one side, and the *chance* of good to be expected from the plan on the other.[75]

It seems odd that such profound disappointment should have engendered so little hope in the camp of the opposition. So deep was the cleavage that even modified positions, the more moderate stances involving concessions to the other side, were fundamentally opposed. If "consolidation" envisioned no states in effect, and if the Articles barely conceived of a national government, then these polar opposites were not much farther apart than were the Virginia and New Jersey Plans. Just as "consolidation" differed only in degree from the Virginia Plan, so the Articles differed only in degree from the New Jersey Plan.

In essence, then, the Virginia and New Jersey plans diverged as sharply as did "consolidation" and the Articles. Both the Virginia Plan and "consolidation" were rooted in the notion of popular sovereignty, whereas the New Jersey Plan and the Articles were based on state sovereignty. Beyond this crucial difference, the Virginia Plan and "consolidation" would have endowed the national government with indefinite, rather than limited, power. The presence or absence of a line delimiting national power in relation to state power constituted, therefore, the core of the difference between the competing positions. The very absence of this line in both the Virginia Plan and "consolidation" made for differences only of degree. National supremacy, based on indefinite national power, could become "consolidation." By the same token, the New Jersey Plan, premised on a line limiting national power *vis-à-vis* the states, could revert to the state supremacy under the Articles.

If these fundamental differences between the nationalists and the would-be Antifederalists appeared less than obvious after the fateful days of July 16 and 17, they were blurred by the effects of the Connecticut Compromise and the substitution of the supremacy clause for the legislative negative. Before the resolution of these issues, debate on equal state representation and on the legislative negative had brought into relatively clear focus basic cleavages — state sovereignty versus popular sovereignty; state supremacy versus national supremacy. The events of July 16 and 17 colored profoundly the rest of the Convention's work. The nationalists were convinced that they had suffered fatal defeats; the opposition, buoyed perhaps by the nationalists' disappointment and flushed by their apparent victories, were lulled into acceptance of the Constitution's most nationalizing provisions.

What emerged from this often ambiguous interplay was a document no less ambiguous. The Constitution reflects the conflicting influences and drives of latter-day Federalists and Antifederalists alike. History abundantly demonstrates the Constitution's incredible flexibility, lending itself to widely divergent interpretations, differences which always seem to turn on the presence or absence of that ubiquitous line purporting to delineate the spheres of national and state power. Antifederalists in the Convention at Philadelphia did not succeed in drawing that line. But their successors have contributed immeasurably to the seemingly endless dispute over its presence.

Men of Little Faith:
The Anti-Federalists on the
Nature of Representative Government

CECELIA M. KENYON

By the early 1950's, Charles Beard's assumption that the Constitution was the product of a conflict between creditors and government bond holders on one hand and debtors and farmers on the other was being attacked by historians who charged him with anachronistically viewing the late eighteenth-century world through Progressive eyes. One of the most important of these post–World War II critics was Cecelia Kenyon, who not only redirected long overdue historical attention to the Antifederalists but shifted the level of analysis from economic interests and motivations to ideas and ideologies — always a healthy antidote to the dangers of anachronism in historical writing. In examining the debates over the Constitution, Kenyon, Professor of Government at Smith College, laid bare the Antifederalists' fears and undermined the Beardian assumption that the Antifederalists were populist majoritarians opposed to the separation of powers and the checks and balances presumably endorsed by Federalists seeking to protect their minority property interests against rampaging legislatures. Whatever may have been the economic and social differences between the Federalists and Antifederalists, Kenyon argued, both shared a common heritage of Whig political thought that deeply mistrusted governmental power of all kinds, legislative as well as executive. Ultimately, she said, what distinguishes the Antifederalists from the Federalists was their lack of faith in the ability of Americans to create and sustain a large-scale continental republic.

One of the gravest defects of the late Charles Beard's economic interpretation of the Constitution is the limited perspective it has encouraged in those who have accepted it, and the block to fruitful investigation of the ideas and institutions of the Revolutionary Age to which it has been conducive. Like many theories influential in both the determination and the interpretation of historical events, Beard's thesis and its implications were

From Cecelia M. Kenyon, "Men of Little Faith: The Anti-Federalists on the Nature of Representative Government," *William and Mary Quarterly,* 3d Ser., 12 (1955), 3–43. Reprinted by permission.

never carefully analyzed either by himself or his followers. As a result, its impact on the study of American history produced certain effects not anticipated, which Beard himself must surely have regretted. The economic interpretation employed by him somewhat tentatively as a tool for analysis and research quickly became a methodological stereotype and led to a stereotypical appreciation of the Constitution and of the historical context in which it was created.

Beard's failure — perhaps it was deliberate refusal — to subject his thesis to rigorous analysis or to define it with precision makes it impossible to label him a clear-cut, thorough-going economic determinist. His position was always ambiguous and ambivalent, and in his later years he explicitly repudiated any monistic theory of causation.[1*] Nevertheless, the thrust of *An Economic Interpretation of the Constitution* and the effects of its thesis as applied have frequently been those of simple and uncritical commitment to a theory of economic determinism.

Of these effects, the most significant has been a disinclination to explore the theoretical foundations of the Constitution. In the chapter entitled "The Constitution as an Economic Document," Beard presented the structure of the government, particularly the system of separation of powers and checks and balances, as the institutional means chosen by the Founding Fathers to protect their property rights against invasion by democratic majorities.[2] This interpretation, or variations of it, has been widely accepted, though it has been frequently challenged both directly and indirectly.[3] Its tendency is to dispose of the institutional thought of the men who framed the Constitution as ideological response to economic interest. The present essay offers yet another challenge to this position, not by further examination of the Constitution or its authors, but by analysis of the Anti-Federalist position of 1787–1788.

Perhaps because theirs was the losing side, the political thought of the Anti-Federalists has received much less attention than that of the Founding Fathers. Since they fought the adoption of a Constitution which they thought to be aristocratic in origin and intent, and which by Beardian criteria was inherently anti-democratic in structure, there has been some tendency to characterize them as spokesmen of eighteenth-century democracy. But their theory of republican government has never been closely analyzed, nor have the areas of agreement and disagreement between them and the Federalists been carefully defined. It is the purpose of this essay to explore these topics. A very large proportion of the people in 1787–1788 *were* Anti-Federalists, and a knowledge of their ideas and attitudes is essential to an understanding of American political thought in the formative years of the republic.

* [See pp. 164–169 for notes to this article. — Ed.]

Implicit in this purpose is the thesis that the ideological context of the Constitution was as important in determining its form as were the economic interests and motivations of its framers, and that the failure of Beard and his followers to examine this context has rendered their interpretation of the Constitution and its origin necessarily partial and unrealistic.

Beard's conclusions rested on two assumptions or arguments. One was that the framers of the Constitution were motivated by their class and perhaps their personal economic interests; a great deal of evidence, drawn from more or less contemporary records, was presented to support this part of the thesis. A second assumption was that the system of separation of powers and checks and balances written into the Constitution was undemocratic. In making this second assumption Beard was more influenced by the ideas of the Populist and Progressive movements of his own time, I think, than by a study of the political beliefs current in 1787. He was preoccupied in 1913 with his period's interest in reforming the structure of the national government to make it more democratic, which by his standards meant more responsible to simple majority rule. Thus he judged an eighteenth-century frame of government by a twentieth-century political doctrine. The effect was to suggest by implication that the men who in 1787–1788 thought the Constitution aristocratic and antagonistic to popular government thought so for the same reasons as Beard.[4] The evidence shows clearly that their reasons were frequently and substantially different. These differences serve to illuminate the context of the Constitution and to illustrate the evolutionary character of American political thought.

At the center of the theoretical expression of Anti-Federalist opposition to increased centralization of power in the national government was the belief that republican government was possible only for a relatively small territory and a relatively small and homogeneous population. James Winthrop of Massachusetts expressed a common belief when he said, "The idea of an uncompounded republick, on an average one thousand miles in length, and eight hundred in breadth, and containing six millions of white inhabitants all reduced to the same standard of morals, of habits, and of laws, is in itself an absurdity, and contrary to the whole experience of mankind."[5] The last part of this statement, at least, was true; history was on the side of the Anti-Federalists. So was the authority of contemporary political thought. The name of Montesquieu carried great weight, and he had taught that republican governments were appropriate for small territories only. He was cited frequently, but his opinion would probably not have been accepted had it not reflected their own experience and inclinations. As colonials they had enjoyed self-government in colony-size packages only and had not sought to extend its operation empire-wise. It is significant that the various proposals for colonial representation in Parliament never grew deep roots during the debate preceding the Revolution. This association of self-government with relatively small geographical units reinforced Montesquieu's doctrine and led to further generalizations. A large republic was impossible, it was argued, because the center of government must necessarily be distant from the people. Their interest would then naturally decrease; and when this happened, "it would not suit the genius of the people to assist in the government," and "Nothing would support the government, in such a case as that, but military coercion." [6] Patrick Henry argued that republican government for a continent was impossible because it was "a work too great for human wisdom." [7]

Associated with the argument regarding size was the assumption that any people who were to govern themselves must be relatively homogeneous in interest, opinion, habits, and mores. The theme was not systematically explored, but it apparently stemmed from the political relativism prevalent at the time,[8] and from the recent experience of conflicts of interest between the colonies and Great Britain, and later between various states and sections of the new confederation.

It is not easy to measure the relative strength of national and state sentiment in either individuals or groups,[9] but it is clear that the Anti-Federalists were conscious of, and emphasized, the cultural diversity of the peoples in the thirteen states. They argued that no one set of laws could operate over such diversity. Said a Southerner, "We see plainly that men who come from New England are different from us." [10] He did not wish to be governed either with or by such men. Neither did the New Englanders wish to share a political roof with Southerners. "The inhabitants of warmer climates are more dissolute in their manners, and less industrious, than in colder countries. A degree of severity is, therefore, necessary with one which would cramp the spirit of the other. . . . It is impossible for one code of laws to suit Georgia and Massachusetts." [11] To place both types of men under the same government would be abhorrent and quite incompatible with the retention of liberty. Either the new government would collapse, or it would endeavor to stamp out diversity and level all citizens to a new uniformity in order to survive. Such was the reasoning of the leading New England publicist, James Winthrop. His indebtedness to Montesquieu is obvious. His failure to grasp the principles of the new federalism is also clear; for the purposes of this argument, and indeed for almost all of their arguments, he and his colleagues refused to consider the proposed government as one of limited, enumerated powers. They constantly spoke and wrote as if the scope and extent of its powers would be the same as those of the respective state governments, or of a unified national government.[12]

In addition to the absence of cultural homogeneity, the Anti-Federalists emphasized the clash of specific economic and political interests. These were primarily sectional,[13] and were of more acute concern in the South than in the North. In Virginia, for example, George Mason expressed the fear that the power of Congress to regulate commerce might be the South's downfall. In Philadelphia he had argued that this power be exercised by a two-thirds majority, and he now feared that by requiring only a simple majority "to make all commercial and navigation laws, the five southern states (whose produce and circumstances are totally different from those of the eight northern and eastern states) will be ruined. . . ." [14] It was also argued in several of the Southern conventions that a majority of the Eastern states might conspire to close the Mississippi,[15] and that they might eventually interfere with the institution of slavery.[16] In New England and the Middle states, there was less feeling that the interests of the entire section were in jeopardy, and therefore less discussion of these concrete issues and their divisive effect. One writer did strike out at the Federalist plea for a transcendent nationalism and repudiated the notion of sacrificing local interests to a presumed general interest as unrealistic and prejudicial to freedom. "It is vain to tell us that we ought to overlook local interests. It is only by protecting local concerns that the interest of the whole is preserved." He went on to stay that men entered into society for egoistic rather than altruistic motives, that having once done so, all were bound to contribute equally to the common welfare, and that to call for sacrifices of local interest was to violate this principle of equality and to subvert "the foundation of free government." [17]

There was much to be said for Winthrop's argument. It was an unequivocal statement of the principle that self-interest is the primary bond of political union. It was also an expression of an attitude which has always played a large part in our national politics: a refusal to sacrifice — sometimes even to subordinate — the welfare of a part to that of the whole. Pursuit of an abstract national interest has sometimes proved dangerous, and there was a healthy toughness in the Anti-Federalist insistence on the importance of local interests. But Winthrop skirted around the really difficult questions raised by his argument, which were also inherent in the Anti-Federalist position that the size of the United States and the diversity which existed among them were too great to be consistent with one republican government operating over the whole. No one would deny that a certain amount of unity or consensus is required for the foundation of popular, constitutional government; not very many people — now or in 1787 — would go as far as Rousseau and insist on virtually absolute identity of interest and opinion. The Anti-Federalists were surprisingly close to Rousseau and to the notions of republicanism which influenced him, but they were sensible, practical men and did not attempt to define their position precisely. Consequently they left untouched two difficult questions: how much, and what kind of unity is required for the foundation of any republican government, large or small; and how, in the absence of perfect uniformity, are differences of opinion and interest to be resolved?

The Anti-Federalist theory of representation was closely allied to the belief that republican government could operate only over a small area. The proposed Constitution provided that the first House of Representatives should consist of sixty-five members, and that afterwards the ratio of representation should not exceed one representative for thirty thousand people. This provision was vigorously criticized and was the chief component of the charge that the Constitution was not sufficiently democratic. The argument was two-fold: first, that sixty-five men could not possibly represent the multiplicity of interests spread throughout so great a country; second, that those most likely to be left out would be of the more democratic or "middling" elements in society. The minority who voted against ratification in the Pennsylvania Convention calculated that the combined quorums of the House and Senate was only twenty-five, and concluded that this number plus the President could not possibly represent "the sense and views of three or four millions of people, diffused over so extensive a territory, comprising such various climates, products, habits, interests, and opinions. . . ." [18] This argument, accompanied with the same calculus, was repeated many times during the ratification debate.

Almost all of the leaders of the opposition laid down what they believed to be the requisites of adequate representation, and there is a remarkable similarity in their definitions. George Mason, speaking in the Virginia Convention against giving the central government the power of taxation, based his argument on the inadequacy of representation as measured by his criteria: "To make representation real and actual, the number of representatives ought to be adequate; they ought to mix with the people, think as they think, feel as they feel, — ought to be perfectly amenable to them, and thoroughly acquainted with their interest and condition." [19] In his *Letters of a Federal Farmer,* Richard Henry Lee developed the same idea further:

> . . . a full and equal representation is that which possesses the same interests, feelings, opinions, and views the people themselves would were they all assembled — a fair representation, therefore, should be so regulated, that every order of men in the community, according to the common course of elections, can have a share in it — in order to allow professional men, merchants, traders, farmers, mechanics, etc. to bring a just proportion of their best informed men respectively into the legislature, the representation must be considerably numerous. [20]

It was the contention of the Anti-Federalists that because of the small size of the House of Representatives, the middle and lower orders in society would not be elected to that body, and that consequently this, the only popular organ of the government, would not be democratic at all. It would, instead, be filled by aristocrats, possibly by military heroes and demagogues.[21] Why should this be? Lee asserted simply that it would be "in the nature of things." Mason seems to have assumed it without any comment or argument. Patrick Henry reasoned that since the candidates would be chosen from large electoral districts rather than from counties, they would not all be known by the electors, and "A common man must ask a man of influence how he is to proceed, and for whom he must vote. The elected, therefore, will be careless of the interest of the electors. It will be a common job to extort the suffrages of the common people for the most influential characters." [22] This argument reflects one of the basic fears of the Anti-Federalists: loss of personal, direct contact with and knowledge of their representatives. They sensed quite accurately that an enlargement of the area of republican government would lead to a more impersonal system, and that the immediate, individual influence of each voter over his representative would be lessened.

The most elaborate explanation of the anticipated results of the electoral process was given by the moderate Anti-Federalist in New York, Melancton Smith. He argued that very few men of the "middling" class would choose to run for Congress, because the office would be "highly elevated and distinguished," the style.of living probably "high." Such circumstances would "render the place of a representative not a desirable one to sensible, substantial men, who have been used to walking in the plain and frugal paths of life." Even if such should choose to run for election, they would almost certainly be defeated. In a large electoral district it would be difficult for any but a person of "conspicuous military, popular, civil, or legal talents" to win. The common people were more likely to be divided among themselves than the great, and "There will be scarcely a chance of their uniting in any other but some great man, unless in some popular demagogue, who will probably be destitute of principle. A substantial yeoman, of sense and discernment, will hardly ever be chosen." [23] Consequently, the government would be controlled by the great, would not truly reflect the interests of all groups in the community, and would almost certainly become oppressive.

Anti-Federalists in Massachusetts were also uneasy about the capacity of the people to elect a legislature which would reflect their opinions and interests. The arguments emphasized geographical as well as class divisions, and expressed the fear and suspicion felt by the western part of the state toward Boston and the other coastal towns. It was predicted that the latter would enjoy a great advantage under the new system, and this prediction was supported by a shrewd analysis in the *Cornelius* Letter:

> The citizens in the seaport towns are numerous; they live compact; their interests are one; there is a constant connection and intercourse between them; they can, on any occasion, centre their votes where they please. This is not the case with those who are in the landed interest; they are scattered far and wide; they have but little intercourse and connection with each other. To concert uniform plans for carrying elections of this kind is entirely out of their way. Hence, their votes if given at all, will be no less scattered than are the local situations of the voters themselves. Wherever the seaport towns agree to centre their votes, there will, of course, be the greatest number. A gentleman in the country therefore, who may aspire after a seat in Congress, or who may wish for a post of profit under the federal government, must form his connections, and unite his interest with those towns. Thus, I conceive, a foundation is laid for throwing the whole power of the federal government into the hands of those who are in the mercantile interest; and for the landed, which is the great interest of this country to lie unrepresented, forlorn and without hope.[24]

What the Anti-Federalists feared, in other words, was the superior opportunities for organized voting which they felt to be inherent in the more thickly populated areas. They shared with the authors of *The Federalist* the fear of party and faction in the eighteenth-century American sense of those words. But they also feared, as the preceding analyses show, the essence of party in its modern meaning, i.e., organizing the vote, and they wanted constituencies sufficiently small to render such organization unnecessary.

This belief that larger electoral districts would inevitably be to the advantage of the well-to-do partially explains the almost complete lack of criticism of the indirect election of the Senate and the President. If the "middling" class could not be expected to compete successfully with the upper class in Congressional elections, still less could they do so in state-wide or nation-wide elections. It was a matter where size was of the essence. True representation — undistorted by party organization — could be achieved only where electoral districts were small.

The conception of the representative body as a true and faithful miniature of the people themselves was the projection of an ideal — almost a poetic one. Very few of its proponents thought it could actually be realized. In the Anti-Federalist attack on the Constitution, it served as a foil for an extraordinary picture of anticipated treachery on the part of the representatives to be elected under the proposed government. No distinction was made on the basis of their method of election, whether directly or indirectly by the people. All were regarded as potential tyrants.

This attack stemmed directly from the Anti-Federalist conception of human nature. They shared with their opponents many of the assumptions regarding the nature of man characteristic of American thought in the late eighteenth century. They took for granted that the dominant motive of human behavior was self-interest, and that this drive found its most extreme political expression in an insatiable lust for power. These were precisely the characteristics with which the authors of *The Federalist Papers* were pre-occupied.[25] Yet the Anti-Federalists chided the Federalists for their excessive confidence in the future virtue of elected officials, and criticized the Constitution for its failure to provide adequate protection against the operation of these tyrannical drives. There is surely an amusing irony to find the Founding Fathers, who prided themselves on their realism, and who enjoy an enviable reputation for that quality today, taken to task for excessive optimism. But they had to meet this charge again and again. Thus Caldwell in the North Carolina Convention found it "remarkable, — that gentlemen, as an answer to every improper part of it [the Constitution], tell us that every thing is to be done by our own representatives, who are to be good men. There is no security that they will be so, or continue to be so." [26] In New York Robert Lansing expressed the same feeling in a passage strikingly reminiscent of the famous paragraph in Madison's *Federalist* 51:

> Scruples would be impertinent, arguments would be in vain, checks would be useless, if we were certain our rulers would be good men; but for the virtuous government is not instituted: its object is to restrain and punish vice; and all free constitutions are formed with two views — to deter the governed from crime, and the governors from tyranny.[27]

This and many other similar statements might have been used interchangeably by either side in the debate, for they symbolized an attitude deeply embedded and widely dispersed in the political consciousness of the age. There were frequent references to "the natural lust of power so inherent in man";[28] to "the predominant thirst of dominion which has invariably and uniformly prompted rulers to abuse their power";[29] to "the ambition of man, and his lust for domination";[30] to rulers who would be "men of like passions," having "the same spontaneous inherent thirst for power with ourselves." [31] In Massachusetts, another delegate said, "we ought to be jealous of rulers. All the godly men we read of have failed; nay, he would not trust a 'flock of Moseses.' " [32]

It is to be noted that this dreadful lust for power was regarded as a universal characteristic of the nature of man, which could be controlled but not eradicated. The Anti-Federalists charged that the authors of the Constitution had failed to put up strong enough barriers to block this inevitably corrupting and tyrannical force. They painted a very black picture indeed of what the national representatives might and probably would do with the unchecked power conferred upon them under the provisions of the new Constitution. The "parade of imaginary horribles" has become an honorable and dependable technique of political debate, but the marvelous inventiveness of the Anti-Federalists has rarely been matched. Certainly the best achievements of their contemporary opponents were conspicuously inferior in dramatic quality, as well as incredibly unimaginative in dull adherence to at least a semblance of reality. The anticipated abuses of power, some real, some undoubtedly conjured as ammunition for debate, composed a substantial part of the case against the Constitution, and they must be examined in order to get at the temper and quality of Anti-Federalist thought as well as at its content. Their source was ordinarily a distorted interpretation of some particular clause.

One clause which was believed to lay down a constitutional road to legislative tyranny was Article I, Section 4: "The times, places, and manner of holding elections for senators and representatives, shall be prescribed in each state by the legislature thereof; but the Congress may, at any time, by law, make or alter such regulations, except as to the places of choosing senators." Here was the death clause of republican government. "This clause may destroy representation entirely," said Timothy Bloodworth of North Carolina.[33] If Congress had power to alter the times of elections, Congress might extend its tenure of office from two years to four, six, eight, ten, twenty, "or even for their natural lives." [34] Bloodworth and his colleagues feared the worst. In Massachusetts, where debate over this clause occupied a day and a half, the primary fear was that Congress, by altering the places of election, might rig them so as to interfere with a full and free expression of the people's choice. Pierce suggested that Congress could "direct that the election for Massachusetts shall be held in Boston," and then by pre-election caucus, Boston and the surrounding towns could agree on a ticket "and carry their list by a major vote." [35] In the same state the delegate who would not trust "a flock of Moseses" argued thus: "Suppose the Congress should say that none should be electors but those worth 50 or a £100 sterling; cannot they do it? Yes, said he, they can; and if any lawyer . . . can beat me out of it, I will give him ten guineas."[36] In Virginia, George Mason suggested that Congress might provide that the election in Virginia should be held only in Norfolk County, or even "go farther, and say that the election for all the states might be had in New York. . . ." [37] Patrick Henry warned, "According to the mode prescribed, Congress may tell you that they have a right to make the vote of one gentleman go as far as the votes of a hundred poor men." [38]

Any of these acts would have been a flagrant abuse of power, but no more so than that which Mason and others predicted under Article II, Section 2, which gave to the President the power to make treaties with the advice and consent of two-thirds of the senators present. This power was believed to be fraught with danger, particularly among Southerners, who feared that the majority of Northern states might use it to give up American rights of navigation on the Mississippi. The North would not have a two-thirds majority of the entire Senate, of course, but Mason suggested that when a "partial" treaty was involved, the President would not call into session senators from distant states, or those whose interests would be affected adversely, but only those he knew to be in favor of it.[39] His colleague, William Grayson, suggested the similarly treacherous prospect of such a treaty's being rushed through while members from the Southern states were momentarily absent from the floor of the Senate: "If the senators of the Southern States be gone but one hour, a treaty may be made by the rest. . . ." [40]

This fear at least had some foundation in fact — there *was* a conflict of interest between North and South over the Mississippi. It would seem that the fear expressed in North Carolina by Abbott on behalf of "the religious part of the society" was pure fantasy: "It is feared by some people, that, by the power of making treaties, they might make a treaty engaging with foreign powers to adopt the Roman Catholic religion in the United States. . . ." [41]

This was not the only provision objected to by "the religious part of the society." They were greatly displeased with the last clause of Article VI, Section 3: "but no religious test shall ever be required as a qualification to any office or public trust under the United States." In the same speech quoted above, Abbott reported, presumably on behalf of his constituents, "The exclusion of religious tests is by many thoughts dangerous and impolitic." For without such, "They suppose . . . pagans, deists, and Mahometans might obtain offices among us, and that the senators and representatives might all be pagans." [42] David Caldwell thought that the lack of a religious qualification constituted "an invitation for Jews and pagans of every kind to come among us," and that since the Christian religion was acknowledged to be the best for making "good members of society . . . those gentlemen who formed this Constitution should not have given this invitation to Jews and heathens." [43] Federalist James Iredell reported a pamphlet in circulation "in which the author states, as a very serious danger, that the pope of Rome might be elected President." [44] This unwittingly placed fresh ammunition at the disposal of the opposition. An Anti-Federalist admitted that he had not at first perceived this danger and conceded that it was not an immediate one. "But," said he, "let us remember that we form a government for millions not yet in existence. I have not the art of divination. In the course of four or five hundred years, I do not know how it will work. This is most certain, that Papists may occupy that chair, and Mahometans may take it. I see nothing against it. There is a disqualification, I believe, in every state in the Union — it ought to be so in this system." [45]

It is to be noted that these fears were fears of the majority of electors as well as of their elected representatives, and that these statements can hardly be said to glow with the spirit of liberty and tolerance. These beliefs were undoubtedly not shared by all Anti-Federalists, but they would not have been expressed so vigorously in the convention debates had they not represented a sizeable segment of constituent opinion.

Another provision, severely and dramatically critized was that which gave to Congress exclusive jurisdiction over the future site of the national capital and other property to be purchased for forts, arsenals, dockyards, and the like.[46] It was predicted that the ten-mile square area would become an enormous den of tyranny and iniquity. In New York George Clinton warned "that the ten miles square . . . would be the asylum of the base, idle, avaricious and ambitious. . . ." [47] In Virginia Patrick Henry pointed out that this provision, combined with the necessary and proper clause, gave Congress a right to pass "any law that may facilitate the execution of their acts," and within the specified area to hang "any man who shall act contrary to their commands . . . without benefit of clergy." [48] George Mason argued that the place would make a perfect lair for hit-and-run tyrants. For if any of the government's "officers, or creatures, should attempt to oppress the people, or should actually perpetuate the blackest deed, he has nothing to do but get into the ten miles square. Why was this dangerous power given?" [49] One man observed that the Constitution did not specify the location of this site, and that therefore Congress was perfectly free to seat itself and the other offices of government in Peking. All in all, a terrible prospect: the Pope as President, operating from a base in Peking, superintending a series of hangings without benefit of clergy! Or worse.

There was no bill of rights in the Constitution. This caused genuine fear for the security of some of the liberties thus left unprotected. The fear itself, though real and well founded, frequently found expression in melodramatically picturesque terms. The Anti-Federalists sometimes mentioned freedom of the press and freedom of conscience,[50] but they were primarily preoccupied with the failure of the Constitution to lay down the precious and venerable common-law rules of criminal procedure. The Constitution guaranteed the right of trial by jury in all criminal cases[51] except impeachment, but it did not list the procedural safeguards associated with that right. There was no specification that the trial should be not merely in the state but in the vicinity where the crime was committed (which was habitually identified with the neighborhood of the accused); there were no provisions made for the selection of the jury or of the procedure to be followed; there were no guarantees of the right to counsel, of the right not to incriminate oneself; there was no prohibition against cruel and unusual punishments. In short, there were few safeguards upon which the citizen accused of crime could rely.[52] Apprehension concerning the latitude left to Congress in this matter was expressed in several conventions;[53] it was Holmes of Massachusetts who painted the most vivid and fearful picture of the possible fate of the unfortunate citizen who ran afoul of federal law. Such an individual might be taken away and tried by strangers far from home; his jury might be handpicked by the sheriff, or hold office for life; there was no guarantee that indictment should be by grand jury only, hence it might be by information of the attorney-general, "in consequence of which the most innocent person in the commonwealth may be . . . dragged from his home, his friends, his acquaintance, and confined in prison. . . ." "On the whole," said Holmes, ". . . we shall find Congress possessed of powers enabling them to institute judicatories little less inauspicious than a certain tribunal in Spain, which has long been the disgrace of Christendom: I mean that diabolical institution, the *Inquisition*. . . . They are nowhere restrained from inventing the most cruel and unheard-of punishments and annexing them to crimes; and there is no constitutional check on them, but that *racks* and *gibbets* may be amongst the most mild instruments of their discipline." [54]

Should Congress have attempted any of these actions, it would have amounted to a virtual *coup d'état* and a repudiation of republicanism.[55] The advocates of the Constitution argued that such abuse of power could not reasonably be expected on the part of representatives elected by the people themselves. This argument was not satisfactory to the Anti-Federalists. They reiterated again and again the universal perfidy of man, especially men entrusted with political power, and emphasized the necessity of providing adequate protection against manifestations of human depravity. They charged that the authors and advocates of the Constitution were about to risk their liberties and those of all of the people on the slim possibility that the men to be elected to office in the new government would be, and would always be, good men.[56]

The Federalists also argued that election would serve as a check, since the people could remove unfaithful or unsatisfactory representatives, and since knowledge of this would make the latter refrain from incurring the displeasure of their constituents. This argument was flatly rejected. Patrick Henry stated his position emphatically during the course of his objection to Congressional power of taxation:

> I shall be told in this place, that those who are to tax us are our repre-
> sentatives. To this I answer, that there is no real check to prevent their
> ruining us. There is no actual responsibility. The only semblance of a
> check is the negative power of not re-electing them. This, sir, is but a
> feeble barrier, when their personal interest, their ambition and avarice,
> come to be put in contrast with the happiness of the people. All checks
> founded on anything but self-love, will not avail.[57]

In North Carolina the same opinion was expressed in a rather remarkable interchange. Taylor objected to the method of impeachment on the ground that since the House of Representatives drew up the bill of indictment, and the Senate acted upon it, the members of Congress themselves would be virtually immune to this procedure. Governor Johnston answered that impeachment was not an appropriate remedy for legislative misrule, and that "A representative is answerable to no power but his constituents. He is accountable to no being under heaven but the people who appointed him." To this, Taylor responded simply, "that it now appeared to him in a still worse light than before." [58] Johnston stated one of the great principles of representative government; it merely deepened Taylor's fear of Congress. He and his fellow Anti-Federalists strongly wished for what Madison had referred to as "auxiliary precautions" against possible acts of legislative tyranny.

These additional safeguards were of two kinds: more explicit limitations written into the Constitution, and more institutional checks to enforce these limitations.

In recent years the Constitution has been much admired for its brevity, its generality, its freedom from the minutiae which characterized nineteenth-century constitutions. These qualities were feared and not admired by the Anti-Federalists. They wanted detailed explicitness which would confine the discretion of Congressional majorities within narrow boundaries. One critic complained of "a certain darkness, duplicity and studied ambiguity of expression running through the whole Constitution. . . ." [59] Another said that "he did not believe there existed a social compact on the face of the earth so vague and so indefinite as the one now on the table." [60] A North Carolinian demanded to know, "Why not use expressions that were clear and unequivocal?" [61] Later, he warned, "Without the most express restrictions, Congress may trample on your rights." [62] Williams of New York expressed the general feeling when he said in that state's convention, "I am, sir, for certainty in the establishment of a constitution which is not only to operate upon us, but upon millions yet unborn." [63] These men wanted everything down in black and white, with no latitude of discretion or interpretation left to their representatives in Congress. It was an attitude which anticipated the later trend toward lengthy constitutions filled with innumerable and minute restrictions on the legislatures.

To no avail did the Federalists argue that if future representatives should indeed prove to be so treacherous and tyrannical as to commit the horrible deeds suggested, then mere guarantees on paper would not stop them for a minute. It is easy to call the Anti-Federalist attitude unrealistic, but to do so is to miss a large part of its significance. Like the Founding Fathers, like all men of their age, they were great constitutionalists. They were also first-generation republicans, still self-consciously so, and aware that their precious form of government was as yet an experiment and had not proved its capacity for endurance. Its greatest enemy was man's lust for power, and the only thing which could hold this in check, they were convinced, was a carefully written and properly constructed constitution. They placed even greater emphasis on the structure of government than did the Founding Fathers, and refused to take for granted, as the latter did, that the "genius" of the country was republican, and that the behavior of the men to be placed in office would in general be republican also.

The Anti-Federalists wanted a more rigid system of separation of powers, more numerous and more effective checks and balances, than the Founding Fathers had provided.[64] They thought this elementary principle of good government, this "political maxim," had been violated, and that corruption leading to tyranny would be the inevitable result. That the doctrine celebrated by Montesquieu did enjoy the status of "maxim" seems unquestionable. Violation of separation of powers was one of George Mason's major objections to the Constitution.[65] Richard Henry Lee made the same protest,[66] and further lamented that there were no "checks in the formation of the government, to secure the rights of the people against the usurpations of those they appoint to govern. . . ." [67] James Monroe said that he could "see no real checks in it." [68] It is no wonder that an obscure member of the Virginia Convention, when he rose with great diffidence to make his only speech, chose safe and familiar grounds to cover:

> That the legislature, executive, and judicial powers should be separate and distinct, in all free governments, is a political fact so well established, that I presume I shall not be thought arrogant, when I affirm that no country ever did, or ever can, long remain free, where they are blended. All the states have been in this sentiment when they formed their state constitutions, and therefore have guarded against the danger; and every schoolboy in politics must be convinced of the propriety of the observation; and yet, by the proposed plan, the legislative and executive powers are closely united. . . .[69]

In Pennsylvania, whose Revolutionary state constitution had embodied very little of separation of powers, an apparent return to Montesquieu's doctrine led to criticism of the Constitution. In the ratifying convention, one of the amendments submitted had for its purpose "That the legislative, executive, and judicial powers be kept separate. . . ." [70] In that same state, the leading Anti-Federalist pamphleteer "Centinel," who is believed to have been either George Bryan, a probable co-author of the 1776 Constitution and formerly in sympathy with the ideas of Tom Paine on this subject, or his son Samuel, now expressed himself in the usual manner:

This mixture of the legislative and executive moreover highly tends to corruption. The chief improvement in government, in modern times, has been the complete separation of the great distinctions of power; placing the *legislative* in different hands from those which hold the *executive;* and again severing the *judicial* part from the ordinary *administrative.* "When the legislative and executive powers (says Montesquieu) are united in the same person, or in the same body of magistrates, there can be no liberty." [71]

The Anti-Federalists were just as unequivocal about the inadequacy of the Constitution's system of checks and balances. Patrick Henry hit his top form when he took up the matter in Virginia: "There will be no checks, no real balances, in this government. What can avail your specious, imaginary balances, your rope-dancing, chain-rattling, ridiculous ideal checks and contrivances?" [72] Later in the Convention he argued that what checks there were had no practical value at all — for reasons which must cloud his reputation as a spokesman for the masses imbued with the radical spirit of Revolutionary democracy: "To me it appears that there is no check in that government. The President, senators, and representatives, all, immediately or mediately, are the choice of the people.[73] His views were echoed by his colleague, William Grayson.[74]

In New York, Melancton Smith returned to the subject several times, arguing, because there would eventually be corruption in Congress. "It is wise to multiply checks to a greater degree than the present state of things requires." [75] In Massachusetts James Winthrop tied up the concept of separation of powers with checks and balances very neatly. "It is now generally understood that it is for the security of the people that the powers of the government should be lodged in different branches. By this means publick business will go on when they all agree, and stop when they disagree. The advantage of checks in government is thus manifested where the concurrence of different branches is necessary to the same act. . . ." [76]

There can be little doubt that the Anti-Federalists were united in their desire to put more checks on the new government. This was natural, since they greatly feared it. Expressions of the opposite opinion were extremely rare. Rawlins Lowndes in South Carolina remarked casually and without elaboration that it was possible to have too many checks on a government.[77] George Clinton and the Pennsylvanian "Centinel" both warned that a government might become so complex that the people could not understand it,[78] but both men expressed the usual fear of abuse of power,[79] and "Centinel" paid his respects to Montesquieu and explicitly criticized the inadequacy of checks by the President or the House of Representatives on the Senate.[80]

Thus no one, so far as I have been able to discover, attacked the general validity of the system of separation of powers and checks and balances. The Anti-Federalists were staunch disciples of Montesquieu on this subject, and they would have found quite unacceptable J. Allen Smith's dictum that "The system of checks and balances must not be confused with democracy; it is opposed to and cannot be reconciled with the theory of popular government."[81]

Although there was much oratory about the Founding Fathers' deviation from Montesquieu's doctrine, there were surprisingly few proposals for specific alterations in the structure of the new government. Of these, the most important was a change in the relationship between President and Senate. The latter's share in the treaty-making and appointing powers was believed to be a dangerous blending of executive and legislative power which ought to have been avoided. Possibly because of their recent memory of the role of the colonial governor's council, possibly because there was no clear provision in the Constitution for an executive cabinet or council, the Anti-Federalists saw the Senate very much in the latter's role and expected it to play a very active and continuous part in giving advice to the President. This was clearly contrary to the doctrine of the celebrated Montesquieu — at least it seemed so to them.

The result would certainly be some form of joint Presidential-Senatorial tyranny, it was argued, but as to which of the two departments would be the stronger of the "partners in crime," the Anti-Federalists were not agreed. Patrick Henry said that the President, with respect to the treaty-making power, "as distinguished from the Senate, is nothing." [82] Grayson, with the North-South division in mind, predicted a *quid pro quo* alliance between the President and "the seven Eastern states." "He will accommodate himself to their interests in forming treaties, and they will continue him perpetually in office." [83] Mason predicted a "marriage" between the President and Senate: "They will be continually supporting and aiding each other: they will always consider their interest as united. . . . The executive and legislative powers, thus connected, will destroy all balances. . . ."[84] "Centinel" of Pennsylvania also feared that the President would not be strong enough to resist pressure from the Senate, and that he would join with them as "the head of the aristocratic junto." [85] Spencer of North Carolina, in support of a remedy in which all of the above men concurred, argued that with an advisory council entirely separate from the legislature, and chosen from the separate states, the President "would have that independence which is necessary to form the intended check upon the acts passed by the legislature before they obtain the sanction of laws." [86]

Although the prevailing opinion thus seemed to be that the President was not strong enough, there were some who believed that he was too strong. George Clinton argued that the extensive powers given to him, combined with his long tenure of office, gave him both "power and time sufficient to ruin his country." Furthermore, since he had no proper council to assist him while the Senate was recessed, he would be without advice, or get it from "minions and favorites" — or "a great council of state will grow out of the principal officers of the great departments, the most dangerous council in a free country." [87]

One man in North Carolina, the only one to the best of my knowledge, departed from the ordinary Anti-Federalist line of attack and criticized the executive veto from a clear majoritarian position. It was Lancaster, who projected the hypothetical case of a bill which passed the House of Representatives unanimously, the Senate by a large majority, was vetoed by the President and returned to the Senate, where it failed to get a two-thirds vote. The House would never see it again, said Mr. Lancaster, and thus, "This is giving a power to the President to overrule fifteen members of the Senate and every member of the House of Representatives." [88]

Except for Lancaster, most Anti-Federalists feared the Senate more than the President, but all feared the two in combination and wanted some checks against them. The separate advisory council for the President was one, and shorter terms and/or compulsory rotation for Senators and President, plus the power of state recall of the former, were others. Direct, popular election of either was *not* proposed.

Since most of the state executives and legislators held office for annual or biennial terms, one would naturally expect the substantially longer tenure of the President and Senate to be severely criticized. There were numerous objections to the six-year term of Senators, some to the four-year term of the President, and a few to the two-year term of members of the House of Representatives. It is to be noted, however, that there was no serious attempt to shorten the length of term of any of these officers, nor was there any attempt to make the tenure of either the President or the Senate correspond with that of the House. It was agreed that the two houses should "afford a mutual check" on each other,[89] and that the "stability" provided by the Senate "was essential to good government." [90]

The most insistent and repeated criticism was the failure of the Constitution to provide for the compulsory rotation of office for Senators and the President. "Nothing is so essential to the preservation of a republican government as a periodical rotation," said George Mason,[91] and Melancton Smith pronounced it "a very important and truly republican institution." [92] They greatly feared that President and Senators would be perpetually re-elected, and in effect hold office for life. Mason, for example, was quite content for the Senate to serve six years, and the President even eight, but he believed that without rotation, the new government would become "an elective monarchy." [93] The President would be able to perpetuate himself forever, it was assumed, because his election would always be thrown into the House of Representatives. In that body, corruption, intrigue, foreign influence, and above all else, the incumbent's use of his patronage, would make it possible for every man, once elected, to hold office for life. Senators would "hold their office perpetually," [94] by corrupting their electors, the state legislatures. In New York, where the subject was debated very thoroughly, the Anti-Federalists were challenged to show how such corruption could take place, and continue for life, among a group which was continuously subject to popular election, and which would presumably not be permanent. To this challenge Lansing replied, "It is unnecessary to particularize the numerous ways in which public bodies are accessible to corruption. The poison always finds a channel, and never wants an object." [95] No distinction as to comparative corruptibility was made between national and state representatives.

To Federalist objections that compulsory rotation constituted an abridgment of the people's right to elect whomsoever they wished. Melancton Smith replied impatiently, "What is government itself but a restraint upon the natural rights of the people? What constitution was ever devised that did not operate as a restraint on their natural liberties?" [96] Lansing conceded that rotation placed a restriction on the people's free choice of rulers, but he thought this beneficial: "The rights of the people will be best supported by checking, at a certain point, the current of popular favor, and preventing the establishment of an influence which may leave to elections little more than the form of freedom." [97]

The power of recall by state legislatures was associated with compulsory rotation as a means of preventing senatorial abuse of power. Not only would it enforce strict responsibility of senators to their electors, but in so doing it would protect the interests and preserve the sovereignty of the separate states. For these reasons, its adoption was strongly pressed in several of the ratifying conventions. Beyond these reasons, which were primary, recall combined with rotation would have a secondary beneficent result. It would serve to prevent the perpetuation of intra-legislative parties and factions — something which the Anti-Federalists feared quite as much as their opponents. Even if the power of recall should not actually be used, said Lansing, it would "destroy party spirit." [98] When his opponents turned this argument against him, and suggested that factions within the state legislatures might use the power to remove good, honorable, and faithful men from the Senate, the answer was that the legislatures had not abused the power under the Articles of Confederation and would almost certainly not do so in the future, and that even if they did, ample opportunity would be provided for the displaced senator to defend himself. The influence of "ambitious and designing men" would be detected and exposed, and the error easily corrected.[99] A curious "Trust them, trust them not" attitude toward the state legislatures is thus revealed. They could not be trusted to refuse re-election to unfaithful or ambitious senators, though they could be trusted to remove the same and to leave in office all those who deserved well of them and of their constituents.

From this it is clear that the Anti-Federalists were not willing to trust either upper or lower house of the proposed national Congress; neither were they willing to trust their own state legislatures completely, though they had less fear of the latter because these could be kept under closer observation.

The same attitude is indicated by Anti-Federalist reaction to the restrictions placed on state legislatures by Article I, Section 10 of the Constitution, and to the then potential review of both state and national legislation by the Supreme Court.

Of the latter prospect, frequently said to have been one of the great bulwarks erected against the democratic majority, very little was said during the ratification debate. There was no explicit provision for judicial review in the Constitution, and it is probably not possible to prove conclusively whether or not its authors intended the Supreme Court to exercise this power. The evidence suggests that they probably assumed it would. Hamilton's *Federalist* 78 supports this view. The issue was never debated in the state conventions, and there are almost no references to it in any of the Anti-Federalist arguments. Since *Federalist* 78 was published before the Virginia, New York, and North Carolina Conventions met, this lack of discussion is significant and would seem to reflect lack of concern. There was severe criticism of Article III, particularly in Virginia, but it centered around the jurisdiction of the lower federal courts to be established by Congress, not around the Supreme Court. The issue was entirely one of state courts versus federal courts, not of courts versus legislatures.

The single direct reference to judicial review made in the Virginia Convention — at least the only one I have found — suggests that this institution was, or would have been, thoroughly congenial to the Anti-Federalists. The statement was made by Patrick Henry:

> Yes, sir, our judges opposed the acts of the legislature. We have this landmark to guide us. They had fortitude to declare that they were the judiciary, and would oppose unconstitutional acts. Are you sure that your federal judiciary will act thus? Is that judiciary as well constructed, and as independent of the other branches, as our state judiciary? Where are your landmarks in this government? I will be bold to say you cannot find any in it. I take it as the highest encomium on this country, that the acts of the legislature, if unconstitutional, are liable to be opposed by the judiciary.[100]

There was nothing equivocal about Henry's attitude. It elicited no comment. Possibly neither side wished to commit itself; more likely the statement was lost and forgotten after brighter flames had issued from the great orator's fire. What is really significant, however, is the complete absence of debate over judicial review. The Anti-Federalists probed the Constitution for every conceivable threat, explicit or implicit, to their conception of free and popular government. If they had considered judicial review such a threat, they would surely have made the most of it, and particularly after *Federalist* 78 was published.

There was also comparatively little attention given to the restrictions which Article I, Section 10 of the Constitution placed on the state legislatures. Among other things, the states were forbidden to coin money, emit bills of credit, make anything but gold or silver legal tender for the payment of debts, or pass any law impairing the obligations of contracts. These are the provisions which recent historians have emphasized as designed to protect the property of the conservative class against the onslaughts of the radical democratic majority. The Anti-Federalists had very little to say about these provisions. The notation of the New York Convention's action is significant: "The committee then proceded through sections 8, 9, and 10, of this article [I], and the whole of the next, with little or no debate." [101] In Virginia and the Carolinas there was more discussion, but nothing like a full-dress debate, and very little indication of any strong or widespread opposition. In fact, Patrick Henry said that the restrictions were "founded in good principles," [102] and William Grayson said of the prohibition against paper money, "it is unanimously wished by every one that it should not be objected to." [103] Richard Henry Lee expressed his preference for paper money to be issued by Congress only.[104] Of the few objections or doubts expressed, these were typical. Henry in Virginia and Galloway in North Carolina both expressed a fear that the contract clause might be interpreted to force the states to redeem their respective shares of the depreciated Continental currency and of state securities at face value.[105] Henry was also angry because of the necessary implication that the states were too "depraved" to be trusted with the contracts of their own citizens.[106] With regard to the prohibition of paper money, two men in North Carolina defended the previous state issue as having been a necessary expedient in troublesome times, but did not seem to object to the prohibition of future issues.[107] One man argued against this clause and the supreme law clause on the ground that the effect might be to destroy the paper money already in circulation and thereby create great confusion.[108] His contention was denied.[109] These remarks, none of which expressed direct opposition, were typical. In South Carolina, however, Rawlins Lowndes came out flatly against this restriction, defended the previous issue of paper money and the right of the state to make further issues in the future.[110] His position appears to have been the exception, at least of those which were expressed openly and publicly on the various convention floors.[111]

The response of the Anti-Federalists to these important limitations on the power of the states can accurately be described, I think, as one of overall approbation tempered by some doubts caused by fear that they would be applied retroactively. This attitude is in rather curious contrast with the extremely jealous reaction to other changes in federal-state relations for which the Constitution provided. There were violent objections to federal control over state militia, to Congressional power to tax and to regulate commerce, to the creation of an inferior system of federal courts. All these things brought forth loud cries that the states would be swallowed up by the national government. These important restrictions on the economic powers of the states were received with relative silence. There was apparently very little objection to these limitations on the power of state legislative majorities.

It remains to consider the extent to which the general Anti-Federalist distrust of their representatives, particularly those who were to serve in the national government but also those who served in their state legislatures, reflected also a distrust of the majorities who elected them, that is to say, of the people themselves. The answer is partly wrapped up in the whole complex of ideas constituting the Anti-Federalist conception of republican government, which I shall attempt to draw together in the concluding section of this essay. Some parts of the answer can be put into the record here.

The attitude of the Anti-Federalists toward the people as distinguished from their representatives, and toward the general problem of majority rule, was not radically different from that of their opponents. It is a curious and remarkable fact that during the course of this great debate in which the most popular national constitution ever framed was submitted to the public for the most popular mode of ratification yet attempted, there was very little tendency on either side to enthrone "the people" or to defer automatically to their judgment. Neither side showed the slightest inclination to use as its slogan, "Vox populi vox Dei." Rather was the contrary true, and some of the Anti-Federalist expressions of this attitude could easily have fitted into the dark picture of human nature presented in *The Federalist*. Indeed, the speeches and essays of the Anti-Federalists were peculiarly lacking in the great expressions of faith in the people which are to be found in the writings of Jefferson, and even occasionally in *The Federalist* itself. This is partly to be accounted for because their position was a negative one; they attacked the proposed system on the ground that it would be destructive of liberty.

It was therefore perhaps natural that they sometimes expressed fear about what may be called the constituent capacity of the people — the capacity of the people to act wisely in the actual choice of a constitution. They were afraid that the people might not see in the proposed new government all of the dangers and defects which they themselves saw. And there were gloomy comments about lack of stability. Said George Clinton in the New York Convention, "The people, when wearied with their distresses, will in the moment of frenzy, be guilty of the most imprudent and desperate measures. . . . I know the people are too apt to vibrate from one extreme to another. The effects of this disposition are what I wish to guard against." [112] His colleague, Melancton Smith, spoke in a similar vein:

> Fickleness and inconstancy, he said, were characteristic of a free people; and, in framing a constitution for them, it was, perhaps, the most difficult thing to correct this spirit, and guard against the evil effects of it. He was persuaded it could not be altogether prevented without destroying their freedom. . . . This fickle and inconstant spirit was the more dangerous in bringing about changes in the government.[113]

It was "Centinel," author or son of the author of Pennsylvania's revolutionary Constitution, who expressed the gravest doubts about the capacity of the people to make a wise choice in the form of government, and who expounded a kind of Burkeian conservatism as the best guarantor of the people's liberties. In a passage apparently aimed at the prestige given to the proposed Constitution by the support of men like Washington and Franklin, "Centinel" wrote that "the science of government is so abstruse, that few are able to judge for themselves." Without the assistance of those "who are competent to the task of developing the principles of government," the people were "too apt to yield an implicit assent to the opinions of those characters whose abilities are held in the highest esteem, and to those in whose integrity and patriotism they can confide. . . ." This was dangerous, because such men might easily be dupes, "the instruments of despotism in the hands of the *artful and designing*." "Centinel" then continued:

> If it were not for the stability and attachment which time and habit gives to forms of government, it would be in the power of the enlightened and aspiring few, if they should combine, at any time to destroy the best establishments, and even make the people the instruments of their own subjugation.
>
> The late revolution having effaced in a great measure all former habits, and the present institutions are so recent, that there exists not that great reluctance to innovation, so remarkable in old communities, and which accords with reason, for the most comprehensive mind cannot foresee the full operation of material changes on civil polity; it is the genius of the common law to resist innovation.[114]

Later in the same series of articles, "Centinel" pronounced "this reluctance to change" as "the greatest security of free governments, and the principal bulwark of liberty." [115] This attitude provides an interesting comparison with the unquestioning assumption in the Federal Convention that the proposed Constitution would be submitted to the people for their verdict, and with the level of popular understanding of political affairs to which the essays of the *Federalist Papers* were addressed.

Serious reservations about the capacity of the people as electors were implicit in several of the arguments noted above. The advocacy of religious qualifications for office-holding indicated a desire to restrict the choice of the electorate to certified Protestants, and the demand for compulsory rotation of senators and President rested on the fear that corruption of both state and national legislatures by the incumbents of those offices could not be prevented by the feeble check of popular election. Perhaps most important was the belief that the people, voting in the large constituencies provided for by the Constitution, would either lose elections to their presumed aristocratic opponents because of the latter's superior capacity for organization, or would themselves let their choice fall on such aristocrats, or be deceived by ambitious and unscrupulous demagogues.

There was no more confidence in the inherent justice of the will of the majority than there was in its electoral capacity. Since the Anti-Federalists were skeptical that constituent opinion would be adequately reflected in the national legislature, they were less inclined than the Federalists to regard the government as the instrument of the people or of the majority. When they did so, there was not the slightest tendency to consider its decisions "right" *because* they were majority decisions. Rather was there always some standard of right and justice, independent of the majority's will, to which that will ought to conform. The Anti-Federalists were perfectly consistent in their conception of political behavior and did not regard a majority as superior to the sum of its parts, that is to say, of individual men motivated by self-interest and subject to a natural lust for power. There was very little discussion of majority rule and minority rights as fundamental principles of representative government, but the general attitude of the Anti-Federalists is, I think, reasonably clear.

They assumed, of course, that in a republican form of government, the majority must rule. But they also assumed that the will of the majority ought to be limited, especially when the "majority" was a legislative one. They demanded a bill of rights, with special emphasis on procedural protections in criminal cases, and vehemently repudiated the somewhat spurious Federalist argument that a bill of rights was not necessary in a government ruled by the people themselves. To this, James Winthrop replied:

> . . . that the sober and industrious part of the community should be defended from the rapacity and violence of the vicious and idle. A bill of rights, therefore, ought to set forth the purposes for which the compact is made, and serves to secure the minority against the usurpation and tyranny of the majority. . . . The experience of all mankind has proved the prevalence of a disposition to use power wantonly. It is therefore as necessary to defend an individual against the majority in a republick as against the king in a monarchy.[116]

The reaction of the Anti-Federalists to the restrictions imposed on state legislative majorities by Article I, Section 10 of the Constitution is also relevant at this point. These provisions were certainly intended to protect the rights of property against legislative invasion by majorities. If there had been any spirit of doctrinaire majoritarianism among the opponents of the Constitution, this would surely have been the occasion to express it, and in quite unequivocal terms. There was very little open criticism of these provisions, none on the grounds that they violated the principle of majority rule or that they were designed to protect the interests of the upper classes.[117] What criticism there was, was expressed largely in terms of practical considerations.

Distrust of majority factions in much the same sense as Madison's was emphatically expressed by the one sector of Anti-Federalism which constituted the most self-conscious minority. Southerners felt keenly the conflict of interest between North and South and were vehemently opposed to surrendering themselves to the majority of the seven Eastern states. One of the reasons for George Mason's refusal to sign the Constitution had been his failure to get adopted a two-thirds majority vote for all laws affecting commerce and navigation. His fears for the South's interests were shared by his fellow Southerners and were frequently expressed in the Convention debates. "It will be a government of a faction," said William Grayson, "and this observation will apply to every part of it; for, having a majority, they may do what they please." [118] Other colleagues in Virginia joined in this distrust of the anticipated Northern majority uniting to oppress the South.[119] In North and South Carolina it was much the same. Bloodworth lamented, "To the north of the Susquehanna there are thirty-six representatives, and to the south of it only twenty-nine. They will always outvote us." [120] In South Carolina, Rawlins Lowndes predicted that "when this new Constitution should be adopted, the sun of the Southern States would set, never to rise again." Why? Because the Eastern states would have a majority in the legislature and would not hesitate to use it — probably to interfere with the slave trade, "because they have none themselves, and therefore want to exclude us from this great advantage." [121]

There was, then, no doctrinaire devotion to majoritarianism. It was assumed that oppression of individuals or of groups might come from majorities of the people themselves as well as from kings or aristocrats.

For a generation the *Economic Interpretation of the Constitution* has exerted a deep and extensive influence over students of American history and government. The conception of the Constitution as the product of a conservative reaction against the ideals of the Revolution has been widely accepted, and Beard's analysis of the document itself commonly followed. According to this interpretation, the Founding Fathers secured their property rights by placing certain restrictions on state legislatures and by setting up a government in which the system of separation of powers, with checks and balances, indirect elections, staggered terms of office, and a national judiciary with the potential power of judicial review, would restrain the force of turbulent, democratic majorities. Surprisingly little attention has been devoted to the Anti-Federalists, but it is implied that they were the true heirs of the Revolutionary tradition — equally devoted to individual liberty and majority rule. The Federalists' desire for strong central government and the Anti-Federalists' fear of such are also considered, but the allegedly undemocratic structure of the national government itself is strongly emphasized. This aspect of the Beard thesis is open to question.

For the objections of the Anti-Federalists were not directed toward the barriers imposed on simple majority rule by the Constitution. Advocates and opponents of ratification may have belonged to different economic classes and been motivated by different economic interests. But they shared a large body of political ideas and attitudes, together with a common heritage of political institutions. For one thing, they shared a profound distrust of man's capacity to use power wisely and well. They believed self-interest to be the dominant motive of political behavior, no matter whether the form of government be republican or monarchical, and they believed in the necessity of constructing political machinery that would restrict the operation of self-interest and prevent men entrusted with political power from abusing it. This was the fundamental assumption of the men who wrote the Constitution, and of those who opposed its adoption, as well.

The fundamental issue over which Federalists and Anti-Federalists split was the question whether republican government could be extended to embrace a nation, or whether it must be limited to the comparatively small political and geographical units which the separate American states then constituted. The Anti-Federalists took the latter view; and in a sense they were the conservatives of 1787, and their opponents the radicals.

The Anti-Federalists were clinging to a theory of representative government that was already becoming obsolete, and would have soon become so even had they been successful in preventing the establishment of a national government. Certainly it was a theory which could never have provided the working principles for such a government. For the Anti-Federalists were not only localists, but localists in a way strongly reminiscent of the city-state theory of Rousseau's *Social Contract*. According to that theory, a society capable of being governed in accordance with the General Will had to be limited in size, population, and diversity. The Anti-Federalists had no concept of a General Will comparable to Rousseau's, and they accepted the institution of representation, where he had rejected it. But many of their basic attitudes were similar to his. Like him, they thought republican government subject to limitations of size, population, and diversity; and like him also, they thought the will of the people would very likely be distorted by the process of representation. In fact, their theory of representation and their belief that republican government could not be extended nation-wide were integrally related.

They regarded representation primarily as an institutional substitute for direct democracy and endeavored to restrict its operation to the performance of that function; hence their plea that the legislature should be an exact miniature of the people, containing spokesmen for all classes, all groups, all interests, all opinions, in the community; hence, too, their preference for short legislative terms of office and their inclination, especially in the sphere of state government, to regard representatives as delegates bound by the instructions of constituents rather than as men expected and trusted to exercise independent judgment. This was a natural stage in the development of representative government, but it contained several weaknesses and was, I think, already obsolete in late eighteenth-century America.

Its major weaknesses were closely akin to those of direct democracy itself, for representation of this kind makes difficult the process of genuine deliberation, as well as the reconciliation of diverse interests and opinions. Indeed, it is notable, and I think not accidental, that the body of Anti-Federalist thought as a whole showed little consideration of the necessity for compromise. The Founding Fathers were not democrats, but in their recognition of the role which compromise must play in the process of popular government, they were far more advanced than their opponents.

It is clear, too, that the same factors limiting the size and extent of direct democracies would also be operative in republics where representation is regarded only as a substitute for political participation by the whole people. Within their own frame of reference, the Anti-Federalists were quite right in insisting that republican government would work only in relatively small states, where the population was also small and relatively homogeneous. If there is great diversity among the people, with many interests and many opinions, then all cannot be represented without making the legislature as large and unwieldy as the citizen assemblies of ancient Athens. And if the system does not lend itself readily to compromise and conciliation, then the basis for a working consensus must be considerable homogeneity in the people themselves. In the opinion of the Anti-Federalists, the American people lacked that homogeneity.[122] This Rousseauistic vision of a small, simple, and homogeneous democracy may have been a fine ideal, but it *was* an ideal even then. It was not to be found even in the small states, and none of the Anti-Federalists produced a satisfactory answer to Madison's analysis of the weaknesses inherent in republicanism operating on the small scale preferred by his opponents.

Associated with this theory of representation and its necessary limitation to small-scale republics was the Anti-Federalists' profound distrust of the electoral and representative processes provided for and implied in the proposed Constitution. Their ideal of the legislature as an "exact miniature" of the people envisaged something not unlike the result hoped for by modern proponents of proportional representation. This was impossible to achieve in the national Congress.[123] There would not and could not be enough seats to go around. The constituencies were to be large — the ratio of representatives to population was not to exceed one per thirty thousand — and each representative must therefore represent not one, but many groups among his electors. And whereas Madison saw in this process of "filtering" or consolidating public opinion a virtue, the Anti-Federalists saw in it only danger. They did not think that a Congress thus elected could truly represent the will of the people, and they particularly feared that they themselves, the "middling class," to use Melancton Smith's term, would be left out.

They feared this because they saw clearly that enlarged constituencies would require more pre-election political organization than they believed to be either wise or safe. Much has been written recently about the Founding Fathers' hostility to political parties. It is said that they designed the Constitution, especially separation of powers, in order to counteract the effectiveness of parties.[124] This is partly true, but I think it worth noting that the contemporary opponents of the Constitution feared parties or factions in the Madisonian sense just as much as, and that they feared parties in the modern sense even more than, did Madison himself. They feared and distrusted concerted group action for the purpose of "centering votes" in order to obtain a plurality, because they believed this would distort the automatic or natural expression of the people's will. The necessity of such action in large electoral districts would work to the advantage of the upper classes, who, because of their superior capacity and opportunity for organization of this kind, would elect a disproportionate share of representatives to the Congress. In other words, the Anti-Federalists were acutely aware of the role that organization played in the winning of elections, and they were not willing to accept the "organized" for the "real" majority. Instead they wanted to retain the existing system, where the electoral constituencies were small, and where organization of this kind was relatively unnecessary. Only then could a man vote as he saw fit, confident that the result of the election would reflect the real will of the people as exactly as possible.

Distrust of the electoral process thus combined with the localist feelings of the Anti-Federalists to produce an attitude of profound fear and suspicion toward Congress. That body, it was felt, would be composed of aristocrats and of men elected from far-away places by the unknown peoples of distant states. It would meet at a yet undesignated site hundreds of miles from the homes of most of its constituents, outside the jurisdiction of any particular state, and protected by an army of its own making. When one sees Congress in this light, it is not surprising that the Anti-Federalists were afraid, or that they had little faith in elections as a means of securing responsibility and preventing Congressional tyranny.[125]

Their demand for more limitations on Congressional power was perfectly natural. These were believed to be necessary in any government because of the lust for power and the selfishness in its use which were inherent in the nature of man. They were doubly necessary in a government on a national scale. And so the Anti-Federalists criticized the latitude of power given to Congress under Article I and called for more detailed provisions to limit the scope of Congressional discretion. We are certainly indebted to them for the movement that led to the adoption of the Bill of Rights, though they were more concerned with the traditional common-law rights of procedure in criminal cases than with the provisions of the First Amendment. They were at the same time forerunners of the unfortunate trend in the nineteenth century toward lengthy and cumbersome constitutions filled with minute restrictions upon the various agencies of government, especially the legislative branch. The generality and brevity which made the national Constitution a model of draftsmanship and a viable fundamental law inspired in the Anti-Federalists only fear.

They repeatedly attacked the Constitution for its alleged departure from Montesquieu's doctrine of separation of powers, emphasized the inadequacy of the checks and balances provided within the governmental structure, and lamented the excessive optimism regarding the character and behavior of elective representatives thus revealed in the work of the Founding Fathers. It is significant, in view of the interpretation long and generally accepted by historians, that *no one* expressed the belief that the system of separation of powers and checks and balances had been designed to protect the property rights of the well-to-do. Their positive proposals for remedying the defects in the system were not numerous. They objected to the Senate's share in the appointive and treaty-making powers and called for a separate executive council to advise the President in the performance of these functions. Shorter terms were advocated for President and Congress, though not as frequently or as strongly as required rotation for senators and President. No one suggested judicial review of Congressional legislation, though Patrick Henry attacked the Constitution because it did not explicitly provide for this safeguard to popular government.

Had the Constitution been altered to satisfy the major structural changes desired by the Anti-Federalists, the House of Representatives would have been considerably larger; there would have been four rather than three branches of the government; the President would have been limited, as he is now, to two terms in office; the senators would have been similarly limited and also subject to recall by their state governments. These changes might have been beneficial. It is doubtful that they would have pleased the late Charles Beard and his followers; it is even more doubtful that they would have facilitated the operation of unrestrained majority rule. Certainly that was not the intention of their proponents.

The Anti-Federalists were not latter-day democrats. Least of all were they majoritarians with respect to the national government. They were not confident that the people would always make wise and correct choices in either their constituent or electoral capacity, and many of them feared the oppression of one section in the community by a majority reflecting the interests of another. Above all, they consistently refused to accept legislative majorities as expressive either of justice or of the people's will. In short, they distrusted majority rule, at its source and through the only possible means of expression in governmental action over a large and populous nation, that is to say, through representation. The last thing in the world they wanted was a national democracy which would permit Congressional majorities to operate freely and without restraint. Proponents of this kind of majority rule have almost without exception been advocates of strong, positive action by the national government. The Anti-Federalists were not. Their philosophy was primarily one of limitations on power, and if they had had their way, the Constitution would have contained more checks and balances, not fewer. Indeed it seems safe to say that the Constitution could not have been ratified at all had it conformed to the standards of democracy which are implicit in the interpretation of Beard and his followers. A national government without separation of powers and checks and balances was not politically feasible. In this respect, then, I would suggest that his interpretation of the Constitution was unrealistic and unhistorical.

The Anti-Federalists may have followed democratic principles within the sphere of state government and possibly provided the impetus for the extension of power and privilege among the mass of the people, though it is significant that they did not advocate a broadening of the suffrage in 1787–1788 or the direct election of the Senate or the President. But they lacked both the faith and the vision to extend their principles nationwide. It was the Federalists of 1787–1788 who created a national framework which would accommodate the later rise of democracy.

The Worthy Against the Licentious

GORDON S. WOOD

*Kenyon's article lifted the debate over the character of the Fed-
eralists and Antifederalists out of the narrow economic context
created by Beard's book. It did not solve, however, the problem
of who the Federalists and Antifederalists were and why they
should have thought as they did. Kenyon had conceded that the
Antifederalists feared the Constitution as an aristocratic document but she did not make this fear central to her analysis. In a
later version of her article, expanded to form an introduction to
a collection of Antifederalist essays,* The Antifederalists *(Indianapolis, 1966), she admitted that the Antifederalist literature
"can easily give the impression that America was on the verge of,
if not actually engaged in, a class war in 1787–88, and that the
issue was in truth one of democracy versus aristocracy. . . ." But,
she added, "it would be a mistake to accept all of the charges and
counter-charges at face value." Why this prevalent class-conscious
rhetoric should be so casually dismissed while other charges by
the Antifederalists are taken at face value is not made clear by
Kenyon. The participants thought they were engaged in a kind of
social war, and it is crucial that we understand what they meant
if we are to understand what the Constitution was all about.*

*Perhaps the meaning of the Federalist and Antifederalist de-
bate can be best discovered by reverting to the Progressive tradition and exploring the social and economic bases of the participants' thought. The most industrious of recent historians seeking
to do just that has been Jackson Turner Main. In his* Political
Parties Before the Constitution *(Chapel Hill, 1973), Main has
surveyed the politics of all the states during the 1780's and by
analyzing roll calls of the state legislatures has discovered in each
state two legislative blocs or "parties," which he has labeled "cos-
mopolitans" and "localists." Although each state had its own
economic and social circumstances, Main found these emerging
political parties to be similar in their composition and attitudes
toward the major issues of the period — government expenditures
and taxes, the return of the Loyalists, paper money, and debtor
relief legislation — and forming in the end the basic alignment
over the proposed federal Constitution.*

*Main's analysis of the economic and social bases of politics helps
to spell out Kenyon's hint of a class war, to substantiate the participants' rhetoric, and in particular to make clear the mistrust
and localism in Antifederalist thought. What is still needed, how-*

*ever, is some explanation of why the Federalists, the heirs of
Main's "cosmopolitan parties" in the states, believed that the new
Constitution would promote their viewpoint and interests.*

How the Federalists expected a new central government to remedy
the vices the individual states had been unable to remedy is the central
question, the answer to which lies at the heart of their understanding of
what was happening in the critical period. In the minds of the Federalists
and of "men of reflection" generally, most of the evils of American society
— the atmosphere of mistrust, the breakdown of authority, the increase of
debt, the depravity of manners, and the decline of virtue — could be reduced to a fundamental problem of social disarrangement. Even the difficulties of the United States in foreign affairs and its weakness as a nation
in the world, as Jay argued in *The Federalist,* Number 3, could be primarily
explained by what the Revolution had done to America's political and
social hierarchy. More than anything else the Federalists' obsession with
disorder in American society and politics accounts for the revolutionary
nature of the nationalist proposals offered by men like Madison in 1787
and for the resultant Federalist Constitution. Only an examination of the
Federalists' social perspective, their fears and anxieties about the disarray
in American society, can fully explain how they conceived of the Constitution as a political device designed to control the social forces the Revolution had released.

The most pronounced social effect of the Revolution was not harmony or stability but the sudden appearance of new men everywhere in
politics and business. "When the pot boils, the scum will rise," James Otis
had warned in 1776; but few Revolutionary leaders had realized just how
much it would rise. By the end of the war men like Governor James
Bowdoin of Massachusetts could "scarcely see any other than new faces," a
change almost "as remarkable as the revolution itself." The emigration of
thousands of Tories, the intensification of interest in politics, the enlargement of the legislatures and the increase in elections, the organization of
new militia and political groups, the breakup of old mercantile combinations and trade circuits, the inflation and profiteering caused by the war —
all offered new opportunities for hitherto unknown but ambitious persons
to find new places for themselves. As John Adams noted, his own deep resentment of his supposed social superiors was being echoed throughout

From Gordon S. Wood, *The Creation of the American Republic, 1776–
1787* (Chapel Hill, 1969), 475–480, 482–499, 506–518. Reprinted by permission.

various levels of the society. For every brilliant provincial lawyer ready to challenge the supremacy of the imperial clique in the colonial metropolis, there were dozens of lesser men, not so brilliant but equally desirous of securing a local magistracy, a captaincy of the militia, some place, however small, of honor and distinction. With the elimination of Crown privilege and appointment men were prepared to take the republican emphasis on equality seriously. The result, as one Baltimore printer declared as early as 1777, was "Whiggism run mad." "When a man, who is only fit 'to patch a shoe,' attempts 'to patch the State,' fancies himself a *Solon* or *Lycurgus*, . . . he cannot fail to meet with contempt." But contempt was no longer enough to keep such men in their place.[1]*

Everywhere *"Specious, interested designing* men," "men, respectable neither for their property, their virtue, nor their abilities," were taking a lead in public affairs that they had never quite had before, courting "the suffrages of the people by tantalizing them with improper indulgences." Thousands of the most respectable people "who obtained their possessions by the hard industry, continued sobriety and economy of themselves or their virtuous ancestors" were now witnessing, so the writings of nearly all the states proclaimed over and over, many men *"whose fathers they would have disdained to have sat with the dogs of their flocks,* raised to immense wealth, or at least to carry the appearance of a haughty, supercilious and luxurious spendthrift." "Effrontery and arrogance, even in our virtuous and enlightened days," said John Jay, "are giving rank and Importance to men whom Wisdom would have left in obscurity." [2] Since "every new election in the States," as Madison pointed out in *The Federalist,* Number 62, "is found to change one half of the representatives," the newly enlarged state legislatures were being filled and yearly refilled with different faces, often with "men without reading, experience, or principle." The Revolution, it was repeatedly charged (and the evidence seems to give substance to the charges), was allowing government to fall "into the Hands of those whose ability or situation in Life does not intitle them to it." [3] Everywhere in the 1780's the press and the correspondence of those kinds of men whose letters are apt to be preserved complained that "a set of unprincipled men, who sacrifice everything to their popularity and private views, seem to have acquired too much influence in all our Assemblies." The Revolution was acquiring a degree of social turbulence that many, for all of their knowledge of revolutions, had not anticipated. Given the Revolutionary leaders' conventional eighteenth-century assumption of a necessary coincidence between social and political authority, many could actually believe that their world was being "turned upside down." [4]

* [See pp. 169–173 for notes to this article. — Ed.]

Beginning well before the Revolution but increasing to a fever pitch by the mid-eighties were fears of what this kind of intensifying social mobility signified for the traditional conception of a hierarchical society ("In due gradation ev'ry rank must be, Some high, some low, but all in their degree") — a conception which the Revolution had unsettled but by no means repudiated. In reaction to the excessive social movement accelerated by the Revolution some Americans, although good republicans, attempted to confine mobility within prescribed channels. Men could rise, but only within the social ranks in which they were born. Their aim in life must be to learn to perform their inherited position with "industry, economy, and good conduct." A man, wrote Enos Hitchcock in his didactic tale of 1793, must not be "elevated above his employment." In this respect republicanism with its emphasis on spartan adversity and simplicity became an ideology of social stratification and control.[5] Over and over writers urged that "the crosses of life improve by retrenching our enjoyments," by moderating "our expectations," and by giving "the heart a mortal disgust to all the gaudy blandishments of sense." Luxury was such a great evil because it confounded "every Distinction between the Poor and the Rich" and allowed "people of the very meanest parentages, or office, if fortune be but a little favourable to them" to "vie to make themselves equal in apparel with the principal people of the place." "Dissipation and extravagance" encouraged even "country-girls in their market carts, and upon their panniered horses," to ride "through our streets with their heads deformed with the plumes of the ostrich and the feathers of other exotick birds." Although many, especially in the South, had expected the Revolution to lessen this kind of social chaos, republicanism actually seemed only to have aggravated it.[6]

Most American leaders, however, were not opposed to the idea of social movement, for mobility, however one may have decried its abuses, lay at the heart of republicanism. Indeed, many like John Adams had entered the Revolution in order to make mobility a reality, to free American society from the artificial constraints Britain had imposed on it, and to allow "Persons of obscure Birth, and Station, and narrow Fortunes" to make their mark in the world. Republicanism represented equality of opportunity and careers open to talent. Even "the reins of state," David Ramsay had said at the outset, "may be held by the son of the poorest man, if possessed of abilities equal to that important station." Ramsay's qualification, however, was crucial to his endorsement of mobility. For all of its emphasis on equality, republicanism was still not considered by most to be incompatible with the conception of a hierarchical society of different gradations and a unitary authority to which deference from lower to higher should be paid. Movement must necessarily exist in a republic, if talent alone were to dominate, if the natural aristocracy were to rule. But such inevitable movement must be into and out of clearly discernible ranks. Those who rose in a republic, it was assumed, must first acquire the attributes of social superiority — wealth, education, experience, and connections — before they could be considered eligible for political leadership. Most Revolutionary leaders clung tightly to the concept of a ruling elite, presumably based on merit, but an elite nonetheless — a natural aristocracy embodied in the eighteenth-century ideal of an educated and cultivated gentleman. The rising self-made man could be accepted into this natural aristocracy only if he had assimilated through education or experience its attitudes, refinements, and style. For all of their earlier criticism of "the better sort of People" in the name of "real Merit," few of the Revolutionary leaders were prepared to repudiate the idea of a dominating elite and the requisite identity of social and political authority. . . .[7]

Throughout all the states spokesmen for "the poor and middling orders" were directly challenging the eighteenth-century assumption that social authority was a necessary prerequisite to the wielding of political power. "Names, families, and connections," wrote Benjamin Austin of Massachusetts, had no real relation to a man's worth and opinion. "Must the poor man be forever debarred from delivering his mind, lest the inquiry should be concerning his *origin*. Are there no observations worthy our attention, unless they are authorized by *family alliances?*" "Elevation in office, and wealth and titles, and political rank and dignity," said William Paca of Maryland, "have no influence at all in making men *good* or *honest*." Even suggestions of degrees of respectability had aristocratic overtones for the most egalitarian. "A democratic government like ours," said John Smilie of Pennsylvania in terms that bluntly denied the traditional belief in a social hierarchy, "admits of no superiority. A virtuous man, be his situation what it may, is respectable." Americans who used other designations of respectability had no basis for them. All such men really had was "more money than their neighbors," and because of this they claimed they were "therefore more respectable." [8]

In South Carolina these kinds of sentiments became particularly pronounced in the eighties; the planters found themselves confronted with widespread challenges to their authority that they had never anticipated in 1776, challenges that came from a new kind of politician, one who, as a defender proudly pointed out, "had no relations or friends, but what his money made for him." In the tense atmosphere of the mid-eighties the case of William Thompson, an unfortunate tavern-keeper who was threatened with banishment from the state by the legislature for allegedly insulting John Rutledge, became a *cause célèbre* and a focal point for the political and social animosities released and aggravated by the Revolution. Thompson's address to the public in April 1784 is a classic expression of American resentment against social superiority, a resentment voiced, as Thompson said, not on behalf of himself but on behalf of the people, or "those more especially, who go at this day, under the opprobrious appellation of, the *Lower Orders of Men.*" Thompson was not simply attacking the few aristocratic "Nabobs" who had humiliated him, but was actually assaulting the entire conception of a social hierarchy ruled by a gentlemanly elite. In fact he turned the prevailing eighteenth-century opinion upside down and argued that the natural aristocracy was peculiarly unqualified to rule. Rather than preparing men for political leadership in a free government, said Thompson, "signal opulence and influence," especially when united "by intermarriage or otherwise," were really "calculated to subvert *Republicanism.*" The "persons and conduct" of the South Carolina "Nabobs" like Rutledge "in *private* life, may be unexceptionable, and even amiable, but their pride, influence, ambition, connections, wealth and political principles, ought in *public* life, ever to exclude them from *public confidence.*" All that was needed in republican leadership was "being *good, able, useful,* and *friends to social equality,*" for in a republican government "consequence is from the *public opinion,* and not from *private fancy.*" In sardonic tones Thompson recounted how he, a tavern-keeper, "a *wretch* of no higher rank in the Commonwealth than that of Common-Citizen," had been debased by "those *self-exalted* characters, who affect to compose the *grand hierarchy* of the State, . . . for having dared to dispute with a *John Rutledge,* or any of the NABOB tribe." The experience had been degrading enough to Thompson as a man, but as a former officer in the army it had been "insupportable" — indicating how Revolutionary military service may have affected the social structure. Undoubtedly, said Thompson, Rutledge had "conceived me his inferior." But Thompson like many others in these years — tavern-keepers, farmers, petty merchants, small-time lawyers, former military officers — could no longer "comprehend the *inferiority.*" [9] The resultant antagonism between those who conceived of such men as their inferiors, unfit to hold public positions, and those who would not accept the imputation of inferiority lay beneath the social crisis of the 1780's — a social crisis which the federal Constitution of 1787 brought to a head.

The division over the Constitution in 1787–88 is not easily analyzed. It is difficult, as historians have recently demonstrated, to equate the supporters or opponents of the Constitution with particular economic groupings. The Antifederalist politicians in the ratifying conventions often possessed wealth, including public securities, equal to that of the Federalists.[10] While the relative youth of the Federalist leaders, compared to the ages of the prominent Antifederalists, was important, especially in accounting for the Federalists' ability to think freshly and creatively about politics, it can hardly be used to explain the division throughout the country.[11] Moreover, the concern of the 1780's with America's moral character was not confined to the proponents of the Constitution. That rabid republican and Antifederalist, Benjamin Austin, was as convinced as any Federalist that "the luxurious living of all ranks and degrees" was "the principal cause of all the evils we now experience." Some leading Antifederalist intellectuals expressed as much fear of "the injustice, folly, and wickedness of the State Legislatures" and of "the usurpation and tyranny of the majority" against the minority as did Madison. In the Philadelphia Convention both Mason and Elbridge Gerry, later prominent Antifederalists, admitted "the danger of the levelling spirit" flowing from "the excess of democracy" in the American republics.[12] There were many diverse reasons in each state why men supported or opposed the Constitution that cut through any sort of class division. The Constitution was a single issue in a complicated situation, and its acceptance or rejection in many states was often dictated by peculiar circumstances — the prevalence of Indians, the desire for western lands, the special interests of commerce — that defy generalization. Nevertheless, despite all of this confusion and complexity, the struggle over the Constitution, as the debate if nothing else makes clear, can best be understood as a social one. Whatever the particular constituency of the antagonists may have been, men in 1787–88 talked as if they were representing distinct and opposing social elements. Both the proponents and opponents of the Constitution focused throughout the debates on an essential point of political sociology that ultimately must be used to distinguish a Federalist from an Antifederalist. The quarrel was fundamentally one between aristocracy and democracy.

Because of its essentially social base, this quarrel, as George Minot of Massachusetts said, was "extremely unequal." To be sure, many Antifederalists, especially in Virginia, were as socially and intellectually formidable as any Federalist. Richard Henry Lee was undoubtedly the strongest mind the Antifederalists possessed, and he sympathized with the Antifederalist cause. Like Austin and other Antifederalists he believed that moral regeneration of America's character, rather than any legalistic manipulation of the constitutions of government, was the proper remedy for America's problems. "I fear," he wrote to George Mason in May 1787, "it is more in vicious manners, than mistakes in form, that we must seek for the causes of the present discontent." [13] Still, such "aristocrats" as Lee or Mason did not truly represent Antifederalism. Not only did they reject the vicious state politics of the 1780's which Antifederalism, by the very purpose of the Constitution, was implicitly if not always explicitly committed to defend, but they could have no real identity, try as they might, with those for whom they sought to speak. Because, as Lee pointed out, "we must recollect how disproportionately the democratic and aristocratic parts of the community were represented" not only in the Philadelphia Convention but also in the ratifying conventions, many of the real Antifederalists, those intimately involved in the democratic politics of the 1780's and consequently with an emotional as well as an intellectual commitment to Antifederalism, were never clearly heard in the formal debates of 1787–88.[14]

The disorganization and inertia of the Antifederalists, especially in contrast with the energy and effectiveness of the Federalists, has been repeatedly emphasized.[15] The opponents of the Constitution lacked both coordination and unified leadership; "their principles," wrote Oliver Ellsworth, "are totally opposite to each other, and their objections discordant and irreconcilable." The Federalist victory, it appears, was actually more of an Antifederalist default. "We had no principle of concert or union," lamented the South Carolina Antifederalist, Aedanus Burke, while the supporters of the Constitution "left no expedient untried to push it forward." Madison's description of the Massachusetts Antifederalists was applicable to nearly all the states: "There was not a single character capable of uniting their wills or directing their measures. . . . They had no plan whatever. They looked no farther than to put a negative on the Constitution and return home." They were not, as one Federalist put it, "good politicians." [16]

But the Antifederalists were not simply poorer politicians than the Federalists; they were actually different kinds of politicians. Too many of them were state-centered men with local interests and loyalties only, politicians without influence and connections, and ultimately politicians without social and intellectual confidence. In South Carolina the up-country opponents of the Constitution shied from debate and when they did occasionally rise to speak apologized effusively for their inability to say what they felt had to be said, thus leaving most of the opposition to the Constitution to be voiced by Rawlins Lowndes, a low-country planter who scarcely represented their interests and soon retired from the struggle. Elsewhere, in New Hampshire, Connecticut, Massachusetts, Pennsylvania, and North Carolina, the situation was similar: the Federalists had the bulk of talent and influence on their side "together with all the Speakers in the State great and small." In convention after convention the Antifederalists, as in Connecticut, tried to speak, but "they were browbeaten by many of those Cicero'es as they think themselves and others of Superior rank." "The presses are in a great measure secured to *their* side," the Antifederalists complained with justice: out of a hundred or more newspapers printed in the late eighties only a dozen supported the Antifederalists, as editors, "afraid to offend the great men, or Merchants, who could work their ruin," closed their columns to the opposition. The Antifederalists were not so much beaten as overawed.[17] In Massachusetts the two leading socially established

Antifederalists, Elbridge Gerry and James Warren, were defeated as delegates to the Ratifying Convention, and Antifederalist leadership consequently fell into the hands of newer, self-made men, of whom Samuel Nasson
was perhaps typical — a Maine shopkeeper who was accused of delivering
ghostwritten speeches in the Convention. Nasson had previously sat in the
General Court but had declined reelection because he had been too keenly
made aware of "the want of a proper Education I feel my Self So Small on
many occasions that I all most Scrink into Nothing Besides I am often
obliged to Borrow from Gentlemen that had advantages which I have not."
Now, however, he had become the stoutest of Antifederalists, "full charged
with Gass," one of those grumblers who, as Rufus King told Madison, were
more afraid of the proponents of the Constitution than the Constitution
itself, frightened that "some injury is plotted against them" because of "the
extraordinary Union in favor of the Constitution in this State of the Wealthy
and sensible part of it." [18]

     This fear of a plot by men who "talk so finely and gloss over matters
so smoothly" ran through the Antifederalist mind. Because the many "new
men" of the 1780's, men like Melancthon Smith and Abraham Yates of New
York or John Smilie and William Findley of Pennsylvania, had bypassed
the social hierarchy in their rise to political leadership, they lacked those
attributes of social distinction and dignity that went beyond mere wealth.
Since these kinds of men were never assimilated to the gentlemanly cast of
the Livingstons or the Morrises, they, like Americans earlier in confronta-
tion with the British court, tended to view with suspicion and hostility the
high-flying world of style and connections that they were barred by their
language and tastes, if by nothing else, from sharing in. In the minds of
these socially inferior politicians the movement for the strengthening of the
central government could only be a "conspiracy" "planned and set to work"
by a few aristocrats, who were at first, said Abraham Yates, no larger in any
one state than the cabal which sought to undermine English liberty at the
beginning of the eighteenth century. Since men like Yates could not quite
comprehend what they were sure were the inner maneuverings of the elite,
they were convinced that in the aristocrats' program, "what was their view
in the beginning" or how "far it was Intended to be carried Must be Collected from facts that Afterwards have happened." Like American Whigs
in the sixties and seventies forced to delve into the dark and complicated
workings of English court politics, they could judge motives and plans "but
by the Event." [19] And they could only conclude that the events of the
eighties, "the treasury, the Cincinnati, and other public creditors, with all
their concomitants," were "somehow or other, . . . inseparably connected,"
were all parts of a grand design "concerted by a few *tyrants*" to undo the
Revolution and to establish an aristocracy in order "to lord it over the rest

of their fellow citizens, to trample the poorer part of the people under their feet, that they may be rendered their servants and slaves." In this climate all the major issues of the Confederation period — the impost, commutation, and the return of the Loyalists — possessed a political and social significance that transcended economic concerns. All seemed to be devices by which a ruling few, like the ministers of the English Crown, would attach a corps of pensioners and dependents to the government and spread their influence and connections throughout the states in order "to dissolve our present Happy and Benevolent Constitution and to erect on the Ruins, a proper Aristocracy." [20]

Nothing was more characteristic of Antifederalist thinking than this obsession with aristocracy. Although to a European, American society may have appeared remarkably egalitarian, to many Americans, especially to those who aspired to places of consequence but were made to feel their inferiority in innumerable, often subtle, ways, American society was distinguished by its inequality. "It is true," said Melancthon Smith in the New York Ratifying Convention, "it is our singular felicity that we have no legal or hereditary distinctions . . . ; but still there are real differences." "Every society naturally divides itself into classes. . . . Birth, education, talents, and wealth, create distinctions among men as visible, and of as much influence, as titles, stars, and garters." Everyone knew those "whom nature hath destined to rule," declared one sardonic Antifederalist pamphlet. Their "qualifications of authority" were obvious: "such as the dictatorial air, the magisterial voice, the imperious tone, the haughty countenance, the lofty look, the majestic mien." In all communities, "even in those of the most democratic kind," wrote George Clinton (whose "family and connections" in the minds of those like Philip Schuyler did not "entitle him to so distinguished a predominance" as the governorship of New York), there were pressures — "superior talents, fortunes and public employments" — demarcating an aristocracy whose influence was difficult to resist.[21]

Such influence was difficult to resist because, to the continual annoyance of the Antifederalists, the great body of the people willingly submitted to it. The "authority of names" and "the influence of the great" among ordinary people were too evident to be denied. "Will any one say that there does not exist in this country the pride of family, of wealth, of talents, and that they do not command influence and respect among the common people?" "The people are too apt to yield an implicit assent to the opinions of those characters whose abilities are held in the highest esteem, and to those in whose integrity and patriotism they can confide; not considering that the love of domination is generally in proportion to talents, abilities and superior requirements." Because of this habit of deference in the people, it was "in the power of the enlightened and aspiring few, if they should combine, at any time to destroy the best establishments, and even make the people the instruments of their own subjugation." Hence, the Antifederalist-minded declared, the people must be awakened to the consequences of their self-ensnarement; they must be warned over and over by popular tribunes, by "those who are competent to the task of developing the principles of government," of the dangers involved in paying obeisance to those who they thought were their superiors. The people must "not be permitted to consider themselves as a grovelling, distinct species, uninterested in the general welfare." [22]

Such constant admonitions to the people of the perils flowing from their too easy deference to the *"natural aristocracy"* were necessary because the Antifederalists were convinced that these "men that had been delicately bred, and who were in affluent circumstances," these "men of the most exalted rank in life," were by their very conspicuousness irreparably cut off from the great body of the people and hence could never share in its concerns nor look after its interests. It was not that these "certain men exalted above the rest" were necessarily "destitute of morality or virtue" or that they were inherently different from other men. "The same passions and prejudices govern all men." It was only that circumstances in their particular environment had made them different. There was "a charm in politicks"; men in high office become habituated with power, "grow fond of it, and are loath to resign it"; "they feel themselves flattered and elevated," enthralled by the attractions of high living, and thus they easily forget the interests of the common people, from which many of them once sprang. By dwelling so vividly on the allurements of prestige and power, by emphasizing again and again how the "human soul is affected by wealth, in all its faculties, . . . by its present interest, by its expectations, and by its fears," these ambitious Antifederalist politicians may have revealed as much about themselves as they did about the "aristocratic" elite they sought to displace.[23] Yet at the same time by such language they contributed to a new appreciation of the nature of society.

In these repeated attacks on deference and the capacity of a conspicuous few to speak for the whole society — which was to become in time the distinguishing feature of American democratic politics — the Antifederalists struck at the roots of the traditional conception of political society. If the natural elite, whether its distinctions were ascribed or acquired, was not in any organic way connected to the "feelings, circumstances, and interests" of the people and was incapable of feeling "sympathetically the wants of the people," then it followed that only ordinary men, men not distinguished by the characteristics of aristocratic wealth and taste, men "in middling circumstances" untempted by the attractions of a cosmopolitan world and thus "more temperate, of better morals, and less ambitious, than the great," could be trusted to speak for the great body of the people, for those who were coming more and more to be referred to as "the middling and lower classes of people." [24] The differentiating influence of the environment was such that men in various ranks and classes now seemed to be broken apart from one another, separated by their peculiar circumstances into distinct, unconnected, and often incompatible interests. With their indictment of aristocracy the Antifederalists were saying, whether they realized it or not, that the people of America even in their several states were not homogeneous entities each with a basic similarity of interest for which an empathic elite could speak. Society was not an organic hierarchy composed of ranks and degrees indissolubly linked one to another; rather it was a heterogeneous mixture of "many different classes or orders of people, Merchants, Farmers, Planter Mechanics and Gentry or wealthy Men." In such a society men from one class or group, however educated and respectable they may have been, could never be acquainted with the "*Situation* and Wants" of those of another class or group. Lawyers and planters could never be "adequate judges of tradesmens concerns." If men were truly to represent the people in government, it was not enough for them to be for the people; they had to be actually of the people. "Farmers, traders and mechanics . . . all ought to have a competent number of their best informed members in the legislature." [25]

Thus the Antifederalists were not only directly challenging the conventional belief that only a gentlemanly few, even though now in America naturally and not artificially qualified, were best equipped through learning and experience to represent and to govern the society, but they were as well indirectly denying the assumption of organic social homogeneity on which republicanism rested. Without fully comprehending the consequences of their arguments the Antifederalists were destroying the great chain of being, thus undermining the social basis of republicanism and shattering that unity and harmony of social and political authority which the eighteenth century generally and indeed most Revolutionary leaders had considered essential to the maintenance of order.

Confronted with such a fundamental challenge the Federalists initially backed away. They had no desire to argue the merits of the Constitution in terms of its social implications and were understandably reluctant to open up the character of American society as the central issue of the debate. But in the end they could not resist defending those beliefs in elitism that lay at the heart of their conception of politics and of their constitutional program. All of the Federalists' desires to establish a strong and respectable nation in the world, all of their plans to create a flourishing commercial economy, in short, all of what the Federalists wanted out of the new central government seemed in the final analysis dependent upon the prerequisite maintenance of aristocratic politics.

At first the Federalists tried to belittle the talk of an aristocracy; they even denied that they knew the meaning of the word. "Why bring into the debate the whims of writers — introducing the distinction of *well-born* from others?" asked Edmund Pendleton in the Virginia Ratifying Convention. In the Federalist view every man was "*well-born* who comes into the world with an intelligent mind, and with all his parts perfect." Was even natural talent to be suspect? Was learning to be encouraged, the Federalists asked in exasperation, only "to set up those who attained its benefits as butts of invidious distinction?" No American, the Federalists said, could justifiably oppose a man "commencing in life without any other stock but industry and economy," and "by the mere efforts of these" rising "to opulence and wealth." If social mobility were to be meaningful then some sorts of distinctions were necessary. If government by a natural aristocracy, said Wilson, meant "nothing more or less than a government of the best men in the community," then who could object to it? Could the Antifederalists actually intend to mark out those "most noted for their virtue and talents . . . as the most improper persons for the public confidence?" No, the Federalists exclaimed in disbelief, the Antifederalists could never have intended such a socially destructive conclusion. It was clear, said Hamilton, that the Antifederalists' arguments only proved "that there are men who are rich, men who are poor, some who are wise, and others who are not; that indeed, every distinguished man is an aristocrat." [26]

But the Antifederalist intention and implication were too conspicuous to be avoided: all distinctions, whether naturally based or not, were being challenged. Robert Livingston in the New York Convention saw as clearly as anyone what he thought the Antifederalists were really after, and he minced no words in replying to Smith's attack on the natural aristocracy. Since Smith had classified as aristocrats not only "the rich and the great" but also "the wise, the learned, and those eminent for their talents or great virtues," aristocrats to the Antifederalists had in substance become all men of merit. Such men, such aristocrats, were not to be chosen for public office, questioned Livingston in rising disbelief in the implications of the Antifederalist argument, "because the people will not have confidence in them; that is, the people will not have confidence in those who best deserve and most possess their confidence?" The logic of Smith's reasoning, said Livingston, would lead to a government by the dregs of society, a monstrous government where all "the unjust, the selfish, the unsocial feelings," where all "the vices, the infirmities, the passions of the people" would be represented. "Can it be thought," asked Livingston in an earlier development of this

argument to the Society of the Cincinnati, "that an enlightened people believe the science of government level to the meanest capacity? That experience, application, and education are unnecessary to those who are to frame
laws for the government of the state?" Yet strange as it may have seemed to
Livingston and others in the 1780's, America was actually approaching the
point where ability, education, and wealth were becoming liabilities, not
assets, in the attaining of public office. "Envy and the ambition of the un-
worthy" were robbing respectable men of the rank they merited. "To these
causes," said Livingston, "we owe the cloud that obscures our internal
governments." [27]

The course of the debates over the Constitution seemed to confirm
what the Federalists had believed all along. Antifederalism represented the
climax of a "war" that was, in the words of Theodore Sedgwick, being
"levied on the virtue, property, and distinctions in the community." The
opponents of the Constitution, despite some, "particularly in Virginia," who
were operating "from the most honorable and patriotic motives," were essentially identical with those who were responsible for the evils the states
were suffering from in the eighties — "narrowminded politicians . . . under
the influence of local views." [28] "Whilst many *ostensible* reasons are assigned" for the Antifederalists' opposition, charged Washington, "the real
ones are concealed behind the Curtains, because they are not of a nature to
appear in open day." "The real object of all their zeal in opposing the
system," agreed Madison, was to maintain "the supremacy of the State Legislatures," with all that meant in the printing of money and the violation of
contracts.[29] The Antifederalists or those for whom the Antifederalists spoke,
whether their spokesmen realized it or not, were "none but the horse-jockey,
the mushroom merchant, the running and dishonest speculator," those "who
owe the most and have the least to pay," those "whose dependence and
expectations are upon changes in government, and distracted times," men
of "desperate Circumstances," those "in Every State" who "have Debts to
pay, Interests to support or Fortunes to make," those, in short, who "wish for
scrambling Times." Apart from a few of their intellectual leaders the Anti-
federalists were thought to be an ill-bred lot: "Their education has been
rather indifferent — they have been accustomed to think on the small scale."
They were often blustering demagogues trying to push their way into office —
"men of much self-importance and supposed skill in politics, who are not of
sufficient consequence to obtain public employment." Hence they were considered to be jealous and mistrustful of "every one in the higher offices of
society," unable to bear to see others possessing "that fancied blessing, to
which, alas! they must themselves aspire in vain." [30] In the Federalist mind
therefore the struggle over the Constitution was not one between kinds of
wealth or property, or one between commercial or noncommercial elements

of the population, but rather represented a broad social division between those who believed in the right of a natural aristocracy to speak for the people and those who did not.

Against this threat from the licentious the Federalists pictured themselves as the defenders of the worthy, of those whom they called "the better sort of people," those, said John Jay, "who are orderly and industrious, who are content with their situations and not uneasy in their circumstances." Because the Federalists were fearful that republican equality was becoming "that *perfect equality* which deadens the motives of industry, and places Demerit on a Footing with Virtue," they were obsessed with the need to insure that the proper amount of inequality and natural distinctions be recognized. "Although there are no nobles in America," observed the French minister to America, Louis Otto, in 1786, "there is a class of men denominated 'gentlemen,' who, by reason of their wealth, their talents, their education, their families, or the offices they hold, aspire to a preeminence which the people refuse to grant them." "How idle . . . all disputes about a technical aristocracy" would be, if only the people would "pay strict attention to the natural aristocracy, which is the institution of heaven. . . . This aristocracy is derived from merit and that influence, which a character for superiour wisdom, and known services to the commonwealth, has to produce veneration, confidence and esteem, among a people, who have felt the benefits. . . ." Robert Morris, for example, was convinced there were social differences — even in Pennsylvania. "What!" he exclaimed in scornful amazement at John Smilie's argument that a republic admitted of no social superiorities. "Is it insisted that there is no distinction of character?" Respectability, said Morris with conviction, was not confined to property. "Surely persons possessed of knowledge, judgment, information, integrity, and having extensive connections, are not to be classed with persons void of reputation or character." [31]

In refuting the Antifederalists' contention "that all classes of citizens should have some of their own number in the representative body, in order that their feelings and interests may be the better understood and attended to," Hamilton in *The Federalist*, Number 35, put into words the Federalists' often unspoken and vaguely held assumption about the organic and the hierarchical nature of society. Such explicit class or occupational representation as the Antifederalists advocated, wrote Hamilton, was not only impractical but unnecessary, since the society was not as fragmented or heterogeneous as the Antifederalists implied. The various groups in the landed interest, for example, were "perfectly united, from the wealthiest landlord down to the poorest tenant," and this "common interest may always be reckoned upon as the surest bond of sympathy" linking the landed representative, however rich, to his constituents. In a like way, the members of the commercial community were "immediately connected" and most naturally represented by the merchants. "Mechanics and manufacturers will always be inclined, with few exceptions, to give their votes to merchants, in preference to persons of their own professions or trades. . . . They know that the merchant is their natural patron and friend; and . . . they are sensible that their habits in life have not been such as to give them those acquired endowments, without which in a deliberative assembly, the greatest natural abilities, are for the most part useless." However much many Federalists may have doubted the substance of Hamilton's analysis of American society, they could not doubt the truth of his conclusion. That the people were represented better by one of the natural aristocracy "whose situation leads to extensive inquiry and information" than by one "whose observation does not travel beyond the circle of his neighbors and acquaintances" was the defining element of the Federalist philosophy.

It was not simply the number of public securities, or credit outstanding, or the number of ships, or the amount of money possessed that made a man think of himself as one of the natural elite. It was much more subtle than the mere possession of wealth: it was a deeper social feeling, a sense of being socially established, of possessing attributes — family, education, and refinement — that others lacked, above all, of being accepted by and being able to move easily among those who considered themselves to be the respectable and cultivated. It is perhaps anachronistic to describe this social sense as a class interest, for it often transcended immediate political or economic concerns, and, as Hamilton's argument indicates, was designed to cut through narrow occupational categories. The Republicans of Philadelphia, for example, repeatedly denied that they represented an aristocracy with a united class interest. "We are of different occupations; of different sects of religion; and have different views of life. No factions or private system can comprehend us all." Yet with all their assertions of diversified interests the Republicans were not without a social consciousness in their quarrel with the supporters of the Pennsylvania Constitution. If there were any of us ambitious for power, their apology continued, then there would be no need to change the Constitution, for we surely could attain power under the present Constitution. "We have already seen how easy the task is for *any character* to rise into power and consequence under it. And there are some of us, who think not so meanly of ourselves, as to dread any rivalship from those who are now in office." [32]

In 1787 this kind of elitist social consciousness was brought into play as perhaps never before in eighteenth-century America, as gentlemen up and down the continent submerged their sectional and economic differences in the face of what seemed to be a threat to the very foundations of society. Despite his earlier opposition to the Order of the Cincinnati,

Theodore Sedgwick, like other frightened New Englanders, now welcomed
the organization as a source of strength in the battle for the Constitution.
The fear of social disruption that had run through much of the writing of
the eighties was brought to a head to eclipse all other fears. Although state
politics in the eighties remains to be analyzed, the evidence from Federalist
correspondence indicates clearly a belief that never had there occurred "so
great a change in the opinion of the best people" as was occurring in the last
few years of the decade. The Federalists were astonished at the outpouring
in 1787 of influential and respectable people who had earlier remained
quiescent. Too many of "the better sort of people," it was repeatedly said,
had withdrawn at the end of the war "from the theatre of public action, to
scenes of retirement and ease," and thus "demagogues of desperate fortunes,
mere adventurers in fraud, were left to act unopposed." [33] After all, it was
explained, "when the wicked rise, men hide themselves." Even the problems
of Massachusetts in 1786, noted General Benjamin Lincoln, the repressor of
the Shaysites, were not caused by the rebels, but by the laxity of "the good
people of the state." But the lesson of this laxity was rapidly being learned.
Everywhere, it seemed, men of virtue, good sense, and property, "almost the
whole body of our enlighten'd and leading characters in every state," were
awakened in support of stronger government. "The scum which was thrown
upon the surface by the fermentation of the war is daily sinking," Benjamin
Rush told Richard Price in 1786, "while a pure spirit is occupying its place."
"Men are brought into action who had consigned themselves to an eve of
rest," Edward Carrington wrote to Jefferson in June 1787, "and the Convention, as a Beacon, is rousing the attention of the Empire." The Antifederalists
could only stand amazed at this "weight of talents" being gathered in support of the Constitution. "What must the individual be who could thus
oppose them united?" [34]

    Still, in the face of this preponderance of wealth and respectability
in support of the Constitution, what remains extraordinary about 1787–88
is not the weakness and disunity but the political strength of Antifederalism.
That large numbers of Americans could actually reject a plan of government
created by a body "composed of the first characters in the Continent" and
backed by Washington and nearly the whole of the natural aristocracy of
the country said more about the changing character of American politics and
society in the eighties than did the Constitution's eventual acceptance.[35] It
was indeed a portent of what was to come. . . .

    If the new national government was to promote the common good
as forcefully as any state government, and if, as the Federalists believed, a
major source of the vices of the eighties lay in the abuse of state power, then
there was something apparently contradictory about the new federal Con-

stitution, which after all represented not a weakening of the dangerous power of republican government but rather a strengthening of it. "The complaints against the separate governments, even by the friends of the new plan," remarked the Antifederalist James Winthrop, "are not that they have not power enough, but that they are disposed to make a bad use of what power they have." Surely, concluded Winthrop, the Federalists were reasoning badly "when they purpose to set up a government possess'd of much more extensive powers . . . and subject to much smaller checks" than the existing state governments possessed and were subject to. Madison for one was quite aware of the pointedness of this objection. "It may be asked," he said, "how private rights will be more secure under the Guardianship of the General Government than under the State Governments, since they are both founded in the republican principle which refers the ultimate decision to the will of the majority." [36] What, in other words, was different about the new federal Constitution that would enable it to mitigate the effects of tyrannical majorities? What would keep the new federal government from succumbing to the same pressures that had beset the state governments? The answer the Federalists gave to these questions unmistakably reveals the social bias underlying both their fears of the unrestrained state legislatures and their expectations for their federal remedy. For all of their desires to avoid intricate examination of a delicate social structure, the Federalists' program itself demanded that the discussion of the Constitution would be inessentially social terms.

The Federalists were not as much opposed to the governmental power of the states as to the character of the people who were wielding it. The constitutions of most of the states were not really at fault. Massachusetts after all possessed a nearly perfect constitution. What actually bothered the Federalists was the sort of people who had been able to gain positions of authority in the state governments, particularly in the state legislatures. Much of the quarrel with the viciousness, instability, and injustice of the various state governments was at bottom social. "For," as John Dickinson emphasized, *the government will partake of the qualities of those whose authority is prevalent.*" The political and social structures were intimately related. "People once respected their governors, their senators, their judges and their clergy; they reposed confidence in them; their laws were obeyed, and the states were happy in tranquility." But in the eighties the authority of government had drastically declined because "men of sense and property have lost much of their influence by the popular spirit of the war." "That exact order, and due subordination, that is essentially necessary in all well appointed governments, and which constitutes the real happiness and well being of society" had been deranged by "men of no genius or abilities" who had tried to run "the machine of government." Since "it cannot be expected

that things will go well, when persons of vicious principles, and loose morals
are in authority," it was the large number of obscure, ignorant, and unruly
men occupying the state legislatures, and not the structure of the governments, that was the real cause of the evils so much complained of.[37]

The Federalist image of the Constitution as a sort of "philosopher's
stone" was indeed appropriate: it was a device intended to transmute base
materials into gold and thereby prolong the life of the republic. Patrick
Henry acutely perceived what the Federalists were driving at. "The Constitution," he said in the Virginia Convention, "reflects in the most degrading
and mortifying manner on the virtue, integrity, and wisdom of the state
legislatures; it presupposes that the chosen few who go to Congress will have
more upright hearts, and more enlightened minds, than those who are members of the individual legislatures." The new Constitution was structurally
no different from the constitutions of some of the states. Yet the powers of
the new central government were not as threatening as the powers of the
state governments precisely because the Federalists believed different kinds
of persons would hold them. They anticipated that somehow the new government would be staffed largely by "the worthy," the naturally social aristocracy of the country. "After all," said Pelatiah Webster, putting his finger
on the crux of the Federalist argument, "the grand secret of forming a good
government, is, to put good men into the administration: for wild, vicious,
or idle men, will ever make a bad government, let its principles be ever so
good." [38]

What was needed then, the Federalists argued, was to restore a
proper share of political influence to those who through their social attributes commanded the respect of the people and who through their enlightenment and education knew the true policy of government. "The people
commonly intend the PUBLIC GOOD," wrote Hamilton in *The Federalist,* but
they did not "always *reason right* about the *means* of promoting it." They
sometimes erred, largely because they were continually beset "by the wiles
of parasites and sycophants, by the snares of the ambitious, the avaricious,
the desperate, by the artifices of men who possess their confidence more than
deserve it, and of those who seek to possess rather than to deserve it." The
rights of man were simple, quickly felt, and easily comprehended: in matters
of liberty, "the mechanic and the philosopher, the farmer and the scholar,
are all upon a footing." But to the Federalists matters of government were
quite different: government was "a complicated science, and requires abilities and knowledge, of a variety of other subjects, to understand it." "Our
states cannot be well governed," the Federalists concluded, "till our old
influential characters acquire confidence and authority." Only if the respected and worthy lent their natural intellectual abilities and their natural

social influence to political authority could governmental order be maintained.[39]

Perhaps no one probed this theme more frenziedly than did Jonathan Jackson in his *Thoughts upon the Political Situation of the United States,* published in 1788. For Jackson the problems of the eighties were not merely intellectual but personal. Although at the close of the Revolution he had been one of the half-dozen richest residents of Newburyport, Massachusetts, by the end of the eighties not only had his wealth been greatly diminished but his position in Newburyport society had been usurped by a newer, less well-educated, less refined group of merchants.[40] His pamphlet, expressing his bitter reaction to this displacement, exaggerated but did not misrepresent a common Federalist anxiety.

Although differences of rank were inevitable in every society, wrote Jackson, "there never was a people upon earth . . . who were in less hazard than the people of this country, of an aristocracy's prevailing — or anything like it, dangerous to liberty." America possessed very little "inequality of fortune." There was "no rank of any consequence, nor hereditary titles." "Landed property is in general held in small portions, even in southern states, compared with the manors, parks and royal demesnes of most countries." And the decay of primogeniture and entail, together with the "diverse" habits and passions between fathers and sons, worked to retard the engrossing of large estates. The only kind of aristocracy possible in America would be an "*aristocracy* of experience, and of the best understandings," a "*natural aristocracy*" that had to dominate public authority in order to prevent America from degenerating into democratic licentiousness, into a government where the people "would be directed by no rule but their own will and caprice, or the interested wishes of a very few persons, who *affect* to speak the sentiments of the people." Tyranny by the people was the worst kind because it left few resources to the oppressed. Jackson explicitly and heatedly denied the assumption of 1776: "that large representative bodies are a great security to publick liberty." Such numerous popular assemblies resembled a mob, as likely filled with fools and knaves as wise and honest men. Jackson went on to question not only the possibility that the general good of the people would be expressed by such large assemblies, but also the advisability of annual elections and rotation of office. The people, Jackson even went so far as to say, "are nearly as unfit to choose legislators, or any of the more important publick officers, as they are in general to fill the offices themselves." There were in fact too many examples in the eighties of men from the people gaining seats in America's public assemblies, men "of good natural abilities and sound understanding, but who had had little or no education, and still less converse with the world." Such men were inevitably suspicious of those "they call the *gentle folks,*" those who were bred in easier circumstances and better endowed with education and worldly experience. Yet without the dominance of these "gentle folks" in the legislatures, the good of the whole society could never be promoted. The central problem facing America, said Jackson, was to bring the natural aristocracy back into use and to convey "authority to those, and those only, who by nature, education, and good dispositions, are qualified for government." It was this problem that the federal Constitution was designed to solve.[41]

In a review of Jackson's pamphlet Noah Webster raised the crucial question. It was commendable, he wrote, that only the wise and honest men be elected to office. "But how can a constitution ensure the choice of such men? A constitution that leaves the choice entirely with the people?" It was not enough simply to state that such persons were to be chosen. Indeed, many of the state constitutions already declared "that senators and representatives *shall* be elected from the *most wise, able,* and *honest* citizens. . . . The truth is, such declarations are *empty things,* as they require *that* to be *done* which cannot be *defined,* much less *enforced.*" It seemed to Webster that no constitution in a popular state could guarantee that only the natural aristocracy would be elected to office. How could the federal Constitution accomplish what the state constitutions like Massachusetts's and Connecticut's had been unable to accomplish? How could it insure that only the respectable and worthy would hold power? [42]

The evils of state politics, the Federalists had become convinced, flowed from the narrowness of interest and vision of the state legislators. "We find the representatives of countries and corporations in the Legislatures of the States," said Madison, "much more disposed to sacrifice the aggregate interest, and even authority, to the local views of their Constituents" than to promote the general good at the expense of their electors. Small electoral districts enabled obscure and designing men to gain power by practicing "the vicious arts by which elections are too often carried." Already observers in the eighties had noticed that a governmental official "standing, not on local, but a general election of the whole body of the people" tended to have a superior, broader vision by "being the interested and natural conservator of the universal interest." "The most effectual remedy for the local biass" of senators or of any elected official, said Madison, was to impress upon their minds "an attention to the interest of the whole Society by making them the choice of the whole Society." If elected officials were concerned with only the interest of those who elected them, then their outlook was most easily broadened by enlarging their electorate.[43] Perhaps nowhere was this contrast between localism and cosmopolitanism more fully analyzed and developed than in a pamphlet written by William Beers of Connecticut. Although Beers wrote in 1791, not to justify the Constitution, his insight into the workings of American politics was precisely that of the Federalists of 1787.

"The people of a state," wrote Beers, "may justly be divided into two classes": those, on one hand, "who are independent in their principles, of sound judgments, actuated by no local or personal influence, and who understand, and ever act with a view to the public good"; and those, on the other hand, who were "the dependent, the weak, the biassed, local party men — the dupes of artifice and ambition." While the independent and worthy were "actuated by a uniform spirit, and will generally unite their views in the same object," they were diffused throughout the whole community. "In particular districts, they bear not an equal proportion to the opposite party, who tho incapable of extending their views throughout the state, find in their particular communities similar objects of union." Thus the best people were often overpowered in small district elections, where "the success of a candidate may depend in a great degree on the quantity of his exertions for the moment," on his becoming "popular, for a single occasion, by qualities and means, which could not possibly establish a permanent popularity or one which should pervade a large community," on his seizing "the occasion of some prevailing passion, some strong impression of separate interest, some popular clamor against the existing administration, or some other false and fatal prejudice" — all the arts which were "well known, by the melancholy experience of this and other nations, to have met, in small circles of election, but too often with triumphant success." But an entire state could not be so deluded. "No momentary glare of deceptive qualities, no intrigues, no exertions will be sufficient to make a whole people lose sight of those points of character which alone can entitle one to their universal confidence." With a large electorate the advance toward public honors was slow and gradual. "Much time is necessary to become the object of general observation and confidence." Only established social leaders would thus be elected by a broad constituency. Narrow the electorate, "and you leave but a single step between the lowest and the most elevated station. You take ambition by the hand, you raise her from obscurity, and clothe her in purple." With respect to the size of the legislative body, the converse was true. Reduce the number of its members and thereby guarantee a larger proportion of the right kind of people to be elected, for "the more you enlarge the body, the greater chance there is, of introducing weak and unqualified men." [44]

Constitutional reformers in the eighties had continually attempted to apply these insights to the states, by decreasing the size of the legislatures and by proposing at-large elections for governors and senators in order to "make a segregation of upright, virtuous, intelligent men, to guide the helm of public affairs." Now these ideas were to be applied to the new federal government with hopefully even more effectiveness. The great height of the new national government, it was expected, would prevent unprincipled and vicious men, the obscure and local-minded men who had gained power in the state legislatures, from scaling its walls. The federal government would act as a kind of sieve, extracting "from the mass of the society the purest and noblest characters which it contains." Election by the people in large districts would temper demagoguery and crass electioneering and would thus, said James Wilson, "be most likely to obtain men of intelligence and uprightness." "Faction," it was believed, "will decrease in proportion to the diminution of counsellors." It would be "transferred from the state legislatures to Congress, where it will be more easily controlled." The men who would sit in the federal legislature, because few in number and drawn from a broad electorate, would be "the best men in the country." "For," wrote John Jay in *The Federalist*, "although town or country, or other contracted influence, may place men in State assemblies, or senates, or courts of justice, or executive departments, yet more general and extensive reputation for talents and other qualifications will be necessary to recommend men to offices under the national government." Only by first bringing these sorts of men, the natural aristocracy of the country, back into dominance in politics, the Federalists were convinced, could Americans begin to solve the pressing foreign and domestic problems facing them. Only then, concluded Jay, would it "result that the administration, the political counsels, and the judicial decisions of the national government will be more wise, systematical, and judicious than those of individual States, and consequently more satisfactory with respect to other nations, as well as more *safe* with respect to us." The key therefore to the prospects of the new federal government, compared to the experience of the confederation of sovereign states, declared Francis Corbin of Virginia in words borrowed from Jean Louis De Lolme, the Genevan commentator on the English constitution, lay in the fact that the federal Constitution "places the remedy in the hands which *feel* the disorder; the other places the remedy in those hands which *cause* the disorder." [45]

In short, through the artificial contrivance of the Constitution overlying an expanded society, the Federalists meant to restore and to prolong the traditional kind of elitist influence in politics that social developments, especially since the Revolution, were undermining. As the defenders if not always the perpetrators of these developments — the "disorder" of the 1780's — the Antifederalists could scarcely have missed the social implications of the Federalist program. The Constitution was intrinsically an aristocratic document designed to check the democratic tendencies of the period, and as such it dictated the character of the Antifederalist response. It was therefore inevitable that the Antifederalists should have charged that the new government was "dangerously adapted to the purposes of an immediate *aristocratic tyranny*." In state after state the Antifederalists reduced the issue to those social terms predetermined by the Federalists themselves: the Constitution was a plan intended to "raise the fortunes and respectability of the *well-born few,* and oppress the plebians"; it was "a continental exertion of the *well-born* of America to obtain that darling domination, which they have not been able to accomplish in their respective states"; it "will lead to an aristocratical government, and establish tyranny over us." Whatever their own particular social standing, the Antifederalist spokesmen spread the warning that the new government would be "in practice a *permanent* ARISTOCRACY" or would soon "degenerate to a compleat Aristocracy." [46] Both George Mason and Richard Henry Lee, speaking not out of the concerns of the social elite to which they belonged but out of a complicated sense of alienation from that elite, expressed as much fear of a "consolidating aristocracy" resulting from the new Constitution as any uncultivated Scotch-Irish upstart. While Lee privately revealed his deep dislike of "the hasty, unpersevering, aristocratic genius of the south" which "suits not my disposition," Mason throughout the duration of the Philadelphia Convention acted as the conscience of an old republicanism he thought his Virginia colleagues had forgotten and continually reminded them of what the Revolution had been about. "Whatever inconveniency may attend the democratic principle," said Mason repeatedly, "it must actuate one part of the Government. It is the only security for the rights of the people." As the Constitution seemed to demonstrate, the "superior classes of society" were becoming too indifferent to the "lowest classes." Remember, he warned his fellow delegates pointedly, "our own children will in a short time be among the general mass." The Constitution seemed obviously "calculated," as even young John Quincy Adams declared, "to increase the influence, power and wealth of those who have it already." Its adoption would undoubtedly be "a grand point gained in favor of the aristocratic party." [47]

Aristocratic principles were in fact "interwoven" in the very fabric of the proposed government. If a government was "so constituted as to admit but few to exercise the powers of it," then it would "according to the natural course of things" end up in the hands of "the natural aristocracy." It went almost without saying that the awesome president and the exalted Senate, "a compound of *monarchy* and *aristocracy*," would be dangerously far removed from the people. But even the House of Representatives, the very body that "should be a true picture of the people, possess a knowledge of their circumstances and their wants, sympathize in all their distresses, and disposed to seek their true interest," was without "a tincture of democracy." Since it could never collect "the interests, feelings, and opinions of three or four millions of people," it was better understood as "an Assistant

Aristocratical Branch" to the Senate than as a real representation of the people.[48] When the number of representatives was "so small, the office will be highly elevated and distinguished; the style in which the members live will probably be high; circumstances of this kind will render the place of a representative not a desirable one to sensible, substantial men, who have been used to walk in the plain and frugal paths of life." While the ordinary people in extensive electoral districts of thirty or forty thousand inhabitants would remain "divided," those few extraordinary men with "conspicuous military, popular, civil or legal talents" could more easily form broader associations to dominate elections; they had family and other connections to "unite their interests." If only a half-dozen congressmen were to be selected to represent a large state, then rarely, argued the Antifederalists in terms that were essentially no different from those used by the Federalists in the Constitution's defense, would persons from "the great body of the people, the middle and lower classes," be elected to the House of Representatives. "The Station is too high and exalted to be filled out [by] the *first Men* in the State in point of Fortune and Influence. In fact no order or class of the people will be represented in the House of Representatives called the Democratic Branch but the rich and wealthy." [49] The Antifederalists thus came to oppose the new national government for the same reason the Federalists favored it: because its very structure and detachment from the people would work to exclude any kind of actual and local interest representation and prevent those who were not rich, well born, or prominent from exercising political power. Both sides fully appreciated the central issue the Constitution posed and grappled with it throughout the debates: whether a professedly popular government should actually be in the hands of, rather than simply derived from, common ordinary people.

Out of the division in 1787–88 over this issue, an issue which was as conspicuously social as any in American history, the Antifederalists emerged as the spokesmen for the growing American antagonism to aristocracy and as the defenders of the most intimate participation in politics of the widest variety of people possible. It was not from lack of vision that the Antifederalists feared the new government. Although their viewpoint was intensely localist, it was grounded in as perceptive an understanding of the social basis of American politics as that of the Federalists. Most of the Antifederalists were majoritarians with respect to the state legislatures but not with respect to the national legislature, because they presumed as well as the Federalists did that different sorts of people from those who sat in the state assemblies would occupy the Congress. Whatever else may be said about the Antifederalists, their populism cannot be impugned. They were true champions of the most extreme kind of democratic and egalitarian politics expressed in the Revolutionary era. Convinced that "it has been the principal care of free governments to guard against the encroachments of the great," the Antifederalists believed that popular government itself, as defined by the principles of 1776, was endangered by the new national government. If the Revolution had been a transfer of power from the few to the many, then the federal Constitution clearly represented an abnegation of the Revolution. For, as Richard Henry Lee wrote in his *Letters from the Federal Farmer,* "every man of reflection must see, that the change now proposed, is a transfer of power from the many to the few." [50]

Although Lee's analysis contained the essential truth, the Federalist program was not quite so simple summed up. It was true that through the new Constitution the Federalists hoped to resist and eventually to avert what they saw to be the rapid decline of the influence and authority of the natural aristocracy in America. At the very time that the organic conception of society that made elite rule comprehensible was finally and avowedly dissolving, and the members of the elite were developing distinct professional, social, or economic interests, the Federalists found elite rule more imperative than ever before. To the Federalists the greatest dangers to republicanism were flowing not, as the old Whigs had thought, from the rulers or from any distinctive minority in the community, but from the widespread participation of the people in the government. It now seemed increasingly evident that if the public good not only of the United States as a whole but even of the separate states were to be truly perceived and promoted, the American people must abandon their Revolutionary reliance on their representative state legislatures and place their confidence in the highmindedness of the natural leaders of the society, which ideally everyone had the opportunity of becoming. Since the Federalists presumed that only such a self-conscious elite could transcend the many narrow and contradictory interests inevitable in any society, however small, the measure of a good government became its capacity for insuring the predominance of these kinds of natural leaders who knew better than the people as a whole what was good for the society.

The result was an amazing display of confidence in constitutionalism, in the efficacy of institutional devices for solving social and political problems. Through the proper arrangement of new institutional structures the Federalists aimed to turn the political and social developments that were weakening the place of "the better sort of people" in government back upon themselves and to make these developments the very source of the perpetuation of the natural aristocracy's dominance of politics. Thus the Federalists did not directly reject democratic politics as it had manifested itself in the 1780's; rather they attempted to adjust to this politics in order to control and mitigate its effects. In short they offered the country an elitist theory of democracy. They did not see themselves as repudiating either the Revo-

lution or popular government, but saw themselves as saving both from
their excesses. If the Constitution were not established, they told themselves
and the country over and over, then republicanism was doomed, the grand
experiment was over, and a division of the confederacy, monarchy, or worse
would result.

Despite all the examples of popular vice in the eighties, the Federalist confidence in the people remained strong. The letters of "Caesar,"
with their frank and violent denigration of the people, were anomalies in
the Federalist literature.[51] The Federalists had by no means lost faith in the
people, at least in the people's ability to discern their true leaders. In fact
many of the social elite who comprised the Federalist leadership were confident of popular election if the constituency could be made broad enough,
and crass electioneering be curbed, so that the people's choice would be
undisturbed by ambitious demagogues. "For if not blind to their own interest, they choose men of the first character for wisdom and integrity."
Despite prodding by so-called designing and unprincipled men, the bulk
of the people remained deferential to the established social leadership —
for some aspiring politicians frustratingly so. Even if they had wanted to,
the Federalists could not turn their backs on republicanism. For it was evident to even the most pessimistic "that no other form would be reconcilable
with the genius of the people of America; with the fundamental principles
of the Revolution; or with that honorable determination which animates
every votary of freedom, to rest all our political experiments on the capacity
of mankind for self-government." Whatever government the Federalists
established had to be "strictly republican" and "deducible from the only
source of just authority — the People." [52]

WHAT WAS THE RELATION OF THE CONSTITUTION TO DEMOCRACY?

The Founding Fathers:
A Reform Caucus in Action

JOHN P. ROCHE

If the Federalists did in fact intend the Constitution to create a high-toned government filled with "better sorts," cosmopolitan sorts, of people, does it follow that they were reactionaries trying to reverse the democratic and populist thrust of the Revolution? This question has been at the center of historical controversy over the Constitution since at least the end of the nineteenth century, and is not easily answered. As John P. Roche, Professor of Politics at Brandeis University, makes clear, the framers of the Constitution were not detached intellectuals free from the responsibilities of power and the constraints of an electorate; they were, in fact, public officials and social leaders fully immersed in the currents of American politics — a politics that would no longer permit the members of an elite to talk only with one another. Whether they liked it or not, the Founding Fathers were "professional politicians in a democratic society," and thus had to adjust their aims and compromise their principles to gain popular acceptance of their revolutionary program — illustrating vividly the continuing problem of the proper relationship between an elite and the populace in a democratic system. Yet it would be a mistake to accept too easily Roche's presentist- and behaviorist-minded essay which tends to dissolve the real distinctions between then and now and to obscure the peculiar ideological issues of the period.

Over the last century and a half, the work of the Constitutional Convention and the motives of the Founding Fathers have been analyzed under a number of different ideological auspices. To one generation of historians, the hand of God was moving in the assembly; under a later dispensation, the dialectic (at various levels of philosophical sophistication) replaced the Deity: "relationships of production" moved into the niche previously reserved for Love of Country. Thus in counterpoint to the Zeitgeist, the Framers have undergone miraculous metamorphoses: at one time acclaimed as liberals and bold social engineers, today they appear in the guise of sound Burkean conservatives, men who in our time would subscribe to *Fortune,* look to Walter Lippmann for political theory, and chuckle patronizingly at the antics of Barry Goldwater. The implicit assumption is that if James Madison were among us, he would be President of the Ford Foundation, while Alexander Hamilton would chair the Committee for Economic Development.

The "Fathers" have thus been admitted to our best circles; the revolutionary ferocity which confiscated all Tory property in reach and populated New Brunswick with outlaws has been converted by the "Miltown School" of American historians into a benign dedication to "consensus" and "prescriptive rights." The Daughters of the American Revolution have, through the ministrations of Professors Boorstin, Hartz, and Rossiter, at last found ancestors worthy of their descendants. It is not my purpose here to argue that the "Fathers" were, in fact, radical revolutionaries; that proposition has been brilliantly demonstrated by Robert R. Palmer in his *Age of the Democratic Revolution.* My concern is with the further position that not only were they revolutionaries, but also they were democrats. Indeed, in my view, there is one fundamental truth about the Founding Fathers that *every* generation of Zeitgeisters has done its best to obscure: they were first and foremost superb democratic politicians. I suspect that in a contemporary setting, James Madison would be Speaker of the House of Representatives and Hamilton would be the *éminence grise* dominating (*pace* Theodore Sorenson or Sherman Adams) the Executive Office of the President. They were, with their colleagues, *political men* — not metaphysicians, disembodied conservatives or Agents of History — and as recent research into the nature of American politics in the 1780s confirms,[1*] they were committed (perhaps willy-nilly) to working within the democratic framework, within a universe

From John P. Roche, "The Founding Fathers: A Reform Caucus in Action," *American Political Science Review*, 55 (1961), 799–816. Reprinted by permission.
* [See pp. 173–178 for notes to this article. — Ed.]

of public approval. Charles Beard *and* the filiopietists to the contrary notwithstanding, the Philadelphia Convention was not a College of Cardinals or a council of Platonic guardians working within a manipulative, predemocratic framework; it was a *nationalist* reform caucus which had to operate with great delicacy and skill in a political cosmos full of enemies to achieve the one definitive goal — popular approbation.

Perhaps the time has come, to borrow Walton Hamilton's fine phrase, to raise the Framers from immortality to mortality, to give them credit for their magnificent demonstration of the art of democratic politics. The point must be reemphasized; they *made* history and did it within the limits of consensus. There was nothing inevitable about the future in 1787; the *Zeitgeist,* that fine Hegelian technique of begging causal questions, could only be discerned in retrospect. What they did was to hammer out a pragmatic compromise which would both bolster the "National interest" and be acceptable to the people. What inspiration they got came from their collective experience as professional politicians in a democratic society. As John Dickinson put it to his fellow delegates on August 13, "Experience must be our guide. Reason may mislead us."

In this context, let us examine the problems they confronted and the solutions they evolved. The Convention has been described picturesquely as a counter-revolutionary junta and the Constitution as a *coup d'etat,*[2] but this has been accomplished by withdrawing the whole history of the movement for constitutional reform from its true context. No doubt the goals of the constitutional elite were "subversive" to the existing political order, but it is overlooked that their subversion could only have succeeded if the people of the United States endorsed it by regularized procedures. Indubitably they were "plotting" to establish a much stronger central government than existed under the Articles, but only in the sense in which one could argue equally well that John F. Kennedy was, from 1956 to 1960, "plotting" to become President. In short, on the fundamental *procedural* level, the Constitutionalists had to work according to the prevailing rules of the game. Whether they liked it or not is a topic for spiritualists — and is irrelevant: one may be quite certain that had Washington agreed to play the De Gaulle (as the Cincinnati once urged), Hamilton would willingly have held his horse, but such fertile speculation in no way alters the actual context in which events took place.

When the Constitutionalists went forth to subvert the Confederation, they utilized the mechanisms of political legitimacy. And the roadblocks which confronted them were formidable. At the same time, they were endowed with certain potent political assets. The history of the United

States from 1786 to 1790 was largely one of a masterful employment of political expertise by the Constitutionalists as against bumbling, erratic behavior by the opponents of reform. Effectively, the Constitutionalists had to induce the states, by democratic techniques of coercion, to emasculate themselves. To be specific, if New York had refused to join the new Union, the project was doomed; yet before New York was safely in, the reluctant state legislature had *sua sponte* to take the following steps: (1) agree to send delegates to the Philadelphia Convention; (2) provide maintenance for these delegates (these were distinct stages: New Hampshire was early in naming delegates, but did not provide for their maintenance until July); (3) set up the special *ad hoc* convention to decide on ratification; and (4) concede to the decision of the *ad hoc* convention that New York should participate. New York admittedly was a tricky state, with a strong interest in a *status quo* which permitted her to exploit New Jersey and Connecticut, but the same legal hurdles existed in every state. And at the risk of becoming boring, it must be reiterated that the *only* weapon in the Constitutionalist arsenal was an effective mobilization of public opinion.

The group which undertook this struggle was an interesting amalgam of a few dedicated nationalists with the self-interested spokesmen of various parochial bailiwicks. The Georgians, for example, wanted a strong central authority to provide military protection for their huge, underpopulated state against the Creek Confederacy; Jerseymen and Connecticuters wanted to escape from economic bondage to New York; the Virginians hoped to establish a system which would give that great state its rightful place in the councils of the republic. The dominant figures in the politics of these states therefore cooperated in the call for the Convention.[3] In other states, the thrust towards national reform was taken up by opposition groups who added the "national interest" to their weapons system; in Pennsylvania, for instance, the group fighting to revise the Constitution of 1776 came out foursquare behind the Constitutionalists, and in New York, Hamilton and the Schuyler *ambiance* took the same tack against George Clinton.[4] There was, of course, a large element of personality in the affair: there is reason to suspect that Patrick Henry's opposition to the Convention and the Constitution was founded on his conviction that Jefferson was behind both, and a close study of local politics elsewhere would surely reveal that others supported the Constitution for the simple (and politically quite sufficient) reason that the "wrong" people were against it.

To say this is not to suggest that the Constitution rested on a foundation of impure or base motives. It is rather to argue that in politics there are no immaculate conceptions, and that in the drive for a stronger general government, motives of all sorts played a part. Few men in the history of mankind have espoused a view of the "common good" or "public interest" that militated against their private status; even Plato with all his reverence for disembodied reason managed to put philosophers on top of the pile. Thus it is not surprising that a number of diversified private interests joined to push the nationalist public interest; what would have been surprising was the absence of such a pragmatic united front. And the fact remains that, however motivated, these men did demonstrate a willingness to compromise their parochial interests in behalf of an ideal which took shape before their eyes and under their ministrations.

As Stanley Elkins and Eric McKitrick have suggested in a perceptive essay,[5] what distinguished the leaders of the Constitutionalist caucus from their enemies was a "Continental" approach to political, economic and military issues. To the extent that they shared an institutional base of operations, it was the Continental Congress (thirty-nine of the delegates to the Federal Convention had served in Congress[6]), and this was hardly a locale which inspired respect for the state governments. Robert de Jouvenal observed French politics half a century ago and noted that a revolutionary Deputy had more in common with a non-revolutionary Deputy than he had with a revolutionary non-Deputy;[7] similarly one can surmise that membership in the Congress under the Articles of Confederation worked to establish a continental frame of reference, that a Congressman from Pennsylvania and one from South Carolina would share a universe of discourse which provided them with a conceptual common denominator *vis à vis* their respective state legislatures. This was particularly true with respect to external affairs: the average state legislator was probably about as concerned with foreign policy then as he is today, but Congressmen were constantly forced to take the broad view of American prestige, were compelled to listen to the reports of Secretary John Jay and to the dispatches and pleas from their frustrated envoys in Britain, France and Spain.[8] From considerations such as these, a "Continental" ideology developed which seems to have demanded a revision of our domestic institutions primarily on the ground that only by invigorating our general government could we assume our rightful place in the international arena. Indeed, an argument with great force — particularly since Washington was its incarnation — urged that our very survival in the Hobbesian jungle of world politics depended upon a reordering and strengthening of our national sovereignty.[9]

Note that I am not endorsing the "Critical Period" thesis; on the contrary, Merrill Jensen seems to me quite sound in his view that for most Americans, engaged as they were in self-sustaining agriculture, the "Critical Period" was not particularly critical.[10] In fact, the great achievement of the Constitutionalists was their ultimate success in convincing the elected representatives of a majority of the white male population that change was imperative. A small group of political leaders with a Continental vision and essentially a consciousness of the United States' *international* impotence, provided the matrix of the movement. To their standard other leaders rallied with their own parallel ambitions. Their great assets were (1) the presence in their caucus of the one authentic American "father figure," George Washington, whose prestige was enormous;[11] (2) the energy and talent of their leadership (in which one must include the towering intellectuals of the time, John Adams and Thomas Jefferson, despite their absence abroad), and their communications "network," which was far superior to anything on the opposition side;[12] (3) the preemptive skill which made "their" issue The Issue and kept the locally oriented opposition permanently on the defensive; and (4) the subjective consideration that these men were spokesmen of a new and compelling credo: *American* nationalism, that ill-defined but nonetheless potent sense of collective purpose that emerged from the American Revolution.

Despite great institutional handicaps, the Constitutionalists managed in the mid-1780s to mount an offensive which gained momentum as years went by. Their greatest problem was lethargy, and paradoxically, the number of barriers in their path may have proved an advantage in the long run. Beginning with the initial battle to get the Constitutional Convention called and delegates appointed, they could never relax, never let up the pressure. In practical terms, this meant that the local "organizations" created by the Constitutionalists were perpetually in movement building up their cadres for the next fight. (The word organization has to be used with great caution: a political organization in the United States — as in contemporary England — generally consisted of a magnate and his following, or a coalition of magnates. This did not necessarily mean that it was "undemocratic" or "aristocratic," in the Aristotelian sense of the word: while a few magnates such as the Livingstons could draft their followings, most exercised their leadership without coercion on the basis of popular endorsement. The absence of organized opposition did not imply the impossibility of competition any more than low public participation in elections necessarily indicated an undemocratic suffrage.)

The Constitutionalists got the jump on the "opposition" (a collective noun: oppositions would be more correct) at the outset with the demand for a Convention. Their opponents were caught in an old political trap: they were not being asked to approve any specific program of reform, but only to endorse a meeting to discuss and recommend needed reforms. If they took a hard line at the first stage, they were put in the position of glorifying the *status quo* and of denying the need for *any* changes. Moreover, the Constitutionalists could go to the people with a persuasive argument for "fair play" — "How can you condemn reform before you know precisely what is involved?" Since the state legislatures obviously would have the final say on any proposals that might emerge from the Convention, the Constitutionalists were merely reasonable men asking for a chance. Besides, since they did not make any concrete proposals at that stage, they were in a position to capitalize on every sort of generalized discontent with the Confederation.

Perhaps because of their poor intelligence system, perhaps because of over-confidence generated by the failure of all previous efforts to alter the Articles,[14] the opposition awoke too late to the dangers that confronted them in 1787. Not only did the Constitutionalists manage to get every state but Rhode Island (where politics was enlivened by a party system reminiscent of the "Blues" and the "Greens" in the Byzantine Empire)[15] to appoint delegates to Philadelphia, but when the results were in, it appeared that they dominated the delegations. Given the apathy of the opposition, this was a natural phenomenon: in an ideologically non-polarized political atmosphere those who get appointed to a special committee are likely to be the men who supported the movement for its creation. Even George Clinton, who seems to have been the first opposition leader to awake to the possibility of trouble, could not prevent the New York legislature from appointing Alexander Hamilton — though he did have the foresight to send two of his henchmen to dominate the delegation. Incidentally, much has been made of the fact that the delegates to Philadelphia were not elected by the people; some have adduced this fact as evidence of the "undemocratic" character of the gathering. But put in the context of the time, this argument is wholly specious: the central government under the Articles was considered a creature of the component states and in all the states but Rhode Island, Connecticut and New Hampshire, members of the national Congress were chosen by the state legislatures. This was not a consequence of elitism or fear of the mob; it was a logical extension of states'-rights doctrine to guarantee that the national institution did not end-run the state legislatures and make direct contact with the people.[16]

With delegations safely named, the focus shifted to Philadelphia. While waiting for a quorum to assemble, James Madison got busy and drafted the so-called Randolph or Virginia Plan with the aid of the Virginia delegation. This was a political master-stroke. Its consequence was that once business got underway, the framework of discussion was established on Madison's terms. There was no interminable argument over agenda; instead the delegates took the Virginia Resolutions — "just for purposes of discussion" — as their point of departure. And along with Madison's proposals, many of which were buried in the course of the summer, went his major premise: a new start on a Constitution rather than piecemeal amendment. This was not necessarily revolutionary — a little exegesis could demonstrate that a new Constitution might be formulated as "amendments" to the Articles of Confederation — but Madison's proposal that this "lump sum" amendment go into effect after approval by nine states (the Articles required unanimous state approval for any amendment) was thoroughly subversive.[17]

Standard treatments of the Convention divide the delegates into "nationalists" and "states'-righters" with various improvised shadings ("moderate nationalists," etc.), but these are a *posteriori* categories which obfuscate more than they clarify. What is striking to one who analyzes the Convention as a case-study in democratic politics is the lack of clear-cut ideological divisions in the Convention. Indeed, I submit that the evidence — Madison's *Notes*, the correspondence of the delegates, and debates on ratification — indicates that this was a remarkably homogeneous body on the ideological level. Yates and Lansing, Clinton's two chaperones for Hamilton, left in disgust on July 10. (Is there anything more tedious than sitting through endless disputes on matters one deems fundamentally misconceived? It takes an iron will to spend a hot summer as an ideological *agent provocateur*.) Luther Martin, Maryland's bibulous narcissist, left on September 4 in a huff when he discovered that others did not share his self-esteem; others went home for personal reasons. But the hard core of delegates accepted a grinding regimen throughout the attrition of a Philadelphia summer precisely because they shared the Constitutionalist goal.

Basic differences of opinion emerged, of course, but these were not ideological; they were *structural*. If the so-called "states'-rights" group had not accepted the fundamental purposes of the Convention, they could simply have pulled out and by doing so have aborted the whole enterprise. Instead of bolting, they returned day after day to argue and to compromise. An interesting symbol of this basic homogeneity was the initial agreement on secrecy: these professional politicians did not want to become prisoners of publicity; they wanted to retain that freedom of maneuver which is only possible when men are not forced to take public stands in the preliminary stages of negotiation.[18] There was no legal means of binding the tongues of the delegates: at any stage in the game a delegate with basic principled objections to the emerging project could have taken the stump (as Luther Martin did after his exit) and denounced the convention to the skies. Yet Madison did not even inform Thomas Jefferson in Paris of the course of the deliberations[19] and available correspondence indicates that the delegates generally observed the injunction. Secrecy is certainly uncharacteristic of any assembly marked by strong ideological polarization. This was noted at the time the *New York Daily Advertiser*, August 14, 1787, commented that the "profound secrecy hitherto observed by the Convention [we consider] a happy omen, as it demonstrates that the spirit of party on any great and essential point cannot have arisen to any height." [20]

Commentators on the Constitution who have read *The Federalist* in lieu of reading the actual debates have credited the Fathers with the invention of a sublime concept called "Federalism."[21] Unfortunately, *The Federalist* is probative evidence for only one proposition: that Hamilton and Madison were inspired propagandists with a genius for retrospective symmetry. Federalism, as the theory is generally defined, was an improvisation which was later promoted into a political theory. Experts on "federalism" should take to heart the advice of David Hume, who warned in his *Of the Rise and Progress of the Arts and Sciences* that "there is no subject in which we must proceed with more caution than in [history], lest we assign causes which never existed and reduce what is merely contingent to stable and universal principles." In any event, the final balance in the Constitution between the states and the nation must have come as a great disappointment to Madison, while Hamilton's unitary views are too well known to need elucidation.

It is indeed astonishing how those who have glibly designated James Madison the "father" of Federalism have overlooked the solid body of fact which indicates that he shared Hamilton's quest for a unitary central government. To be specific, they have avoided examining the clear import of the Madison-Virginia Plan,[22] and have disregarded Madison's dogged inch-by-inch retreat from the bastions of centralization. The Virginia Plan envisioned a unitary national government effectively freed from and dominant over the states. The lower house of the national legislature was to be elected directly by the people of the states with membership proportional to population. The upper house was to be selected by the lower and the two chambers would elect the executive and choose the judges. The national government would be thus cut completely loose from the states.[23]

The structure of the general government was freed from state control in a truly radical fashion, but the scope of the authority of the national sovereign as Madison initially formulated it was breathtaking — it was a formulation worthy of the Sage of Malmesbury himself. The national legislature was to be empowered to disallow the acts of state legislatures,[24] and the central government was vested, in addition to the powers of the nation under the Articles of Confederation, with plenary authority wherever "the separate States are incompetent or in which the harmony of the United States may be interrupted by the exercise of individual legislation."[25] Finally, just to lock the door against state intrusion, the national Congress was to be given the power to use military force on recalcitrant states.[26] This was Madison's "model" of an ideal national government, though it later received little publicity in *The Federalist*.

The interesting thing was the reaction of the Convention to this militant program for a strong autonomous central government. Some delegates were startled, some obviously leery of so comprehensive a project of reform,[27] but nobody set off any fireworks and nobody walked out. Moreover, in the two weeks that followed, the Virginia Plan received substantial endorsement *en principe;* the initial temper of the gathering can be deduced from the approval "without debate or dissent," on May 31, of the Sixth Resolution which granted Congress the authority to disallow state legislation "contravening *in its opinion* the Articles of Union." Indeed, an amendment was included to bar states from contravening national treaties.[28]

The Virginia Plan may therefore be considered, in ideological terms, as the delegates' Utopia, but as the discussions continued and became more specific, many of those present began to have second thoughts. After all, they were not residents of Utopia or guardians in Plato's Republic who could simply impose a philosophical ideal on subordinate strata of the population. They were practical politicians in a democratic society, and no matter what their private dreams might be, they had to take home an acceptable package and defend it — and their own political futures — against predictable attack. On June 14 the breaking point between dream and reality took place. Apparently realizing that under the Virginia Plan, Massachusetts, Virginia and Pennsylvania could virtually dominate the national government — and probably appreciate that to sell this program to "the folks back home" would be impossible — the delegates from the small states dug in their heels and demanded time for a consideration of alternatives. One gets a graphic sense of the inner politics from John Dickinson's reproach to Madison: "You see the consequence of pushing things too far. Some of the members from the small States wish for two branches in the General Legislature and are friends to a good National Government; but we would sooner submit to a foreign power than . . . be deprived of an equality of suffrage in both branches of the Legislature, and thereby be thrown under the domination of the large States." [29]

The bare outline of the *Journal* entry for Tuesday, June 14, is suggestive to anyone with extensive experience in deliberative bodies. "It was moved by Mr. Patterson [*sic,* Paterson's name was one of those consistently misspelled by Madison and everybody else] seconded by Mr. Randolph that the further consideration of the report from the Committee of the whole House [endorsing the Virginia Plan] be postponed til tomorrow, and before the question for postponement was taken. It was moved by Mr. Randolph seconded by Mr. Patterson that the House adjourn." [30] The House adjourned by obvious prearrangement of the two principals: since the preceding Saturday when Brearley and Patterson of New Jersey had announced their fundamental discontent with the representational features of the Virginia Plan, the informal pressure had certainly been building up to slow down the streamroller. Doubtless there were extended arguments at the Indian Queen between Madison and Patterson, the latter insisting that events were moving rapidly towards a probably disastrous conclusion, towards a political suicide pact. Now the process of accommodation was put into action smoothly — and wisely, given the character and strength of the doubters. Madison had the votes, but this was one of those situations where the enforcement of mechanical majoritarianism could easily have destroyed the objectives of the majority: the Constitutionalists were in quest of a qualitative as well as a quantitative consensus. This was hardly from deference to local Quaker custom; it was a political imperative if they were to attain ratification.

According to the standard script, at this point the "states'-rights" group intervened in force behind the New Jersey Plan, which has been characteristically portrayed as a reversion to the *status quo* under the Articles of Confederation with but minor modifications. A careful examination of the evidence indicates that only in a marginal sense is this an accurate description. It is true that the New Jersey Plan put the states back into the institutional picture, but one could argue that to do so was a recognition of political reality rather than an affirmation of states'-rights. A serious case can be made that the advocates of the New Jersey Plan, far from being ideological addicts of states'-rights, intended to substitute for the Virginia Plan a system which would both retain strong national power and have a chance of adoption in the states. The leading spokesman for the project asserted quite clearly that his views were based more on counsels of expediency than on principle; said Paterson on June 16: "I came here not to speak my own sentiments, but the sentiments of those who sent me. Our object is not such a Governmt. as may be best in itself, but such a one as our Constituents have authorized us to prepare, and as they will approve." [31] This is Madison's version; in Yates' transcription, there is a crucial sentence following the remarks above: "I believe that a little practical virtue is to be preferred to the finest theoretical principles, which cannot be carried into effect." [32] In his preliminary speech on June 9, Paterson had stated "to the public mind we must accommodate ourselves," [33] and in his notes for this and his later effort as well, the emphasis is the same. The *structure* of government under the Articles should be retained:

> 2. Because it accords with the Sentiments of the People
>   [Proof:] 1. Coms. [Commissions from state legislatures defining the jurisdiction of the delegates]
>   2. News-papers — Political Barometer. Jersey never would have sent Delegates under the first [Virginia] Plan —
> Not here to sport Opinions of my own. Wt. [What] can be done. A little practicable Virtue preferrable to Theory.[34]

This was a defense of political acumen, not of states'-rights. In fact, Paterson's notes of his speech can easily be construed as an argument for attaining the substantive objectives of the Virginia Plan by a sound political route, *i.e.,* pouring the new wine in the old bottles. With a shrewd eye, Paterson queried:

> Will the Operation and Force of the [central] Govt. depend upon the mode of Representn. — No — it will depend upon the Quantum of Power lodged in the leg. ex. and judy. Departments — Give [the existing] Congress the same Powers that you intend to give the two Branches, [under the Virginia Plan] and I apprehend they will act with as much Propriety and more Energy. . . .[35]

In other words, the advocates of the New Jersey Plan concentrated their fire on what they held to be the *political liabilities* of the Virginia Plan — which were matters of institutional structure — rather than on the proposed scope of national authority. Indeed, the Supremacy Clause of the Constitution first saw the light of day in Paterson's Sixth Resolution; the New Jersey Plan contemplated the use of military force to secure compliance with national law; and finally Paterson made clear his view that under either the Virginia or the New Jersey systems, the general government would "act on individuals and not on states." [36] From the states'-rights viewpoint, this was heresy: the fundament of that doctrine was the proposition that any central government had as its constituents the states, not the people, and could only reach the people through the agency of the state government.

Paterson then reopened the agenda of the Convention, but he did so within a distinctly nationalist framework. Paterson's position was one of favoring a strong central government in principle, but opposing one which in fact *put the big states in the saddle.* (The Virginia Plan, for all its abstract merits, did very well by Virginia.) As evidence for this speculation, there is a curious and intriguing proposal among Paterson's preliminary drafts of the New Jersey Plan:

> Whereas it is necessary in Order to form the People of the U.S. of America in to a Nation, that the States should be consolidated, by which means all the Citizens thereof will become equally intitled to and will equally participate in the same Privileges and Rights . . . it is therefore resolved, that all the Lands contained within the Limits of each state individually, and of the U.S. generally be considered as constituting one Body or Mass, and be divided into thirteen or more integral parts.
>
> Resolved, That such Divisions or integral Parts shall be styled Districts.[37]

This makes it sound as though Paterson was prepared to accept a strong unified central government along the lines of the Virginia Plan if the existing states were eliminated. He may have gotten the idea from his New Jersey colleague Judge David Brearley, who on June 9 had commented that the only remedy to the dilemma over representation was "that a map of the U.S. be spread out, that all the existing boundaries be erased, and that a new partition of the whole be made into 13 equal parts." [38] According to Yates, Brearley added at this point, "then a government on the present [Virginia Plan] system will be just." [39]

This proposition was never pushed — it was patently unrealistic — but one can appreciate its purpose: it would have separated the men from the boys in the large-state delegations. How attached would the Virginians have been to their reform principles if Virginia were to disappear as a component geographical unit (the largest) for representational purposes? Up to this point, the Virginians had been in the happy position of supporting high ideals with that inner confidence born of knowledge that the "public interest" they endorsed would nourish their private interest. Worse, they had shown little willingness to compromise. Now the delegates from the small states announced that they were unprepared to be offered up as sacrificial victims to a "national interest" which reflected Virginia's parochial, ambition. Caustic Charles Pinckney was not far off when he remarked sardonically that "the whole [conflict] comes to this": "Give N. Jersey an equal vote, and she will dismiss her scruples, and concur in the Natil. system." [40] What he rather unfairly did not add was that the Jersey delegates were not free agents who could adhere to their private convictions; they had to take back, sponsor and risk their reputations on the reforms approved by the Convention — and in New Jersey, not in Virginia.

Paterson spoke on Saturday, and one can surmise that over the weekend there was a good deal of consultation, argument, and caucusing among the delegates. One member at least prepared a full length address: on Monday Alexander Hamilton, previously mute, rose and delivered a six-hour oration.[41] It was a remarkably apolitical speech; the gist of his position was that *both* the Virginia and New Jersey Plans were inadequately centralist, and he detailed a reform program which was reminiscent of the Protectorate under the Cromwellian *Instrument of Government* of 1653. It has been suggested that Hamilton did this in the best political tradition to emphasize the moderate character of the Virginia Plan,[42] to give the cautious delegates something *really* to worry about; but this interpretation seems somehow too clever. Particularly since the sentiments Hamilton expressed happened to be completely consistent with those he privately — and sometimes publicly — expressed throughout his life. He wanted, to take a striking phrase from a letter to George Washington, a "strong well mounted government";[43] in essence, the Hamilton Plan contemplated an elected life monarch, virtually free of public control, on the Hobbesian ground that only in this fashion could strength and stability be achieved. The other alternatives, he argued, would put policy-making at the mercy of the passions of the mob; only if the sovereign was beyond the reach of selfish influence would it be possible to have government in the interests of the whole community.[44]

From all accounts, this was a masterful and compelling speech, but (aside from furnishing John Lansing and Luther Martin with ammunition for later use against the Constitution) it made little impact. Hamilton was simply transmitting on a different wave-length from the rest of the delegates; the latter adjourned after his great effort, admired his rhetoric, and then returned to business.[45] It was rather as if they had taken a day off to attend the opera. Hamilton, never a particularly patient man or much of a negotiator, stayed for another ten days and then left, in considerable disgust, for New York.[46] Although he came back to Philadelphia sporadically and attended the last two weeks of the Convention, Hamilton played no part in the laborious task of hammering out the Constitution. His day came later when he led the New York Constitutionalists into the savage imbroglio over ratification — an arena in which his unmatched talent for dirty political infighting may well have won the day. For instance, in the New York Ratifying Convention, Lansing threw back into Hamilton's teeth the sentiments the latter had expressed in his June 18 oration in the Convention. However, having since retreated to the fine defensive positions immortalized in *The Federalist,* the Colonel flatly denied that he had ever been an enemy of the states, or had believed that conflict betwen states and nation was inexorable! As Madison's authoritative *Notes* did not appear until 1840, and there had been no press coverage, there was no way to verify his assertions, so in the words of the reporter, " . . . a warm personal altercation between [Lansing and Hamilton] engrossed the remainder of the day [June 28, 1788]." [47]

On Tuesday morning, June 19, the vacation was over. James Madison led off with a long, carefully reasoned speech analyzing the New Jersey Plan which, while intellectually vigorous in its criticisms, was quite conciliatory in mood. "The great difficulty," he observed, "lies in the affair of Representation; and if this could be adjusted, all others would be surmountable." [48] (As events were to demonstrate, this diagnosis was correct.) When he finished, a vote was taken on whether to continue with the Virginia Plan as the nucleus for a new constitution: seven states voted "Yes"; New York, New Jersey, and Delaware voted "No"; and Maryland, whose position often depended on which delegates happened to be on the floor, divided.[49] Paterson, it seems, lost decisively; yet in a fundamental sense he and his allies had achieved their purpose: from that day onward, it could never be forgotten that the state governments loomed ominously in the background and that no verbal incantations could exorcise their power. Moreover, nobody bolted the convention: Paterson and his colleagues took their defeat in stride and set to work to modify the Virginia Plan, particularly with respect to its provisions on representation in the national legislature. Indeed, they won an immediate rhetorical bonus; when Oliver Ellsworth of Connecticut rose to move that the word "national" be expunged from the Third Virginia Resolution ("Resolved that a *national* Government ought to be established consisting of a *supreme* Legislative, Executive and Judiciary" [50]), Randolph agreed and the motion passed unanimously.[51] The process of compromise had begun.

For the next two weeks, the delegates circled around the problem of legislative representation. The Connecticut delegation appears to have evolved a possible compromise quite early in the debates, but the Virginians and particularly Madison (unaware that he would later be acclaimed as the prophet of "federalism") fought obdurately against providing for equal representation of states in the second chamber. There was a good deal of acrimony and at one point Benjamin Franklin — of all people — proposed the institution of a daily prayer; practical politicians in the gathering, however, were mediating more on the merits of a good committee than on the utility of Divine intervention. On July 2, the ice began to break when through a number of fortuitous events[52] — and one that seems deliberate[53] — the majority against equality of representation was converted into a dead tie. The Convention had reached the stage where it was "ripe" for a solution (presumably all the therapeutic speeches had been made), and the South Carolinians proposed a committee. Madison and James Wilson wanted none of it, but with only Pennsylvania dissenting, the body voted to establish a working party on the problem of representation.

The members of this committee, one from each state, were elected by the delegates — and a very interesting committee it was. Despite the fact that the Virginia Plan had held majority support up to that date, neither Madison nor Randolph was selected (Mason was the Virginian) and Baldwin of Georgia, whose shift in position had resulted in the tie, was chosen. From the composition, it was clear that this was not to be a "fighting" committee: the emphasis in membership was on what might be described as "second-level political entrepreneurs." On the basis of the discussions up to that time, only Luther Martin of Maryland could be described as a "bitter-ender." Admittedly, some divination enters into this sort of analysis, but one does get a sense of the mood of the delegates from these choices — including the interesting selection of Benjamin Franklin, despite his age and intellectual wobbliness, over the brilliant and incisive Wilson or the sharp, polemical

Gouverneur Morris, to represent Pennsylvania. His passion for conciliation was more valuable at this juncture than Wilson's logical genius, or Morris' acerbic wit.

There is a common rumor that the Framers divided their time between philosophical discussions of government and reading the classics in political theory. Perhaps this is as good a time as any to note that their concerns were highly practical, that they spent little time canvassing abstractions. A number of them had some acquaintance with the history of political theory (probably gained from reading John Adams' monumental compilation *A Defense of the Constitutions of Government*,[54] the first volume of which appeared in 1786), and it was a poor rhetorician indeed who could not cite Locke, Montesquieu, or Harrington *in support* of a desired goal. Yet up to this point in the deliberations, no one had expounded a defense of states'-rights or the "separation of powers" on anything resembling a theoretical basis. It should be reiterated that the Madison model had no room either for the states or for the "separation of powers": effectively *all* governmental power was vested in the national legislature. The merits of Montesquieu did not turn up until *The Federalist;* and although a perverse argument could be made that Madison's ideal was truly in the tradition of John Locke's *Second Treatise of Government*,[55] the Locke whom the American rebels treated as an honorary president was a pluralistic defender of vested rights,[56] not of parliamentary supremacy.

It would be tedious to continue a blow-by-blow analysis of the work of the delegates; the critical fight was over representation of the states and once the Connecticut Compromise was adopted on July 17, the Convention was over the hump. Madison, James Wilson, and Gouverneur Morris of New York (who was there representing Pennsylvania!) fought the compromise all the way in a last-ditch effort to get a unitary state with parliamentary supremacy. But their allies deserted them and they demonstrated after their defeat the essentially opportunist character of their objections — using "opportunist" here in a non-pejorative sense, to indicate a willingness to swallow their objections and get on with the business. Moreover, once the compromise had carried (by five states to four, with one state divided), its advocates threw themselves vigorously into the job of strengthening the general government's substantive powers — as might have been predicted, indeed, from Paterson's early statements. It nourishes an increased respect for Madison's devotion to the art of politics, to realize that this dogged fighter could sit down six months later and prepare essays for *The Federalist* in contradiction to his basic convictions about the true course the Convention should have taken.

Two tricky issues will serve to illustrate the later process of accommodation. The first was the institutional position of the Executive. Madison argued for an executive chosen by the National Legislature and on May 29 this had been adopted with a provision that after his seven-year term was concluded, the chief magistrate should not be eligible for reelection. In late July this was reopened and for a week the matter was argued from several different points of view. A good deal of desultory speech-making ensued, but the gist of the problem was the opposition from two sources to election by the legislature. One group felt that the states should have a hand in the process; another small but influential circle urged direct election by the people. There were a number of proposals: election by the people, election by state governors, by electors chosen by state legislatures, by the National Legislature (James Wilson, perhaps ironically, proposed at one point that an Electoral College be chosen by lot from the National Legislature!), and there was some resemblance to three-dimensional chess in the dispute because of the presence of two other variables, length of tenure and reeligibility. Finally, after opening, reopening, and re-reopening the debate, the thorny problem was consigned to a committee for resolution.

The Brearley Committee on Postponed Matters was a superb aggregation of talent and its compromise on the Executive was a masterpiece of political improvisation. (The Electoral College, its creation, however, had little in its favor as an *institution* — as the delegates well appreciated.) The point of departure for all discussion about the presidency in the Convention was that in immediate terms, the problem was non-existent; in other words, everybody present knew that under any system devised, George Washington would be President. Thus they were dealing in the future tense and to a body of working politicians the merits of the Brearley proposal were obvious: everybody got a piece of cake. (Or to put it more academically, each viewpoint could leave the Convention and argue to its constituents that it had *really* won the day.) First, the state legislatures had the right to determine the mode of selection of the electors; second, the small states received a bonus in the Electoral College in the form of a guaranteed minimum of three votes while the big states got acceptance of the principle of proportional power; third, if the state legislatures agreed (as six did in the first presidential election), the people could be involved directly in the choice of electors; and finally, if no candidate received a majority in the College, the right of decision passed to the National Legislature with each state exercising equal strength. (In the Brearley recommendation, the election went to the Senate, but a motion from the floor substituted the House; this was accepted on the ground that the Senate already had enough authority over the executive in its treaty and appointment powers.)

This compromise was almost too good to be true, and the Framers snapped it up with little debate or controversy. No one seemed to think well of the College as an *institution;* indeed, what evidence there is suggests that there was an assumption that once Washington had finished his tenure as

President, the electors would cease to produce majorities and the chief executive would usually be chosen in the House. George Mason observed casually that the selection would be made in the House nineteen times in twenty and no one seriously disputed this point. The vital aspect of the Electoral College was that it got the Convention over the hurdle and protected everybody's interests. The future was left to cope with the problem of what to do with this Rube Goldberg mechanism.

In short, the Framers did not in their wisdom endow the United States with a College of Cardinals — the Electoral College was neither an exercise in applied Platonism nor an experiment in indirect government based on elitist distrust of the masses. It was merely a jerry-rigged improvisation which has subsequently been endowed with a high theoretical content. When an elector from Oklahoma in 1960 refused to cast his vote for Nixon (naming Byrd and Goldwater instead) on the ground that the Founding Fathers intended him to exercise his great independent wisdom, he was indulging in historical fantasy. If one were to indulge in counter-fantasy, he would be tempted to suggest that the Fathers would be startled to find the College still in operation — and perhaps even dismayed at their descendants' lack of judgment or inventiveness.[57]

The second issue on which some substantial practical bargaining took place was slavery. The morality of slavery was, by design, not at issue;[58] but in its other concrete aspects, slavery colored the arguments over taxation, commerce, and representation. The "Three-Fifths Compromise," that three-fifths of the slaves would be counted both for representation and for purposes of direct taxation (which was drawn from the past — it was a formula of Madison's utilized by Congress in 1783 to establish the basis of state contributions to the Confederation treasury) had allayed some Northern fears about Southern over-representation (no one then foresaw the trivial role that direct taxation would play in later federal financial policy), but doubts still remained. The Southerners, on the other hand, were afraid that Congressional control over commerce would lead to the exclusion of slaves or to their excessive taxation as imports. Moreover, the Southerners were disturbed over "navigation acts," i.e., tariffs, or special legislation providing, for example, that exports be carried only in American ships; as a section depending upon exports, they wanted protection from the potential voracity of their commercial brethren of the Eastern states. To achieve this end, Mason and others urged that the Constitution include a proviso that navigation and commercial laws should require a two-thirds vote in Congress.

These problems came to a head in late August and, as usual, were handed to a committee in the hope that, in Gouverneur Morris' words, "these things may form a bargain among the Northern and Southern states." [59] The Committee reported its measures of reconciliation on August

25, and on August 29 the package was wrapped up and delivered. What occurred can best be described in George Mason's dour version (he anticipated Calhoun in his conviction that permitting navigation acts to pass by majority vote would put the South in economic bondage to the North — it was mainly on this ground that he refused to sign the Constitution):

> The Constitution as agreed to till a fortnight before the Convention rose was such a one as he would have set his hand and heart to. . . . [Until that time] The 3 New England States were constantly with us in all questions . . . so that it was these three States with the 5 Southern ones against Pennsylvania, Jersey and Delaware. With respect to the importation of slaves, [decision-making] was left to Congress. This disturbed the two Southern-most States who knew that Congress would immediately suppress the importation of slaves. Those two States therefore struck up a bargain with the three New England States. If they would join to admit slaves for some years, the two Southern-most States would join in changing the clause which required the ⅔ of the Legislature in any vote [on navigation acts]. It was done.[60]

On the floor of the Convention there was a virtual love-feast on this happy occasion. Charles Pinckney of South Carolina attempted to overturn the committee's decision, when the compromise was reported to the Convention, by insisting that the South needed protection from the imperialism of the Northern states. But his Southern colleagues were not prepared to rock the boat and General C. C. Pinckney arose to spread oil on the suddenly ruffled waters; he admitted that:

> It was in the true interest of the S [outhern] States to have no regulation of commerce; but considering the loss brought on the commerce of the Eastern States by the Revolution, their liberal conduct towards the views of South Carolina [on the regulation of the slave trade] and the interests the weak Southn. States had in being united with the strong Eastern states, he thought it proper that no fetters should be imposed on the power of making commercial regulations; *and that his constituents, though prejudiced against the Eastern States, would be reconciled to this liberality.* He had himself prejudices agst the Eastern States befòre he came here, but would acknowledge that he had found them as liberal and candid as any men whatever. (Italics added)[61]

Pierce Butler took the same tack, essentially arguing that he was not too happy about the possible consequences, but that a deal was a deal.[62] Many Southern leaders were later — in the wake of the "Tariff of Abominations" — to rue this day of reconciliation; Calhoun's *Disquisition on Government* was little more than an extension of the argument in the Convention against permitting a congressional majority to enact navigation acts.[63]

Drawing on their vast collective political experience, utilizing every weapon in the politician's arsenal, looking constantly over their shoulders, at their constituents, the delegates put together a Constitution. It was a make-shift affair; some sticky issues (for example, the qualification of voters) they ducked entirely; others they mastered with that ancient instrument of political sagacity, studied ambiguity (for example, citizenship), and some they just overlooked. In this last category, I suspect, fell the matter of the power of the federal courts to determine the constitutionality of acts of Congress. When the judicial article was formulated (Article III of the Constitution), deliberations were still in the stage where the legislature was endowed with broad power under the Randolph formulation, authority which by its own terms was scarcely amenable to judicial review. In essence, courts could hardly determine when "the separate States are incompetent or . . . the harmony of the United States may be interrupted"; the National Legislature, as critics pointed out, was free to define its own jurisdiction. Later the definition of legislative authority was changed into the form we know, a series of stipulated powers, *but the delegates never seriously reexamined the jurisdiction of the judiciary under this new limited formulation*.[64] All arguments on the intention of the Framers in this matter are thus deductive and *a posteriori*, though some obviously make more sense than others.[65]

The Framers were busy and distinguished men, anxious to get back to their families, their positions, and their constituents, not members of the French Academy devoting a lifetime to a dictionary. They were trying to do an important job, and do it in such a fashion that their handiwork would be acceptable to very diverse constituencies. No one was rhapsodic about the final document, but it was a beginning, a move in the right direction, and one they had reason to believe the people would endorse. In addition, since they had modified the impossible amendment provisions of the Articles (the requirement of unanimity which could always be frustrated by "Rogues Island") to one demanding approval by only three-quarters of the states, they seemed confident that gaps in the fabric which experience would reveal could be rewoven without undue difficulty.

So with a neat phrase introduced by Benjamin Franklin (but devised by Gouverneur Morris) [66] which made their decision sound unanimous, and an inspired benediction by the Old Doctor urging doubters to doubt their own infallibility, the Constitution was accepted and signed. Curiously, Edmund Randolph, who had played so vital a role throughout, refused to sign, as did his fellow Virginian George Mason and Elbridge Gerry of Massachusetts. Randolph's behavior was eccentric, to say the least — his excuses for refusing his signature have a factitious ring even at this late date; the best explanation seems to be that he was afraid that the Constitution would prove to be a liability in Virginia politics, where Patrick Henry was burning up the countryside with impassioned denunciations. Presumably, Randolph wanted to check the temper of the populace before he risked his reputation, and perhaps his job, in a fight with both Henry and Richard Henry Lee.[67] Events lend some justification to this speculation: after much temporizing and use of the conditional subjunctive tense, Randolph endorsed ratification in Virginia and ended up getting the best of both worlds.

Madison, despite his reservations about the Constitution, was the campaign manager in ratification. His first task was to get the Congress in New York to light its own funeral pyre by approving the "amendments" to the Articles and sending them on to the state legislatures. Above all, momentum had to be maintained. The anti-Constitutionalists, now thoroughly alarmed and no novices in politics, realized that their best tactic was attrition rather than direct opposition. Thus they settled on a position expressing qualified approval but calling for a second Convention to remedy various defects (the one with the most demagogic appeal was the lack of a Bill of Rights). Madison knew that to accede to this demand would be equivalent to losing the battle, nor would he agree to conditional approval (despite wavering even by Hamilton). This was an all-or-nothing proposition: national salvation or national impotence with no intermediate positions possible. Unable to get congressional approval, he settled for second best: a unanimous resolution of Congress transmitting the Constitution to the states for whatever action they saw fit to take. The opponents then moved from New York and the Congress, where they had attempted to attach amendments and conditions, to the states for the final battle.[68]

At first the campaign for ratification went beautifully: within eight months after the delegates set their names to the document, eight states had ratified. Only in Massachusetts had the result been close (187–168). Theoretically, a ratification by one more state convention would set the new government in motion, but in fact until Virginia and New York acceded to the new Union, the latter was a fiction. New Hampshire was the next to ratify; Rhode Island was involved in its characteristic political convulsions (the Legislature there sent the Constitution out to the towns for decision by popular vote and it got lost among a series of local issues);[69] North Carolina's convention did not meet until July and then postposed a final decision. This is hardly the place for an extensive analysis of the conventions of New York and Virginia. Suffice it to say that the Constitutionalists clearly outmaneuvered their opponents, forced them into impossible political positions, and won both states narrowly. The Virginia Convention could serve as a classic study in effective floor management: Patrick Henry had to be contained, and a reading of the debates discloses a standard two-stage technique. Henry would give a four- or five-hour speech denouncing some section of the Constitution on every conceivable ground (the federal district, he averred at one point, would become a haven for convicts escaping from state authority!);[70] when Henry subsided, "Mr. Lee of Westmoreland" would rise and literally poleaxe him with sardonic invective (when Henry complained about the militia power, "Lighthorse Harry" really punched below the belt: observing that while the former Governor had been sitting in Richmond during the Revolution, *he* had been out in the trenches with the troops and thus felt better qualified to discuss military affairs).[71] Then the gentlemanly Constitutionalists (Madison, Pendleton and Marshall) would pick up the matters at issue and examine them in the light of reason.

Indeed, modern Americans who tend to think of James Madison as a rather dessicated character should spend some time with this transcript. Probably Madison put on his most spectacular demonstration of nimble rhetoric in what might be called "The Battle of the Absent Authorities." Patrick Henry in the course of one of his harangues alleged that Jefferson was known to be opposed to Virginia's approving the Constitution. This was clever; Henry hated Jefferson, but was prepared to use any weapon that came to hand. Madison's riposte was superb: First, he said that with all due respect to the great reputation of Jefferson, he was not in the country and therefore could not formulate an adequate judgment; second, no one should utilize the reputation of an outsider — the Virginia Convention was there to think for itself; third, if there were to be recourse to outsiders, the opinions of George Washington should certainly be taken into consideration; and finally, he knew from privileged personal communications from Jefferson that in fact the latter *strongly favored* the Constitution.[72] To devise an assault route into this rhetorical fortress was literally impossible.

The fight was over; all that remained now was to establish the new frame of government in the spirit of its framers. And who were better qualified for this task than the Framers themselves? Thus victory for the Constitution meant simultaneous victory for the Constitutionalists; the anti-Constitutionalists either capitulated or vanished into limbo — soon Patrick Henry would be offered a seat on the Supreme Court [73] and Luther Martin would be known as the Federalist "bull-dog." [74] And irony of ironies, Alexander Hamilton and James Madison would shortly accumulate a reputation as the formulators of what is often alleged to be our political theory, the concept of "federalism." Also, on the other side of the ledger, the arguments would soon appear over what the Framers "really meant"; while these disputes have assumed the proportions of a big scholarly business in the last century, they began almost before the ink on the Constitution was dry. One of the best early ones featured Hamilton versus Madison on the scope of presidential power, and other Framers characteristically assumed positions in this and other disputes on the basis of their political convictions.

Probably our greatest difficulty is that we know so much more about what the Framers *should have meant* than they themselves did. We are intimately acquainted with the problems that their Constitution should have been designed to master; in short, we have read the mystery story backwards. If we are to get the right "feel" for their time and their circumstances, we must in Maitland's phrase, "think ourselves back into a twilight." Obviously, no one can pretend completely to escape from the solipsistic web of his own environment, but if the effort is made, it is possible to appreciate the past roughly on its own terms. The first step in this process is to abandon the academic premise that because we can ask a question, there must be an answer.

Thus we can ask what the Framers meant when they gave Congress the power to regulate interstate and foreign commerce, and we emerge, reluctantly perhaps, with the reply that (Professor Crosskey to the contrary notwithstanding) [75] they may not have known what they meant, that there may not have been any semantic consensus. The Convention was not a seminar in analytic philosophy or linguistic analysis. Commerce was *commerce* — and if different interpretations of the word arose, later generations could worry about the problem of definition. The delegates were in a hurry to get a new government established; when definitional arguments arose, they characteristically took refuge in ambiguity. If different men voted for the same proposition for varying reasons, that was politics (and still is); if later generations were unsettled by this lack of precision, that would be their problem.

There was a good deal of definitional pluralism with respect to the problems the delegates did discuss, but when we move to the question of extrapolated intentions, we enter the realm of spiritualism. When men in our time, for instance, launch into elaborate talmudic exegesis to demonstrate that federal aid to parochial schools is (or is not) in accord with the intentions of the men who established the Republic and endorsed the Bill of Rights, they are engaging in historical Extra–Sensory Perception. (If one were to join this ESP contingent for a minute, he might suggest that the hard-boiled politicians who wrote the Constitution and Bill of Rights would chuckle scornfully at such an invocation of authority: obviously a politician would chart his course on the intentions of the living, not of the dead, and count the number of Catholics in his constituency.)

The Constitution, then, was not an apotheosis of "constitutionalism," a triumph of architectonic genius; it was a patch-work sewn together under the pressure of both time and events by a group of extremely talented democratic politicians. They refused to attempt the establishment of a strong, centralized sovereignty on the principle of legislative supremacy for the excellent reason that the people would not accept it. They risked their political fortunes by opposing the established doctrines of state sovereignty because they were convinced that the existing system was leading to national impotence and probably foreign domination. For two years, they worked to get a convention established. For over three months, in what must have seemed to the faithful participants an endless process of give-and-take, they reasoned, cajoled, threatened, and bargained amongst themselves. The result was a Constitution which the people, in fact, by democratic processes, did accept, and a new and far better national government was established.

Beginning with the inspired propaganda of Hamilton, Madison and Jay, the ideological build-up got under way. *The Federalist* had little impact on the ratification of the Constitution, except perhaps in New York, but this volume had enormous influence on the image of the Constitution in the minds of future generations, particularly on historians and political scientists who have an innate fondness for theoretical symmetry. Yet, while the shades of Locke and Montesquieu *may* have been hovering in the background, and the delegates *may* have been unconscious instruments of a transcendent *telos*, the careful observer of the day-to-day work of the Convention finds no over-arching principles. The "separation of powers" to him seems to be a by-product of suspicion, and "federalism" he views as a *pis aller*, as the farthest point the delegates felt they could go in the destruction of state power without themselves inviting repudiation.

To conclude, the Constitution was neither a victory for abstract theory nor a great practical success. Well over half a million men had to die on the battlefields of the Civil War before certain constitutional principles could be defined — a baleful consideration which is somehow overlooked in our customary tributes to the farsighted genius of the Framers and to the supposed American talent for "constitutionalism." The Constitution was, however, a vivid demonstration of effective democratic political action, and of the forging of a national elite which literally persuaded its countrymen to hoist themselves by their own boot straps. American proconsuls would be wise not to translate the Constitution into Japanese, or Swahili, or treat it as a work of semi-Divine origin; but when students of comparative politics examine the process of nation-building in countries newly freed from colonial rule, they may find the American experience instructive as a classic example of the potentialities of a democratic elite.

Democracy and *The Federalist*

Martin Diamond

*In this selection, Martin Diamond, Professor of Political Science
at Claremont College, directly confronts the relationship between the Constitution and popular government, seeing in the
Constitution — as the Federalists did — "a republican remedy for
the diseases most incident to republican government." Although
the Founding Fathers in creating the Constitution may have intended to curb the popular excesses released by the Revolution,
the language and principles they used to defend the Constitution
were decidedly popular. Indeed, most of the Federalists felt they
had little choice in their use of rhetoric. The proponents of the
Constitution did not need John Dickinson to warn them that
"when this plan goes forth, it will be attacked by the popular
leaders. Aristocracy will be the watchword; the Shibboleth among
its adversaries." Precisely because the Antifederalists, as Alexander
Hamilton observed in the New York ratifying convention, did
talk "so often of an aristocracy," the Federalists were continually
compelled in the debates over ratification to minimize, even to
disguise, the elitist elements in the Constitution. And because the
Constitution seemed so novel and so contrary to the localist ideas
of republican government embedded in the faith of '76, its supporters were forced over and over again to show how and why the
new system was "strictly republican." In formulating this popular
defense of the Constitution, the Federalists helped to create a new
science of politics.*

*It is in this context that the most famous defense of the Con-
stitution, The Federalist, should be read. Despite their divided
authorship and piecemeal creation, Diamond argues that The
Federalist papers reveal a remarkable consistency of thought underlying a new appreciation of republican government. Separation of powers, representation, and the extended sphere of
government, were all devised to control the great evil of republican government, majoritarian factionalism, and to preserve
popular government against its own excesses. Yet beneath all this
popular language and republican theorizing ran the basic socio-
logical insight breaking through in paper after paper of The
Federalist: that the new government would work because its extended structure would result "in the substitution of representatives whose enlightened views and virtuous sentiments render
them superior to local prejudices and to schemes of injustice."*

Immediately after the 1787 federal convention Alexander Hamilton turned to the difficult task of securing New York's ratification of the proposed Constitution. As part of his strategy, he planned a series of short essays to expound the virtues of the Constitution. Hamilton secured the collaboration of John Jay and, ironically only after several others declined his invitation, of James Madison as well. *The Federalist* was published serially in groups of two and four essays in the New York City press. The essays were intended to influence the election of delegates to the state ratifying convention and, since for this election universal manhood suffrage was adopted, the essays were therefore addressed "to the People of the State of New York." But *The Federalist* was further intended to instruct and inspirit favorable delegates and to persuade or mollify unfavorable delegates to the convention. To this end, even before completion of serial publication in the press, the essays were published as a book and circulated to leading supporters of the Constitution throughout the country. Thus *The Federalist* was at once addressed to the widest electorate but also to those able and educated men who actually would determine the fate of the Constitution. It seems clear that its authors also looked beyond the immediate struggle and wrote with a view to influencing later generations by making their work the authoritative commentary on the meaning of the Constitution. While *The Federalist* was the most immediate kind of political work, a piece of campaign propaganda, it spoke also to thoughtful men then and now, with a view to the permanence of its argument.

The reading of *The Federalist* is further complicated by the fact that it was written by two men (Jay's small contribution may be disregarded here) whose individual opinions and subsequent careers radically diverged.[1]* This fact has encouraged many readers to see fundamental inconsistencies in the work where they do not exist, on the presumption that a work written jointly by Hamilton and Madison must contradict itself. Like the belief that *The Federalist* was merely a propaganda piece, the belief that it was the inconsistent work of incompatible authors has depreciated *The Federalist* as a theoretical writing. But *The Federalist* presents itself as the work of one Publius who claims to supply a consistent, comprehensive, and true account of the Constitution and of the regime it was calculated to engender. As will be seen, Publius makes good his claim.

Apart from the fact that Hamilton and Madison had motive and capacity to achieve a remarkably consistent Publius, *The Federalist* has a

Martin Diamond, "The Federalist," in Leo Strauss and Joseph Cropsey, (Ed.), *History of Political Philosophy,* © 1963 by Rand McNally and Company, Chicago, pp. 573–593.
* [See pp. 178–179 for notes to this article. — Ed.]

literary character which made it possible for them to agree quite easily on much of what had to be said. *The Federalist* deals largely with factual matters. Whatever their differences, Hamilton and Madison could agree as to what the convention had done and what kind of country would be the result. Similarly they could readily agree on how to make the Constitution seem most attractive or least noxious to those they were seeking to persuade. *The Federalist* was a commentary on and a plea for a constitution. Its authors were therefore not *primarily* obliged to deal with the most controversial subject, namely, the standard by which they themselves deemed the Constitution good. This is, of course, not to say that Publius stays only at the surface or says only what his readers want to hear. In fact, Hamilton and Madison go very far, as Publius, in suggesting the theoretical grounds upon which a wise acceptance of the Constitution should rest. That is what makes *The Federalist* an illuminating work. But the literary character of *The Federalist* did not oblige them to push so far in the discussion as to lay bare their ultimate differences. Unfortunately, what helps explain Publius' consistency explains also why *The Federalist* falls short of those great works in which theoretical matters are pressed to their proper, that is, farthest limits.

One last observation on Publius leads directly to the teaching of *The Federalist*. We know that Hamilton took his pseudonyms seriously; they were meant to convey the character of his argument.[2] Shortly before Publius appeared, a series of essays in support of the Constitution had been initiated under the pseudonym "Caesar." It has often been thought that Hamilton was also Caesar, but scholarship has now made this seem unlikely. In any event, Caesar's first two essays were very poorly received and the series was abandoned by its author. The choice of "Publius" is especially revealing when compared with the ill-fated Caesar essays, whether the latter were written by Hamilton or not. Publius, the educated reader knew, was the Publius Valerius Publicola described in Plutarch. Publius like Caesar was a "strong man," but between them there was one enormous difference: Caesar destroyed a republic, Publius saved one. Unlike Caesar, Publius makes his contribution to the republic in a way compatible with its continued existence. He brings to its salvation qualities it cannot itself supply, but leaves it essentially intact after his efforts. Whoever wrote them, the Caesar papers had to founder. The Constitution was in fact not Caesarist, and the public to be persuaded was then profoundly hostile to a Caesarist appeal. The character of Publius on the contrary was exactly appropriate to the situation and perfectly characterized the argument of *The Federalist*. Publius, with a capacity and knowledge that the people cannot themselves supply, brings to the people the constitution that will preserve, indeed will safely found the republic.

In the first essay Publius supplies the outline of the work.

[1] *The utility of the UNION to your political prosperity* — [2] *The insufficiency of the present Confederation to preserve that Union* — [3] *The necessity of a government at least equally energetic with the one proposed, to the attainment of this object* — [4] *The conformity of the proposed Constitution to the true principles of republican government* — [5] *Its analogy to your own State constitution* — and lastly, [6] *The additional security which its adoption will afford to the preservation of that species of government, to liberty, and to property.*[3]

Publius then finds it necessary to explain the order of his work. "It may perhaps be thought superfluous to offer arguments to prove the utility of the UNION," he says, since it is thought that it "has no adversaries." Publius justifies his opening theme on the ground that there are in fact secret adversaries. But apart from this peculiar justification, it is possible to see Publius' other grounds for the organization of his work. In particular it is clear why he begins with the utility of the union. For one thing, he gets off on the right foot by beginning with a subject on which he is in accord with nearly all his readers. Further, a proper and full statement of the agreed end of union turns out, as a full statement of the end always does, to contain the clearest implications for what must be done to achieve the end. Therefore, by the time Publius has fully stated the value of union, he has introduced all his major arguments on disputed matters in the amiable context of the undisputed end. Rightly stated, the end of union is palpably inconsistent with the "imbecility" (*i.e.*, weakness) of the Confederation and requires an "energetic" government. Publius wants to extort from the "general assent to the abstract proposition"[4] that union is good and the Confederation inadequate, acquiescence in what is necessary to sustain the union. Publius is able to convert "general assent" into intelligent and detailed assent by instructing his readers on what is logically implied in their vague commitment to union. The first three branches of Publius' work therefore make this argument: to desire union is necessarily to despise the present Confederation and to welcome the energetic government union needs. All that remains is to show that the union under this energetic government, the proposed Constitution, is satisfactorily republican. Hence Publius must teach a republican way more fully to enjoy the "utility of Union" than hitherto thought possible.

This, as will be seen, is both Publius' most difficult political task and his most important theoretical teaching. A closer look at the organization of the work reveals its importance. The work is actually divided among the six "branches of the inquiry" in the following way: (1) "the utility of Union" — 14 papers; (2) "the insufficiency of the present Confederation" — 8 papers; (3) the necessity of energetic government — 14 papers; (4) the republicanism of the Constitution — 48 papers; (5) and (6) — 1 paper. By the time he has reached the last paper, Publius claims to have "so fully anticipated and exhausted" the last two branches that he only brings together the appropriate arguments and concludes the work. The book is therefore written in fact under four "heads." But the organization may be stated still more simply. As has been seen, the first three heads deal with one theme, the immediate political question of what is to be done about the union — showing why it is good, what is inadequate in the Articles of Confederation, and what kind of government will be adequate to the end of union. The proposed Constitution being adequate to that end, all that remains is to show that this Constitution conforms to the *true* principles of republican government. And this is the work of the fourth, and by far the largest branch of the inquiry. The organization of the essays stated in its simplest form therefore is: union and republicanism. The organization of the essays perfectly conveys *The Federalist*'s teaching. *The Federalist* teaches a new and true republicanism which involves crucially a new view of the problem of union.[5]

Americans were already living under republican governments, and under a confederal union of these republics; but, in the view of *The Federalist*, the principle of these republics and their confederal union was old and false. The Confederation was therefore necessarily foundering, and the individual republics were tending to "the mortal diseases under which popular governments have everywhere perished." [6] The Constitution contains the new and true principle of republican union which will rescue republican government in America. The proud conclusion of the famous tenth essay summarizes the teaching: "*In the extent and proper structure of the Union*, therefore, we behold a *republican* remedy for the diseases most incident to republican government." (Italics supplied.)

The Federalist is remarkable for the conjunction it achieves between discussion of the most urgent political matters and of theoretical matters. This is nowhere more evident than in the treatment of republican union. The right arrangement of union was the first political problem of the day; but what *The Federalist* has to say on this practical question is based on its most novel and important theoretical teaching. The opposition to the Constitution also rested upon a theoretical view. Indeed, one of the remarkable features of the debate over the Constitution was the extraordinary intrusion of theoretical considerations into the settlement of the practical question. The great attack on the Constitution was the charge that the new union was antirepublican. Certain features of the Constitution were regarded as specifically antirepublican, but the main thrust of the opposition resulted from the more general argument that only the state governments, not some huge central government, could be made effectively free and republican.

This rested on a widely held belief, popularized in the way men understood Montesquieu, that only small countries could enjoy republican government. The reasoning that *The Federalist* had to oppose ran as follows.

Large countries necessarily turn to despotism. For one thing, large countries need despotic rule simply in consequence of largeness; political authority in the parts breaks down without more forceful government than the republican form admits. Further, large countries, usually wealthy and populous, are warlike or are made warlike by envious neighbors; the conduct of wars inevitably nurtures despotic rule. And even if large countries try to be republican, they cannot succeed. To preserve their rule, the people must be patriotic, vigilant, and informed. This requires that the people give loving attention to public things, and that the affairs of the country be on a scale commensurate with popular understanding. But in large countries the people are baffled and rendered apathetic by the complexity of public affairs, and at last become absorbed in their own pursuits. Finally, even the alert citizenry of a large republic must allow a few men actually to conduct the public business; far removed from the localities and possessed of the instruments of coercion, the trusted representatives would inevitably subvert the republican rule to their own passions and interests. Such was the traditional and strongly held view of the necessity that republics be small. It followed that such small republics could only combine for limited purposes into confederacies which respect the primacy of the member states. But its opponents regarded the Constitution not as a proper confederacy, but as "calculated ultimately to make the states one consolidated government," which is to say, one large republic; hence the Constitution was *necessarily* antirepublican. That is, the Constitution was denounced as resting on a novel and false view of republican union.

The Federalist, understandably then, asks its readers to "hearken not to the voice which petulantly tells you that the form of government recommended for your adoption is a novelty in the political world; that it has never yet had a place in the theories of the wildest projectors; that it rashly attempts what it is impossible to accomplish." [7]

While the readers are urged to hearken not, *The Federalist* does not deny the charge of novelty; on the contrary, it extols novelty as "the glory of the people of America."

> Happily for America, happily, we trust for the whole human race, [the leaders of the revolution did not fear to depart from old ways but rather] pursued a new and more noble course. They accomplished a revolution which has no parallel in the annals of human society. They reared the fabrics of government which have no model on the face of the globe. They formed the design of a great Confederacy, which it is incumbent on their successors to improve and perpetuate. [8]

But one must expect, we are immediately told, some flaws in these achievements. It turns out that "they erred most in the structure of the Union." But this was to be expected because *"this was the work most difficult to be executed."* (Italics supplied.) The right republican union, then, is a more difficult work to accomplish than a revolution without parallel and the creation of state governments without previous model. But the Constitution will accomplish this most difficult work. It will fulfill and therefore save "the new and more noble" way of life America has brought to the world. This "more perfect Union" rests upon the new and true republicanism which it is Publius' task to expound.

Publius states his most important claim in the conclusion of the famous tenth essay: he presents "a republican remedy for the diseases most incident to republican government." Again, Publius praises Thomas Jefferson for displaying equally "a fervent attachment to republican government and an enlightened view of the dangerous propensities against which it ought to be guarded." [9] Publius thus claims to be the wholehearted but cool-headed partisan of republicanism. But the word republican does not tell us enough about the kind of regime which Publius advocates. That is, the question immediately arises: what *kind* of republic? How may Publius' republic be fitted into the traditional distinction of three kinds of rule, by the one, few, or many? The answer is obvious: Publius espouses a *democratic* republic. Indeed, what is remarkable is the extent to which Publius gives the word republic, in the key passages, an exclusively democratic content. For example, "the republican principle . . . enables the majority to defeat [a minority faction's] sinister views by regular vote." And this must be a majority "derived from the great body of the society, not from an inconsiderable proportion, or a favored class of it." [10] While it is true that the word republic always meant the absence of monarchy and implied the importance of the whole body of citizens, it did not imply universal or nearly universal manhood suffrage: earlier usage always distinguished between aristocratic or oligarchic republics and democratic republics. But Publius' exclusively democratic idea of republicanism obliges him explicitly to deny the appellation republic to all those aristocratic and oligarchic regimes formerly so styled.[11] In short, in so far as it accepts the old three-fold distinction of regimes, *The Federalist* treats its republican regime as belonging overwhelmingly to the democratic kind of rule. However much of its regime departs from the character of a "pure democracy," *The Federalist* emphatically and rightly denies that the departure removes the Constitution from the class of democratic governments into the monarchical or aristocratic class.

Publius' new and true republicanism is therefore a new and true democratic teaching. For many reasons, which cannot be discussed here, the democratic character of *The Federalist,* and of the Constitution it expounded, has been obscured. This has been to miss the most important thing about *The Federalist.* It is necessary and appropriate, however, to examine one argument frequently made in support of the view that Publius' Constitution did not establish a democratic regime. In a famous passage in the tenth essay, Publius is thought himself to have radically distinguished republics from democracies, and hence himself to have withdrawn the Constitution from the democratic class. This is not quite accurate. Publius distinguishes a republic from "a *pure* democracy," [12] and that is a very different thing. By a pure democracy, Publius says he means "a society consisting of a small number of citizens, who assemble and administer the government in person." As Publius compares the two, a republic "varies from a pure democracy" only in that it is "a government in which the scheme of representation takes place." This and this alone is the distinction Publius makes. The perfect synonym for Publius' use of republic is therefore representative democracy. The principle of representation, however, introduces an impurity into the republican form from the point of view of pure democracy. But this does not mean that republics are opposed in kind to democracies; rather, republics are, so to speak, "impure" democracies.

On the crucial question of where sovereignty is lodged, namely, with the many, republics and pure democracies alike belong to a more inclusive class. The apparent difficulty raised by *The Federalist's* distinction between republics and pure democracies is resolved when we see that this larger class or genus is what Publius calls *popular* government. And by popular government Publius means what is meant today by the term democracy. That is, Publius sees popular government as including all the forms of rule by the many, as distinguished from the various forms of rule by the few or the one. We may seek aid in understanding Publius from Madison and Hamilton individually. On the crucial question of the locus of political authority, Publius, Madison, and Hamilton all speak of a republic, democracy, and popular government interchangeably. Publius in the tenth essay speaks identically of a *republican* remedy for the disease of faction, and a remedy that will "preserve the spirit and form of *popular* government." On June 6 at the federal convention, Madison discussed the identical remedy as "the only defense against the inconveniences of *democracy* consistent with the *democratic* form of government." Hamilton styled the republic created by the Constitution a *"representative democracy."* [13] Publius must be understood, then, as having undertaken, in the fine phrase G. L. Pierson applied to Tocqueville, to "make democracy safe for the world." This is how Publius' greatest claim is to be understood. To save popular government from its "mortal diseases" while preserving both "the spirit and the form of popular government is . . . the great object . . . [of] our inquiries." Publius claims to rescue "this form of government . . . from the opprobrium under which it has so long labored," and therefore to recommend it "to the esteem and adoption of mankind." [14]

The foregoing is not intended, however, to depreciate the importance of Publius' distinction between republic and pure democracy. On the contrary, the peculiar property of a republic, that it is a *representative* democracy, is the foundation of *The Federalist*'s teaching; it "promises the cure for which we are seeking." [15] But the democratic character of *The Federalist*'s republicanism must be emphasized in order to grasp its central contention. Publius claims to cure the hitherto incurable ills of popular government, while remaining perfectly consistent with the principle of popular government, that is, lodging sovereignty with the many.

Publius helps us to see what is new in his teaching. In the fourteenth essay, which continues the assault on "the error which limits republican government to a narrow district," [16] Publius explains why men so long committed that error. What Publius now knows about republicanism was hitherto veiled from men by both the ancient and modern examples of it. The possibilities latent in the popular republican form were veiled because "most of the popular governments of antiquity were of the democratic species." While

> in modern Europe, to which we owe the great principle of representation, no example is seen of a government *wholly popular,* and founded, at the same time, wholly on that principle. If Europe has the merit of discovering this great mechanical power in government, by the simple agency of which the will of the largest political body may be concentred, and its force directed to any object which the public good requires, *America* can claim the merit of making the discovery the basis of *unmixed* and *extensive* republics. It is only to be lamented that any of her citizens should wish to deprive her of the additional merit of displaying its full efficacy in the establishment of the comprehensive system now under her consideration.[17]

The ancients had many wholly popular governments but mostly of the *pure* democratic species, that is, of the direct, not the representative kind. The Europeans have partly or wholly representative governments, but none at once wholly representative and wholly of the popular kind. It has remained for America to innovate the combination: governments wholly popular and wholly based upon the representative principle. The word "unmixed" must be read in its full force. The American states were not *mixed regimes*; as wholly popular states, they had no significant admixture of aristocratical or monarchical elements. And they were not small republics as that term had been traditionally understood; they were already *extensive* republics. All that is needed, Publius concludes, is to display the "full efficacy" of the representative principle in the unmixed and still more extensive republic proposed by the Constitution. But Publius' mild speech is deceptive; as we have seen, all that remains to be done is "the work most difficult to be executed."

Publius understandably treats gently the pride and affection of his readers for their state governments. The state governments are fine, he seems to say, and the Constitution will be even finer. He says that "the valuable improvements made by the American constitutions on the popular models, both ancient and modern, cannot certainly be too much admired." [18] This sentence can be read in two ways; the amount of praise it bestows is uncertain. How does Publius actually regard the "valuable improvements" in the state government? The state governments, for all their improvements, fail utterly to solve the problem of faction which is *the* problem of popular government. The state governments will founder on this rock as all previous democracies have foundered. They will founder because they do not have a sufficient "number of citizens and extent of territory." They are "extensive republics," but not extensive enough.

The ancient popular governments obscured the possibilities latent in republicansim, we were told, because "most" of them lacked the representative principle. But something else was lacking in antiquity. Publius therefore comes back to this very question many essays later. Now he warns "that the position concerning the ignorance of the ancient governments on the subject of representation, is by no means precisely true in the latitude commonly given to it." [19] He now gives a considerable list of ancient representative institutions. True, none of the ancient republics was based wholly on the representative principle as are the American states. And this was a defect. But it was a trivial defect; they suffered from a much worse ill. "It cannot be believed, that any form of representative government could have succeeded within the narrow limits occupied by the democracies of Greece." [20] The utility of the representative principle, then, which offers "the cure for which we are seeking," depends entirely upon the size of country. Even the relatively large American states will not suffice; only a union of the magnitude and character envisaged by the Constitution will solve the problem of popular government.

"The enlightened friends to liberty" would have had to abandon the cause of republican government as "indefensible" if this new solution had not been found. The solution rests upon the "science of politics," which "like most other sciences, has received great improvement. The efficacy of various principles is now well understood, which were either not known at all, or imperfectly known to the ancients."

The regular distribution of power into distinct departments; the introduction of legislative balances and checks; the institution of courts composed of judges holding their offices during good behavior; the representation of the people in the legislature by deputies of their own election: these are wholly new discoveries, or have made their principal progress towards perfection in modern times. They are means, and powerful means, by which the excellences of republican government may be retained and its imperfections lessened or avoided. To this catalogue of circumstances that tend to the amelioration of popular systems of civil government, I shall venture, however novel it may appear to some, to add one more, on a principle which has been made the foundation of an objection to the new Constitution; I mean the ENLARGEMENT of the ORBIT within which such systems are to revolve, either in respect to the dimensions of a single State, or to the consolidation of several smaller States into one great Confederacy.[21]

Publius is thus the spokesman for the new "science of politics," the previous teachers of which he does not name, who has himself made an important addition to the science, namely the possibility of a very large republic. Further, everything in that modern science of politics is seen now in a democratic light; if the earlier teachers of the new science only tended in a democratic direction, or suggested only partly democratic regimes, Publius takes the new science of politics and enlarges upon it and uses it for the amelioration of a "wholly popular" system of civil government. Finally, through Publius, the moment has come for the new science to cease being merely a teaching and to become a great political actuality.

Publius sees the problem of representative popular government as threefold. First, there is the possibility that the people will lose control of their government, that the representative rulers will subvert the regime. Second, there is the possibility that popular majorities, through compliant representatives, will rule oppressively. Third, there is the possibility that majorities, through compliant representatives, will rule not oppressively, but foolishly, failing to do the things necessary for the strength and stability of the government.

Protecting the people is the simplest task. "The whole power of the proposed government is to be in the hands of the representatives *of the people*." [22] The actual rulers will have no warrant ultimately save as they are "the objects of popular choice." [23] This guards against subversion by the representative rulers; making the representatives wholly dependent upon the people "is the essential, and, after all, only efficacious security for the rights and privileges of the people, which is attainable in civil society." [24] Although the regime is now to be wholly popular and wholly representative, there is nothing new thus far; democracy's oldest claim is that the right of suffrage guards the society against the oppression of its rulers. The new science of politics, however, offers an additional safeguard to the rights of the people. Separation of powers, "the regular distribution of power into distinct departments," lessens the threat that the rulers will be able to concert and execute schemes of oppression. The liberty of the people generally and the rights of individuals are secured by "the improbability of . . . a mercenary and perfidious combination of the several members of government, standing on as different foundations as republican principles will well admit, and at the same time accountable to the society over which they are placed." [25] This is what was sought in separation of powers by Jefferson, who feared above all oppression of the people by their rulers. How separation of powers will supply this protection can be better understood when we see how separation of powers mitigates the other evils Publius feared.

It is not enough, Publius argues, to guard society against the oppression of the representative rulers, it is necessary also "to guard one part of the society against the injustice of the other part." [26] In plain words, the problem is to guard against "overbearing" popular majorities. This is a far greater problem than the unconstitutional treachery of representatives because "the form of popular government" permits a popular majority "to execute and mask its violence under the forms of the Constitution." [27] In this sentence Publius boldly displays the democratic nature of the regime he expounds: the many rule and therefore can legally do oppressive things. Unlike Jefferson's "elective despotism," this evil occurs, not when the representatives are unfaithful to their constituents, but when they too faithfully heed the oppressive wishes of popular majorities. The great danger Publius sees is that popular majorities will demand oppressive measures and that their elected representatives will only too readily oblige. Publius seeks to solve the problem at both levels, among the people and among their representatives. "Multiplicity" of factions is his famous answer to the problem of the oppressive majority itself. But first we must consider how separation of powers solves the problem at the level of the representatives.

Publius is aware of two other respectable ways of preventing majorities from oppressing minorities. One is to create "a will in the community independent of the majority — that is, of the society itself." [28] But this is the monarchical solution which Publius rejects. The other is exemplified in the Roman republic where the legislative authority was divided into two "distinct and independent legislatures," [29] which enabled the patrician minority constitutionally to resist the plebeian majority. This may be taken to illustrate the traditional idea of the mixed republic which is excluded in Publius' "unmixed" republic, in which "all authority . . . will be derived from and dependent on the society." [30] The problem of oppressive majorities cannot be solved in a wholly popular regime by means belonging to the monarchical or mixed regimes. Publius finds in the new science of politics, which is not necessarily democratic, a solution which can be grafted onto democracy: separation of powers. Perhaps there is even a deeper kinship between separation of powers and democracy. In any event, Publius employs separation of powers, as he does all other things in the new science, so as "to preserve the spirit and the form of popular government."

Separation of powers mitigates the evil of oppressive majorities at the level of the government. In a republic without separation of powers, where a single body of representatives performs all the functions of government, there would be nothing in the machinery of government that could stay the will of an oppressive popular majority. But this is precisely what separation of powers is designed to do: to create a distance 'twixt the majority's cup and lip. Separation of powers takes the old distinction of the legislative, executive, and judicial functions of governing and makes it a distinction of the legislative, executive, and judicial personnel. This means, then, to create some representatives who will resist the wrong desires of the people to which other representatives are supinely yielding, or which they are even demagogically arousing. When the governing power is distributed into distinct departments, it is clear which are the representatives who may resist and which are those who will yield to popular demands. "In republican government, the legislative authority necessarily predominates." [31] "The legislative department" as the sad experience of the state governments had shown, "is everywhere extending the sphere of its activity, and drawing all power into its impetuous vortex." [32] As it were, it is against the legislature that the force of separation needs especially to be directed. "The great security against a gradual concentration of the several powers in the same department, consists in giving to those who administer each department the necessary constitutional means and personal motives to resist encroachment of the others." [33]

Publius had reason to speak blandly but his meaning is clear. The executive and the judiciary must have the means and personal motives to resist the legislature. For example, "when occasions present themselves, in which the interests of the people are at variance with their inclinations"; or when the legislators, who "commonly have the people on their side," are bent on oppression, then "the Executive should be in a situation to dare to act his own opinion with vigor and decision." [34] Separation of powers creates authorities who, despite their independence upon the people and their lack of any independent title to rule, are yet likely to resist and stay the legislature when it is yielding to the wrong demands of the populace, the constitutional master of all three branches of government.

Publius shows quite easily how the executive and the judiciary will have the "means" to stave off oppressive legislation; the veto, the president's legislative initiative, his discretion in the enforcement of the laws, judicial review, and the judges' discretion in the adjudication of individual cases, all give to the other two branches the constitutional means temporarily to void or to moderate oppressive legislation. But it is more difficult to see why the executive and the judiciary will have the "personal motives" to resist the legislature. Why will they collaborate with the legislature in good actions, without which collaboration government would be reduced to the imbecility Publius despised, and collide with the legislature in its bad actions? Publius gives us two reasons. First, "ambition must be made to counteract ambition. The interest of the man must be connected with the constitutional rights of the place." [35] If the government is properly arranged, presidents and judges will defend their offices against the legislature because their pride, love of power or fame, even avarice, will lead them to identify their self-interest with the integrity of their offices. But there is a crucial assumption here. Publius assumes that oppressive legislation necessarily or at least ordinarily derogates from the dignity of the executive and judicial offices. Publius appears to assume that oppressive legislation requires servile execution and servile adjudication; and that servile executives and judges enjoy no dignity, no power, no fame, and ultimately not even pecuniary rewards. Hence Publius expects the executive and judiciary, for reasons of private interest and passion, to resist the legislature when it is oppressive. Separation of powers supplies democracy with governors who, without the traditional motives of family distinction or wealth, simply because of the jobs they hold and their self-regarding attachment to them, will tend to rule in the best interest of the democracy.

Publius' second reason for believing that 'the other branches will resist oppressive legislation desired by a popular majority is also based on his assumption that oppressive legislation ordinarily derogates from the integrity of the executive and judicial offices. But he appears further to assume that presidents and judges will resist oppressive legislation, not only because of interested attachment to their offices, but also out of a decent regard for the proper fulfillment of their duties. As reasonably decent men doing a job, they will have the motives, as it were the professional motives, to resist oppressive legislation because it tends to violate the arts they serve, and to subordinate the executive and judicial offices.

This last consideration leads to an understanding of how Publius expected separation of powers to help solve the third problem of popular government, not the oppressiveness but the ineptitude of popular rule. Again, Publius is confronting the traditional criticism of popular government which was that it gave over government into the hands of the many, which is to say the unwise. The very principle of representation itself may be a step in the right direction. The effect of representation may be to refine and enlarge the public views, by passing them through the medium of a chosen body of citizens, whose wisdom may best discern the true interest of their country, and whose patriotism and love of justice will be least likely to sacrifice it to temporary or partial considerations. . . . It may well happen that the public voice, pronounced by the representatives of the people, will be more consonant to the public good than if pronounced by the people themselves, convened for the purpose.[36]

But we know that Publius does not count much on the wisdom and courage of the legislature alone. It is those other representatives of the people, the executive and the judiciary, who are crucial to elevating the whole representation of the people. (It should be noted that much of what is said here of separation of powers applies as well to "legislative checks and balances," that is, those checks imposed by the existence of the Senate.) The executive and judiciary are elected and appointed at some remove from the immediate opinion of the people, but democratically, that is, not upon any authority outside the sovereignty of the people. They serve for longer terms and serve larger constituencies; the nature of their duties thrusts more forcefully upon them awareness of what is necessary for the interest of the whole. They come to want to do their jobs well. Separation of powers creates offices which of themselves tend to make the men who occupy them worthy of the offices.

Moreover, separation of powers aids in securing for the executive and judiciary the men most likely to acquit themselves well; that is, it influences beneficially the majority choice. Separation of powers, one can see, supplies a superb rhetorical mode to those who are concerned with the ineptitude of popular rule. Publius has the courage — and it says something about his audience that he felt he could dare — to ask the many to select for their rulers men who are their superiors in wisdom and virtue. Every people ought "to obtain for rulers men who possess most wisdom to discern, and most virtue to pursue, the common good." [37] Separation of powers gives Publius a framework within which to press the people to seek wisdom and virtue in their rulers. He can present the executive and judiciary (and the Senate) as having, so to speak, a list of job specifications, qualities which are necessary to the performance of the functions and which approximate wisdom and virtue. It is politically easier and more effective to ask the people to select the right man for the specific job, especially a people with the "commercial character of America." [38] More willing to vote for superior men when superiority is presented in the guise of job qualifications, the people are also instructed in how to choose the better men; the job specifications supply them with a kind of simple checklist to guide choice to better rather than poorer men.

Publius shows how separation of powers, legislative checks and balances, and numerous practical embellishments upon these make possible for the first time a sound popular regime, a system of popular rule which will be less oppressive and wiser in the art of government than any before. But we must now see that this achievement depends utterly upon the last item in Publius' science, the enlargement of the republican orbit.

Separation of powers is a refinement of the representative principle. It would have no place in a pure democracy. Separation guards against that "accumulation of all powers, legislative, executive, and judiciary, in the same hands, whether of one, a few, or many, and whether hereditary, self-appointed, or elective [which] may justly be pronounced the very definition of tyranny." [39] But a pure democracy, by Publius' definition, is precisely the accumulation of all powers in the hands of the many. Hence it is only in a representative democracy that the rulers can be separated into distinct departments. But just as it is not enough to have a representative democracy, so it is not enough even to have properly separated representatives. It must be remembered that Publius said that the small ancient democracies could not have been helped by "*any* form of representative government"; they fatally lacked the advantages of an extensive territory and a numerous population. The representative principle is meant to supply rulers who can govern the people better than the people can govern themselves directly. But in small republics, the representative rulers are so immediately under the scrutiny and influence of a compacted popular majority that the representatives constitute no independent presence in the regime, but are merely the tools of the majority. Hence the representative principle is useless in a small republic.[40] Nor can separation of powers save the small republic. The immediate influence there of popular majorities, sufficient to awe a single representative body, is sufficient also to make of separated departments the mere agents of popular will. Only when there is a distance between the people and their government will there be that difference between the ultimate authority of the people and the immediate authority of their representatives which is the decisive condition for the advantages supplied by the principle of both representation and separation of powers. Not even in those large republics, the states, but only in a very large republic, the union, will the representative principle and its corollary, separation of powers, work "to the amelioration of popular systems of civil government."

The representative principle, reinforced by separation of powers, is meant to deny the authority of the government to oppressive popular majorities *after* they have formed. But Publius was aware that this was not enough, even in large republics. If a majority comes to have the same oppressive passion or interest and holds to it for only four to six years, it will find the means to triumph over separation of powers, checks and balances, the not so difficult amending procedure, and all the contrivances of the Constitution. These devices were designed, and could be designed, only to stay the will of the majority. This is not to depreciate the importance of the legal barriers; they have enormous efficacy in tempering the force Publius feared. But that efficacy depends ultimately upon a prior weakening of the force applied against them, upon the majority having been deflected from its "schemes of oppression." This is why Publius calls the problem of the popular majority itself *the* problem of popular government.

Publius therefore seeks to solve the problem of the oppressive and unwise rule of popular systems by trying to deal with the popular majority itself. Again everything depends upon the novel conception of a very large republic and, as we shall see, a certain kind of very large republic. The problem is dealt with in the famous tenth essay on the problem of "violence of faction."

Publius is not concerned with the problem of faction generally; he devotes only two sentences in the whole essay to the dangers of minority factions. The real problem in popular government is majority faction, or, more precisely, *the* majority faction, *i.e.,* the great mass of the little propertied and the unpropertied. If the people is the sovereign, the many are the sovereign, and the many may desire to oppress the few; it is the many therefore from whom can come the greatest harm. Publius emphasizes one harm in particular, the harm which results from the struggle between the rich and the poor and which made the ancient democracies short-lived "spectacles of turbulence and contention." *The* problem for the friend of popular government is how to avoid the "domestic convulsion" which results when the rich and the poor, the few and the many, as is their wont, are at each others' throats. Always before in popular governments the many, armed with political power, precipitated such convulsions. The many can be diverted from this natural course, Publius says, by one of two means only.

> Either the existence of the same passion or interest in a majority at the same time must be prevented, or the majority, having such co-existent passion or interest, must be rendered, by their number and local situation, unable to concert and carry into effect schemes of oppression.[41]

But "we well know that neither moral nor religious motives can be relied on" as a control if such a majority forms and concerts its action. The "circumstance principally" which will provide both defenses against oppressive majorities is the "greater number of citizens and extent of territory which may be brought within the compass" of very large republican governments.

The smaller the society, the fewer probably will be the distinct parties and interests composing it; the fewer the distinct parties and interests, the more frequently will a majority be found of the same party; and the smaller the number of individuals composing a majority, and the smaller the compass within which they are placed, the more easily will they concert and execute their plans of oppression. Extend the sphere and you take in a greater variety of parties and interests; you make it less probable that a majority of the whole will have a common motive to invade the rights of other citizens; or if such a common motive exists, it will be more difficult for all who feel it to discover their own strength, and to act in unison with each other.[42]

In a small republic the many poor come to see themselves as a single interest arrayed against the single interest of the few rich; accordingly, the politics of the small republic is the fatal politics of class struggle. That is what is important here about smallness. In the small republic, the many are divided into but a few trades and callings; further, it can be suggested, the smallness of the country makes instantly visible to anyone that these few differences among the many are trivial as compared with the massive difference between all the poor and all the rich. In a small republic, the divisions among the many are insufficient to prevent them from conceiving their lot in common and uniting in fatal struggle against the common enemy. In a large republic, however, distinctions arise among the many, sufficiently numerous and divisive to prevent the forming and concerting of such majorities. But clearly, largeness is not as such decisive; there can be large countries in which the poor are undifferentiated, poor only in a few ways. Only a certain kind of large republic holds out the prospect of the right kind of divisiveness. Publius tells us where this occurs. The properly divisive host of interests grows up "of necessity in civilized nations, and divide[s] them into different classes, actuated by different sentiments and views." Strikingly, as it does in Adam Smith, "civilized nations" means large nations devoted to the commercial life. The largeness of the large republic offers a remedy for the republican disease only if the large republic is also a modern commercial republic.

Publius' republican remedy depends entirely upon achieving the right kind of political divisions. Now Publius sees more than one source of division; for example, he clearly relies upon the presence of a "multiplicity of [religious] sects."[43] But he is well known to emphasize primarily the economic. "The possession of different *degrees* and *kinds* of property . . . [influences] the sentiments and views of the respective proprietors . . . [and produces the] division of the society into different interests and parties." Although other causes of division must not be overlooked, "the most common and durable source of factions has been the *various* and *unequal* distribution of property." (Italics supplied.) It is important to notice that in both statements Publius distinguishes two kinds of divisions which result from property: men differ according to the *amount* of property they hold, but also according to the *kind* of property they hold. The difference according to amount of property, between rich and poor, was the basis of the fatal class struggles of small republics. But Publius sees in the large commercial republic the possibility for the first time of subordinating the difference over amount of property to the difference over kind of property. In such a republic the hitherto fatal class struggle is replaced by the safe, even salutary struggle among different kinds of propertied interests. In such a republic, a man will regard it as more important to himself to further the immediate advantage of his specialized trade, or his specialized calling within a trade, than to advance the general cause of the poor or the rich. The struggle of the various interests veils the difference between the few and the many. In particular, the interest of the many as such can be fragmented into sundry narrower, more limited interests, each seeking immediate advantage. In such a republic and with such citizens, "you make it less probable that a majority of the whole will have a common motive to invade the rights of other citizens." In such a republic, popular majorities will still rule but now "among the great variety of interests, parties, and sects which it embraces, a coalition of a majority of the whole society could seldom take place on any other principles than those of justice and the general good." [44]

Publius is aware of what is involved in his novel teaching regarding the large commercial republic. His doctrine moves in directions which carry it beyond those manifestly political concerns with which we have dealt. Publius sees, as does Adam Smith, the connection between a very large area of trade and the possibility of division of labor, which in turn is so closely connected with the saving multiplicity of faction. This is why Publius so desperately seeks to preserve, render vastly more intimate, and strengthen the union. Publius also knows that his solution to the problem of popular majorities requires that the country be profoundly democratic, that is, that all men must be equally free and equally encouraged to seek their immediate gain and to associate with others in the process. There must be no rigid barriers which bar men from the pursuit of their immediate interest. Indeed, it is especially the lowly, from whom so much is to be feared, who must feel barred from opportunity and most sanguine about their chances. Further, his solution requires a country that achieves commercial success, a wealthy country. That is, the limited and immediate gains must be real; the fragmented interests must achieve real gains from time to time, else the scheme ceases to beguile or mollify. Further, the laws, and especially the fundamental law, must look to the protection of the property of all, of the little propertied so that they may cleave to their little as their fundamental concern, and of the much propertied so as to make their property seem beyond the reach of envy. The fundamental law must also render difficult especially those most likely oppressive acts such as the states' tampering with the value of money or impairing the obligation of contracts.

And Publius is aware that his scheme involves an enormous reliance on the ceaseless striving after immediate private gains; the commercial life must be made honorable and universally practiced. Publius counts on a portion of patriotism and wisdom in the people and especially in their representative rulers. But precisely in his discussion of separation of powers, that device for securing enlightened rulers, he returns to his primary emphasis. Enlightened though they may be, it is primarily their private passions and interests that render them useful to the public. In perhaps the most remarkable and revealing single sentence of the book, Publius speaks of "this policy of supplying, by opposite and rival interests, the defect of better motives, [which] might be traced through the whole system of human affairs, private as well as public." [45] To understand fully how Publius understands "the defect of better motives," and how he seeks to make up for the defect by founding a regime in which the art of government is made commensurate with the capacity of men when their passions and interests are rightly arranged, is to understand Publius' contribution to the new "science of politics" and to understand the American republic he had so large a hand in framing.

NOTES

The Nationalists of 1781–1783 and the Economic
Interpretation of the Constitution, E. JAMES FERGUSON

1 Modern studies that bring out the implications of the Nationalist movement most explicitly are Clarence L. Ver Steeg, *Robert Morris: Revolutionary Financier: With an Analysis of his Earlier Career* (Philadelphia, 1954); Merrill Jensen, *The New Nation: A History of the United States During the Confederation, 1781–1789* (New York, 1950), and E. James Ferguson, *The Power of the Purse: A History of American Public Finance, 1776–1790* (Chapel Hill, 1961). The economic phases of the movement are implicit throughout Robert A. East, *Business Enterprise in the American Revolutionary Era* (New York, 1938); and the political aspects are treated in George Bancroft, *History of the Formation of the Constitution of the United States* (2 vols., New York, 1882).

2 Worthington C. Ford, ed., *Journals of the Continental Congress, 1774–1789* (34 vols., Washington, 1904–1937), XV, 1019–20. On the constitutional point, see James Madison to Thomas Jefferson, May 6, 1780, Edmund C. Burnett, ed., *Letters of Members of the Continental Congress* (8 vols., Washington, 1921–1936), V, 128–29.

3 The affinity between central government and political elitism is the central theme of Merrill Jensen, *The Articles of Confederation: An Interpretation of the Social-Constitutional History of the United States* (Madison, 1940). This is made explicit in his concluding statement, pp. 239–45. The same phenomenon in late colonial times is discussed in Edmund S. and Helen M. Morgan, *The Stamp Act Crisis: Prologue to Revolution* (Chapel Hill, 1953), 11–20. With his talent for the pungent and invidious phrase, Gouverneur Morris supposed in 1774 (as paraphrased by his biographer) that an American central government would "restrain the democratic spirit, which the constitutions and local circumstances of the country had so long fostered in the minds of the people." Jared Sparks, *Life of Gouverneur Morris . . . in the Political History of the United States* (3 vols., Boston, 1832), I, 27.

4 On the magnitude of confiscations, see Ferguson, *Power of the Purse*, 57–64.

5 Oscar and Mary F. Handlin, "Revolutionary Economic Policy in Massachusetts," *William and Mary Quarterly*, IV (Jan. 1947), 3–26; East, *Business Enterprise*, 195–212. See also Curtis P. Nettels, *The Emergence of a National Economy: 1775–1815* (New York: 1962), 27–29.

6 East, *Business Enterprise*, 207, describes the repudiation of paper currency in 1781 as a victory for the "rising conservative movement" in which the viewpoint of merchants and lawyers figured prominently. Robert Morris, who frequently expressed himself on this point, looked forward in 1781 to the time when, by the removal of the "detestable tribe" of economic restrictions, people would possess "that freedom for which they are contending." Robert Morris to the Governors of North Carolina, South Carolina, and Georgia, Dec. 19, 1781, Francis Wharton, ed., *The Revolutionary Diplomatic Correspondence of the United States* (6 vols., Washington, 1889), V, 58–59.

7 Alexander Hamilton to James Duane, Sept. 3, 1780, Harold C. Syrett, ed., Jacob E. Cooke, assoc. ed., *The Papers of Alexander Hamilton* (13 vols., New York, 1961–   ), II, 406.

8 "Original Documents: A Hartford Convention in 1780," *Magazine of American History*, VIII (Oct. 1882), 688–89; Bancroft, *History of the . . . Constitution*, I, 14–16; Ferguson, *Power of the Purse*, 149–52.

9 Jensen, *New Nation*, 45–53; East, *Business Enterprise*, 207–12; Jennings B. Sanders, *Evolution of Executive Departments of the Continental Congress, 1774–1789* (Chapel Hill, 1935), 3–5.

10 Robert Morris is entitled to a place in the line of succession that includes Hamilton and Albert Gallatin. Although Ver Steeg in his excellent study compares Robert Morris with Hamilton, he does not give Morris enough credit. Ver Steeg, *Robert Morris*, 193–99.

11 Foreign loans became an important resource for Congress only in 1781 as the fighting drew to a close. Ferguson, *Power of the Purse*, 125–31, 333n.

12 *Journals*, XVIII, 1033–36, XIX, 110–13; Madison to Edmund Pendleton, May 29, 1781, Burnett, ed., *Letters*, VI, 103–04. The grant of the impost was to be coextensive with the existence of the Revolutionary debt.

13 Ferguson, *Power of the Purse*, 29–31, 140–41, 221–28.

14 *Ibid.*, 141–44, 180–83, 203–04.

15 Robert Morris to Governors of Massachusetts, Rhode Island, New York, Delaware, Maryland, and North Carolina, July 27, 1781, Wharton, ed., *Diplomatic Correspondence*, IV, 608.

16 Robert Morris to Nathaniel Appleton, April 16, 1782, *ibid.*, V, 311. Robert Morris exempted the federal debt from the general expenses of the Revolution which were to be apportioned on the states. Robert Morris to President of Congress, Aug. 28, 1781, *ibid.*, IV, 674–75. At his insistence, Congress refused to allow the states credit for payments they had made to their own lines in the Continental army. Robert Morris to Governor of Rhode Island, June 26, 1782, *ibid.*, V, 524; Robert Morris to Daniel of St. Thomas Jenifer, March 12, 1782; Report on the New Jersey Memorial, Sept. 27, 1782; to Receivers of the several States, Oct. 5, 1782, Official Letterbook C, 97–99, Official Letterbook D, 231–34, 277–78, Robert Morris Papers (Manuscript Division, Library of Congress); *Journals*, XXIII, 629–31. Congress backed down from this position, April 13, 1785. *Ibid.*, XXVIII, 261.

17 *Journals*, XXII, 82–86.

18 *Ibid.*, XXIV, 206–10. See Ferguson, *Power of the Purse*, 156–57.

19 The foreign debt of about $11,000,000 was generally conceded to be a federal obligation and did not affect constitutional issues. On the foreign debt in the postwar era, see Ferguson, *Power of the Purse*, 234–38.

20 The quotation is out of context. It is taken from a comment on Hamilton's funding program by Oliver Wolcott, Jr. Hamilton to Oliver Wolcott, Sr., March 27, 1790, George Gibbs, ed., *Memoirs of the Administration of Washington and Adams From the Papers of Oliver Wolcott* (2 vols., New York, 1846), I, 43.

21 Robert Morris to President of Congress, Aug. 5, 1782, *Journals*, XXII, 432. His report was dated July 29, 1782. Robert Morris expected the Bank of North America to create the same kind of unifying appeal. Robert Morris to John Jay, July 13, 1781, Wharton, ed., *Diplomatic Correspondence*, IV, 563, 568–69; Robert Morris to Benjamin Franklin, July 13, 1781, *ibid.*, IV, 568–69.

22 Robert Morris' report, dated July 29, 1782, is the fullest theoretical exposition of his views. *Journals*, XXII, 429–46; Wharton, ed., *Diplomatic Correspondence*, V, 619–34. He was thinking not only of the existing loan office debt but also of the enlarged federal debt that would result from the settlement of claims already under way. In his last official communication before he retired from office, he expressed his confidence that the debt would one day be funded and added that it was "a commercial problem which admits of absolute demonstration that the punctual payment of interest on our debts will produce a clear annual gain of more than such interest can possibly amount to." Robert Morris to President of Congress, Sept. 30, 1784, *ibid.*, VI, 822.

23 Robert Morris to Robert Smith, July 17, 1781, Wharton, ed., *Diplomatic Correspondence*, IV, 582; Alexander Hamilton to James Duane, Sept. 3, 1780, Syrett, ed., *Papers of Alexander Hamilton*, II, 415.

24 For an appraisal of colonial experience with paper money and a bibliography of the subject up to the date of publication, see E. James Ferguson, "Currency Finance: An Interpretation of Colonial Monetary Practices," *William and Mary Quarterly*, X (April 1953),

153–80. The reorientation of scholarly opinion as to colonial monetary practices has become pretty general. It has been embraced with particular enthusiasm by the new economic historians, who are highly interested in the function of colonial currency and land banks in promoting economic development. See Ralph L. Andreano, ed., *New Views on Economic Development: A Selective Anthology of Recent Work* (Cambridge, Mass., 1965), 41–56. The current reappraisal is judiciously stated by Curtis P. Nettels, who writes that in the middle colonies land banks were prudently managed and "realized the benefits claimed for them," but that serious depreciation took place in Massachusetts, Rhode Island, and South Carolina. (He might have added that the depreciation was at an early date in South Carolina and that for forty-five years before the Revolution the colony's currency was stable.) Nettels concludes by saying that it was the depreciation that occurred during the Revolution that evoked "impassioned opposition" to paper money during the 1780s — the main reason being that creditors no longer trusted the legislatures. Nettels, *Emergence of a National Economy*, 80–81.

25 For an expression of these ideas, see *Journals*, XVIII, 1157–64, in which a committee report of December 18, 1780, envisages a bank note currency; also, Robert Morris to Franklin, July 13, 1781; Robert Morris to Governors of the States, Sept. 4, 1781, Wharton, ed., *Diplomatic Correspondence*, IV, 562–63, 693; Madison to Pendleton, Feb. 25, 1782, Burnett, ed., *Letters*, VI, 305–06; Hamilton to Robert Morris, April 30, 1781, Syrett, ed., *Papers of Alexander Hamilton*, II, 620, 623–24, 627–30.

26 *Journals*, XX, 545–48. Wharton, ed., *Diplomatic Correspondence*, IV, 565–68; *Journals*, XXI, 1187–90.

27 Employing federal securities as bank stock was proposed in Congress, April 12, 1781, *Journals*, XIX, 381. In the plan for a bank which he submitted to Robert Morris, Hamilton suggested that land be accepted as partial payment for shares. Robert Morris replied that he had thought of "interweaving a security" in the bank's capital, but had given up the idea as too risky. Hamilton to Robert Morris, April 30, 1781; Robert Morris to Hamilton, May 26, 1781, Syrett, ed., *Papers of Alexander Hamilton*, II, 621–22, 645–46. See also the plan of a bank Hamilton sent to Duane, Sept. 3, 1780, *ibid.*, II, 400–18. Businessmen already employed securities like money in making payments to one another. In his statement of accounts published in 1785, Robert Morris expressed his continuing faith in the potential economic uses of the public debt, saying: "A due provision for the public debts would at once convert those debts into a real medium of commerce. The possessors of certificates, would then become the possessors of money. And of course, there would be no want of it among those who having property wish to borrow provided that the laws and administration are such, as to compel the punctual payment of debts." Robert Morris, *A Statement of the Accounts of the United States of America During the Administration of the Superintendent of Finance* (Philadelphia, 1785), ix.

28 On the plans, see Robert Morris to Jay, July 13, 1781; Robert Morris to Franklin, July 13, 1781, Wharton, ed., *Diplomatic Correspondence*, IV, 562–65, 568–71. Nettels is perceptive, but no more perceptive than Robert Morris himself, in seeing the implications of the flotation of currency. Nettels, *Emergence of a National Economy*, 32–33. See Robert Morris to Hamilton, Oct. 5, 1782, Syrett, ed., *Papers of Alexander Hamilton*, III, 177–79.

29 Robert Morris to President of Congress, Aug. 26, 1783, Papers of the Continental Congress, No. 137, III, 33–40 (National Archives); Ferguson, *Power of the Purse*, 209–10.

30 Jefferson among others, was hopeful of the impost's adoption. Jefferson to Madison, May 7, 1783, Julian P. Boyd, ed., *The Papers of Thomas Jefferson* (17 vols., Princeton, 1952–   ), VI, 265–67.

31 The analysis that follows is based on Ferguson, *Power of the Purse*, 220–42.

32 *Journals*, XXX, 439–44; James Monroe to Madison, Sept. 12, 1786, James Madison Papers (Manuscript Division, Library of Congress).

33 Committee report of Aug. 17, 1786, *Journals*, XXXI, 521–23. See John Henry to Governor of Maryland, Aug. 30, 1786, Burnett, ed., *Letters*, VIII, 455–56.

34 For a discussion of federal regulation of trade, see Nettels, *Emergence of a National Economy*, 66–75.

35 Duties on exports were excepted. In the struggle over ratification, the Antifederalists tried to limit congressional taxing power. Every state convention that attached amendments to its ratification requested that federal revenues be restricted to indirect taxes in the first instance, that additional sums be raised by requisitions, and that federal collection of taxes within the states be permitted only if the states themselves did not deliver the money. This proposal was considered by the first Congress, along with other amendments, but voted down thirty-nine to nine in the House of Representatives and not included among the amendments sent out to the states for ratification. Jonathan Elliot, ed., *The Debates in the Several State Conventions on the Adoption of the Federal Constitution* (2nd ed., 5 vols., Philadelphia, 1861), I, 175–77, 322–23, 325, 326, 336, II, 545; U.S. Congress, *Annals of Congress: The Debates and Proceedings in the Congress of the United States* (42 vols., Washington, 1834–1856), I, 773–77. See "Luther Martin's Letter on the Federal Convention of 1787," in Elliot, ed., *Debates*, I, 368–69.

36 Elliot, ed., *Debates*, III, 29.

37 Ferguson, *Power of the Purse*, 284–85. Most of the largest holders were brokers who did not own all the securities registered in their names; hence, the figures might seem to overstate the degree of concentration. However, nearly all the records relative to $18,000,000 (out of a total of about $40,000,000) have been almost completely destroyed. These were of securities registered at the treasury, in which the really great interstate speculators, foreign as well as domestic, tended to invest. If these records were available, the degree of concentration would undoubtedly appear much higher than is suggested by the figures given here.

38 For a powerful summary of the economic effects of the establishment of the national government, see Nettels, *Emergence of a National Economy*, 89–108.

39 Writing in 1796, Gallatin, leading spokesman of the Republicans on financial matters, said that Republicans had never disputed the necessity of funding the debt, although he suggested mildly that they would have preferred a discrimination between creditors. He himself had no objection to the way the debt was funded. Gallatin, "Sketch of the Finances," Adams, ed., *Writings of Gallatin*, III, 128, 148.

40 "The situation of our public debts and the very great embarrassments which attended all our concerns on that account, were the *principal* causes, of that revolution which has given us the Constitution." Letter on Hamilton's funding proposals dated New York, Feb. 3, 1790, *Maryland Journal and Baltimore Advertiser*, Feb. 12, 1790.

The Progress of Constitutional Theory Between the Declaration of Independence and the Meeting of the Philadelphia Convention,
EDWARD S. CORWIN

1 See, *e.g.*, R. L. Schuyler, *Constitution of the United States*, p. 5. Professor Schuyler voices the opinion (p. 6) that "the Constitution is not to be regarded as in any true sense an original creative act of the Convention at Philadelphia, which framed it." It is interesting to oppose to this sentiment the following passage from Professor Roscoe Pound's *Interpretations of Legal History*, p. 127: "Except as an act of omnipotence, creation does not mean the making of something out of nothing. Creative activity takes materials and gives them form so that they may be put to uses for which the materials unformed are not adopted." Professor Schuyler's sweeping statement would probably be quite as near the truth if the word "not" were omitted from it.

2 *Writings*, ed. Ford, X, 254, 256.

3 See Farrand, *Records of the Federal Convention*, I, 83–84, 134–135, 137, 139, 151–152, 161, 254, 285 ff., 304 ff., 317, 356, 398 ff., 426 ff., 437–438, 444–449, 451, etc. The lessons of the past, its successes and failures, are cited for the most part. The term "political science" is used by Mercer, *ibid.*, II, 284, while "the science of politics" is Hamilton's expression in

Federalist, no. 9 (ed. Lodge). This, he says, "has undergone great improvement." The entire passage is worth perusal in this connection. See also Madison in *Federalist*, nos. 14 and 47, and Adams's preface to his *Defence (Works*, IV. 283–298).

4 *Ancient Law* (New York, 1888), p. 226.

5 Farrand, I. 133–134.

6 *Ibid.*, I. 48, 255, 424, 525, 533, II. 285.

7 See W. C. Webster, "State Constitutions of the American Revolution," in *Annals of the American Academy of Political and Social Science*, May, 1897.

8 Niles, *Principles and Acts of the Revolution*, p. 234; from an address by Dr. Benjamin Rush delivered at Philadelphia on July 4, 1787, before members of the Convention and others. The address testifies throughout to the importance of the governmental situation in the states as a problem before the Convention.

9 See *Federalist*, no. 47.

10 See 11 (second edition, ed. Lewis).

11 See *Laws of New Hampshire*, ed. Batchellor, V. *passim*. Some of the less usual items are those on pp. 21, 66, 89, 90–91, 110–111, 125–126, 130–131, 167–168, 243, 320–321, 334–335, 363, 395–396, 400–401, 404–406, 411–412, 417–418, 455–456, 485, 499, 522. The volume is crowded with acts "restoring" a defeated or defaulting party "to his law," "any usage, custom, or law to the contrary notwithstanding."

12 See the references I have collected in my *Doctrine of Judicial Review*, pp. 69–71; also Baldwin, *The American Judiciary*, ch. II.

13 McIlwain, *The High Court of Parliament and its Supremacy*, ch. III.

14 Baldwin, *op. cit.*, ch. I.

15 See, *e.g.*, *Messages from the Governors* (of New York), ed. Lincoln, I. 55.

16 A good summary of legislative persecution of the Loyalists appears in Van Tyne, *American Revolution*, pp. 255 ff.

17 *Two Centuries' Growth of American Law*, pp. 129–133.

18 Cooley, *Constitutional Limitations*, ch. V.

19 *Writings*, Memorial ed., II. 163–164. See to the same effect Chief Justice Pendleton's words in 4 Call 5, 17 (Va., 1782).

20 In *Federalist*, no. 47, Madison also declares that "the entire legislature [*i.e.*, Parliament] can perform no judiciary act." This assertion is based on his readings of Montesquieu, but it is untrue even of Parliament to-day. Stephen, *Commentaries* (eleventh ed.), IV. 283; Pollard, *Evolution of Parliament*, p. 239.

21 Iredell's perusal of Blackstone produced an entire change in his theory of the basis of judicial review. Compare McRee, *Life and Correspondence of James Iredell*, II. 172–173; and Calder *v.* Bull, 3 Dallas 386, 398. One aspect of Marshall's thinking on the same matter is touched upon briefly in note 40, *infra*.

22 Niles, *op. cit.*, p. 47.

23 *Life and Works*, VI. 94–97; Morse, *The Federalist Party in Massachusetts*, pp. 68–69.

24 *History* (New York, 1892), V. 329.

25 Hart, *Slavery and Abolition*, p. 153. See also G. H. Moore, *Slavery in Massachusetts*.

26 Hart, *op. cit.*, p. 154.

27 Moore, *Diary of the American Revolution*, p. 362. See also *Works of Alexander Hamilton*, Constitutional ed. IV. 232.

28 This seems to have been the origin of the American distrust of legislatures, upon which Bryce comments in his *American Commonwealth*, I. 427, 451 (second ed.).

29 D. W. Brown, *The Commercial Power of Congress*, ch. II.; A. A. Giesecke, *American Commercial Legislation before 1789.*

30 McLaughlin, *The Confederation and the Constitution*, ch. IX.

31 *Writings*, Memorial ed., II: 160 ff.

32 *Proceedings relative to the calling of the Conventions of 1776 and 1790* (Harrisburg, 1825), pp. 83 ff. For a contemporary criticism of the report, see *Federalist*, no. 49.

33 *Works*, IV. 273 ff. The quotation is from p. 587.

34 *The English Constitution* (New York, 1906), p. 296.

35 F. J. Stimson, *Federal and State Constitutions*, sect. 304.

36 Austin Scott, "Holmes *v.* Walton, the New Jersey Precedent," in *Am. Hist. Rev.*, IV. 456 ff.

37 See generally my *Doctrine of Judicial Review*, pp. 71–75, and references there given.

38 Holland, *Elements of Jurisprudence*, thirteenth ed., pp. 19–21, 32–34, 41–45.

39 See note 37, above; also Varnum's contemporary pamphlet on the case. The case was the first and last case of judicial review of the sort under the old charter.

40 Compare in this connection Luther Martin's "Genuine Information," in Farrand's *Records*, III. 230, with Hamilton's argument for judicial review in *Federalist*, no. 78, and Marshall's opinion in Marbury *v.* Madison, 1 Cranch 129. The former regards political authority as a *cessio* from the people to the government which "never devolves back to them" except in events amounting to a dissolution of government. The latter regard it as a revocable *translatio* to agents by a principal who is by no means bound to act through agents.

41 See my "Basic Doctrine of American Constitutional Law," in *Michigan Law Review*, XII. 256, 260.

42 Bk. IV., ch. 14.

43 *Institutes*, IV. 70, 71; 12 *Reports* 63.

44 *Institutes*, IV. 23, 26, 36.

45 *Second Treatise on Civil Government*, ch. XI., sect. 136.

46 *Spirit of Laws* (trans. Pritchard), bk. XI., ch. 6.

47 *Commentaries*, I. 44, 46, 58, 160–161, 267, 269.

48 Broom, *Maxims* (fifth American ed.), p. 105 and citations; pp. 140–141 of the original edition.

49 See note 43, *supra*.

50 *Commentaries*, I. 69–71.

51 1 Martin 42.

52 McRee, *Life and Correspondence of Iredell*, II, 145–149.

53 See especially *Federalist*, no. 15.

54 McLaughlin, *op. cit.*, ch. XI.

55 Van Tyne, "Sovereignty in the American Revolution," in *Am. Hist. Rev.*, XII. 529 ff.

56 *Journals of the Continental Congress*, ed. Hunt, XVIII. 936–937; Wharton, *Revolutionary Diplomatic Correspondence*, V. 88–89; New York Historical Society, *Collections*, 1878, pp. 138–139; J. C. Welling in Am. Hist. Assoc., *Papers*. III. 167 ff.

57 *Works of James Wilson*, ed. J. D. Andrews, I. 558 ff.

58 MacDonald, *Documentary Source Book*, pp. 207–208.

59 See H. B. Dawson's pamphlet on the case; also Coxe's and Haines's well-known volumes. Hamilton had the year previous been a member of a committee of Congress which had the subject of violations of the treaty of peace under consideration. For the report of this committee, see *Journals of the American Congress* (Washington, 1823), IV. 224–225.

60 Allan McLane Hamilton, *Intimate Life of Alexander Hamilton*, pp. 457, 460–461. "Our sovereignty began by a Federal act," he asserts (p. 459).

61 See *Works*, Constitutional ed., IV. 238–240.

62 *Secret Journals of Congress* (Boston, 1821), IV. 185–287.

63 Jefferson's letter of May 29, 1792, to the British minister Hammond, gives all the facts. *Writings*, Memorial ed., XVI. 183–277.

64 *Federalist*, no. 40.

65 D. W. Brown, *op. cit.*, ch. II.

66 *Political Writings of Thomas Paine* (1835), I. 45–46.

67 *Works*, Constitutional ed., I. 213.

68 See the credentials, Elliot's *Debates*, second ed., I. 159 ff.

69 Beveridge, *Life of John Marshall*, vol. I., ch. 8.

70 *Writings*, ed. Hunt, II. 361 ff.

71 *Cf.* Farrand, II. 73–80; and *Federalist*, no. 78.

The Constitutional Convention, ALPHEUS THOMAS MASON

1 *Independent Gazetteer* (Philadelphia), April 13, 1787. Quoted in Jackson T. Main, *The Antifederalists: Critics of the Constitution, 1781-1788* (Chapel Hill, 1961), p. 115.

2 *Continental Journal* (Boston), May 31, 1787. Quoted in Main, *ibid.*

3 Max Farrand, *The Framing of the Constitution of the United States* (New Haven, Conn.: Yale University Press, 1913), II, 10.

4 *Id.*, 28.

5 Madison to Randolph, April 8, 1787, in Gaillard Hunt, ed., *The Writings of James Madison* (New York, 1900-1910), II, pp. 336-40.

6 *Ibid.*

7 *Ibid.*

8 Max Farrand, ed., *The Records of the Federal Convention* (New Haven, Conn.: Yale University Press, 1911), I, pp. 33-34. Cited hereafter as Farrand.

9 *Id.*, 42.

10 *Id.*, 34.

11 *Id.*, 42-43.

12 Farrand, III, 23.

13 *Id.*, 24.

14 *Id.*, 30.

15 Farrand, I, 164-165.

16 *Id.*, 165.

17 *Id.*

18 *Id.*, 166.

19 *Id.*, 177-179.

20 *Id.*, 180.

21 *Id.*, 179.

22 For a comparison of the purpose of the two plans, see *id.*, 20 (Virginia Plan), and *id.*, 242 (New Jersey Plan).

23 *Id.*, 20-22.

24 *Id.*, 242-44. For James Wilson's point-by-point comparison of the two plans, see *id.*, 252-53.

25 *Id.*, 242.

26 *Id.*, 551.

27 *Id.*, 321.

28 *Id.*, 251.

29 *Id.*, 250.

30 *Id.*, 347.

31 *Id.*, 359.

32 *Id.*, 436.

33 *Id.*, 445.

34 *Id.*, 444.

35 *Id.*, 460.

36 *Id.*, 461-62.

37 *Id.*, 463.

38 *Id.*, 464.

39 *Id.*, 475-76.

40 *Id.*, 483.

41 *Id.*, 526.

42 *Id.*, 529.

43 *Id.*, 527.

44 *Id.*, 529-30.

45 Farrand, II, 5.

46 *Id.*

47 *Id.*

48 *Id.*, 7.

49 *Id.*, 10.

50 *Id.*, 5.

51 *Id.*, 25.

52 Farrand, I, 54.

53 *Id.*, 168.

54 *Supra*, note 6.

55 *Supra*, note 16.

56 Farrand, II, 27-28.

57 *Id.*, 28.

58 Jefferson to Madison, June 20, 1787, Julian P. Boyd, ed., *The Papers of Thomas Jefferson* (Princeton, 1950–), XI, 480-81.

59 *Supra*, note 58. See also Sherman on August 23, Farrand, II, 390.

60 Farrand, II, 589.

61 *Id.*, 347.

62 *Id.*, 349.

63 Farrand, I, 214.

64 *Id.*, 122-23.

65 Farrand, II, 92.

66 *Id.*, 93.

67 Farrand, I, 214.

68 Farrand, II, 93-94.

69 *Id.*, 476. Gerry also advocated state ratification at this time; see *id.*, 478.

70 *Id.*, 476.

71 Madison to Jefferson, September 6, 1787, in Farrand, II, 77.

72 Farrand, II, 391.

73 *Id.*, 479. Randolph, of course, later suggested a second Convention for precisely the opposite reasons. See his speech of September 10, *id.*, 564, where he deplores, among other things, the dangerous extent of national power, including the implied powers.

74 *Id.*, 317.

75 *Id.*, 645-46 (emphasis added).

Men of Little Faith: The Anti-Federalists on the
Nature of Representative Government, CECELIA M. KENYON

1 A critical and definitive study of Beard as an historian has not yet been done. Interesting commentaries on the ambiguity to be found in Beard's thesis are Max Lerner's "Charles A. Beard," in his *Ideas Are Weapons* (New York, 1939), pp. 161–162, and Richard Hofstadter's "Charles Beard and the Constitution," in *Charles A. Beard: An Appraisal*, edited by Howard K. Beale (University of Kentucky Press, 1954). Hofstadter also cites the different attitudes toward the Constitution and its framers reflected in the Beard's *The Rise of American Civilization* (1927) and their *Basic History of the United States* (1944). Beale's essay in the same collection, "Charles Beard: Historian," recounts in broad terms the shifts in Beard's historiographical thought throughout his career. It is with the Beard of the earlier period that this essay is concerned, for this was the period of his most influential works.

2 Charles A. Beard, *An Economic Interpretation of the Constitution* (New York, 1913), Ch. VI, especially pp. 154–164. See also the succinct statement in *The Economic Basis of Politics* (New York, 1922), pp. 66–67: "Under the circumstances the framers of the Constitution relied, not upon direct economic qualification, but upon checks and balances to secure the rights of property — particularly personal property — against the assaults of the farmers and the proletariat." In Charles and Mary Beard's *The Rise of American Civilization* (New York, 1927), the theme is continued: "Almost unanimous was the opinion that democracy was a dangerous thing, to be restrained, not encouraged, by the Constitution, to be given as little voice as possible in the new system, to be hampered by checks and balances." (p. 315; cf. p. 326). It was this position which the Beards had apparently abandoned by the 1940's. The attitude of *The Republic* (1942), and of *The Basic History* (1944), is one of appreciation of the authors of the Constitution, not condemnation.

3 In 1936 Maurice Blinkoff published a study of the influence of Beard on American historiography and came to the conclusion that authors of college history textbooks had adopted Beard's views "with virtual unanimity." *The Influence of Charles A. Beard upon American Historiography*, University of Buffalo Studies, XII (May, 1936), p. 36. I have not conducted a comprehensive survey, but it seems to me that Blinkoff's conclusions would probably not be accurate for today.

For challenges to the Beard position, the reader may consult the survey of reviews of *An Economic Interpretation of the Constitution* cited in Blinkoff, as well as some of the selections in the *Amherst Problems in American Civilization* series; Earl Latham, editor, *The Declaration of Independence and the Constitution* (Boston, 1949), though this collection is, in the opinion of the author, biased in favor of the Beard interpretation. See also B. F. Wright, "The Origin of Separation of Powers in America," *Economica*, May, 1933; and "The Federalist on the Nature of Political Man," *Ethics*, Vol. LIX, No. 2, Part II (January, 1949); and Douglass Adair, "The Tenth Federalist Revisited," *William and Mary Quarterly*, 3d Series, Vol. VIII (January, 1951).

4 There is no doubt at all that many of the Anti-Federalists did regard the Constitution as dangerous and aristocratic, and its framers and supporters likewise. They were acutely suspicious of it because of its class origin and were on the lookout for every evidence of bias in favor of the "aristocrats" who framed it. Note, for example, the attitude of Amos Singletary expressed in the Massachusetts ratifying convention: "These lawyers, and men of learning and moneyed men, that talk so finely, and gloss over matters so smoothly, to make us poor illiterate people swallow down the pill, expect to get into Congress themselves; they expect to be managers of this Constitution, and get all the power and all the money into their own hands, and then they will swallow up all us little folks like the great *Leviathan;* yes, just as the whale swallowed up Jonah!" Jonathan Elliot, *The Debates in the Several State Conventions on the Adoption of the Federal Constitution as Recommended by the General Convention at Philadelphia, in 1787*, Second Edition, 5 vols. (Philadelphia, 1896), II, p. 102. See also reference to this attitude in a letter from Rufus King to James Madison, January 27, 1888. This letter is to be found in the *Documentary History of the*

Constitution of the United States of America, 1780–1870 (Washington, 1894–1905), 5 vols.; IV, p. 459. A similar feeling was reported to exist in the New Hampshire convention. See John Langdon to George Washington, February 28, 1788, *ibid.*, p. 524.

5 The *Agrippa* Letters in Paul Leicester Ford, *Essays on the Constitution of the United States* (Brooklyn, 1892), p. 65. See also pp. 91–92.

6 Elliot, IV, p. 52.

7 Elliot, III, p. 164; cf. III, pp. 607 ff.; II, pp. 69, 335; the *Centinel* Letters in John Bach McMaster and Frederick D. Stone, editors, *Pennsylvania and the Federal Constitution, 1787–1788* (Historical Society of Pennsylvania, 1888), p. 572; R. H. Lee, "Letters of a Federal Farmer," in Paul Leicester Ford, *Pamphlets on the Constitution of the United States* (Brooklyn, 1888), p. 288; George Clinton, *Cato*, in Ford, *Essays*, pp. 256 ff.

8 Political relativism had long been a part of the colonial heritage. Seventeenth-century Puritans, who were sure that God had regulated many aspects of life with remarkable precision, believed that He had left each people considerable freedom in the choice of their form of government. The secularized legacy of this belief prevailed throughout the era of framing state and national constitutions. Fundamental principles derived from natural law were of course universally valid, and certain "political maxims" regarding the structure of the government very nearly so, but the embodiment of these general truths in concrete political forms was necessarily determined by the nature and circumstances of the people involved.

9 On this subject see John C. Ranney, "The Bases of American Federalism," *William and Mary Quarterly*, Series 3, Vol. III, No. 1 (January, 1946).

10 Elliot, IV, p. 24.

11 From the *Agrippa* Letters, Ford, *Essays*, p. 64.

12 It was this misunderstanding of the proposed new system which Madison attempted to remove in *Federalist* 39.

13 Curiously enough, the Big-Little State fight, which almost broke up the Convention, played very little part in the ratification debates. And ironically one of the evidences of ideological unity which made the "more perfect union" possible was the similarity of arguments put forth by the Anti-Federalists in their respective states.

14 "Objections," Ford, *Pamphlets*, p. 331.

15 Elliot, III, p. 326.

16 Elliot, IV, pp. 272–273.

17 *Agrippa* Letters, Ford, *Essays*, p. 73.

18 "Address and Reasons of Dissent of the Minority of the Convention of Pennsylvania to their Constituents," reprinted in McMaster and Stone, *Pennsylvania and the Constitution*, p. 472.

19 Elliot, III, p. 32.

20 Ford, *Pamphlets*, pp. 288–289.

21 This idea appeared frequently in Anti-Federalist arguments. See, for example, the "Address and Dissent of the Minority. . . ," McMaster and Stone, *Pennsylvania and the Constitution*, pp. 472, 479; Lee, "Letters of a Federal Farmer," Ford, *Pamphlets*, p. 295, Elliot, III, pp. 266–267, 426 (George Mason).

22 Elliot, III, p. 322.

23 Elliot, II, p. 246.

24 The *Cornelius* Letter is reprinted in Samuel Bannister Harding, *The Contest over the Ratification of the Federal Constitution in the State of Massachusetts* (New York, 1896). See pp. 123–124.

25 See B. F. Wright. "*The Federalist* on the Nature of Political Man," *Ethics* (January, 1949).

26 Elliot, IV, p. 187; cf. pp. 203–204, and III, p. 494. Caldwell's statement is very similar to Madison's comment in *Federalist* 10: "It is in vain to say that enlightened statesmen will be able to adjust these clashing interests, and render them all subservient to the public good. Enlightened statesmen will not always be at the helm."

27 Elliot, II, pp. 295–296. Madison's declaration was this: "But what is government itself,

but the greatest of all reflections on human nature? If men were angels, no government would be necessary. If angels were to govern men, neither external nor internal controls on government would be necessary. In framing a government which is to be administered by men over men, the great difficulty lies in this: you must first enable the government to control the governed; and in the next place oblige it to control itself."

28 Mason in Virginia, Elliot, III, p. 32.

29 Henry in Virginia, *ibid.*, p. 436.

30 "Letters of Luther Martin," Ford, *Essays*, p. 379.

31 Barrell in Massachusetts, Elliot, II, p. 159.

32 White in Massachusetts, Elliot, II, p. 28.

33 Elliot, IV, p. 55.

34 Elliot, IV, pp. 51–52, 55–56, 62–63, 87–88.

35 Elliot, II, p. 22.

36 Elliot, II, p. 28.

37 Elliot, III, pp. 403–404.

38 Elliot, III, p. 175. Cf. *Centinel*, McMaster and Stone, *Pennsylvania and the Constitution*, p. 598, and James Winthrop in the *Agrippa* Letters, Ford, *Essays*, p. 105.

39 Elliot, III, p. 499.

40 Elliot, III, p. 502.

41 Elliot, IV, pp. 191–192. Abbott was not an Anti-Federalist, but was, according to L. I. Trenholme, in *The Ratification of the Federal Constitution in North Carolina* (New York, 1932), something of an independent. See p. 178. He voted for ratification.

42 Elliot, IV, p. 192.

43 *Ibid.*, p. 199.

44 *Ibid.*, p. 195.

45 *Ibid.*, p. 215. This quotation transmits a sense of the method of Anti-Federalist debate admirably. A similar statement by Amos Singletary of Massachusetts gives something of the flavor of the thinking done by the honest and pious patriots of the back country, in which opposition to the Constitution was strong: "The Hon. Mr. Singletary thought we were giving up all our privileges, as there was no provision that men in power should have any *religion*, and though he hoped to see Christians, yet by the Constitution, a Papist, or an Infidel, was as eligible as they. It had been said that men had not degenerated; he did not think that men were better now than when men after God's own heart did wickedly. He thought, in this instance, we were giving great power to we know not whom." Elliot, II, p. 44.

46 Article I, Section 8.

47 The *Cato* Letters; reprinted in Ford, *Essays*, p. 265.

48 Elliot, III, p. 436.

49 *Ibid.*, p. 431.

50 The expressed fear that Roman Catholicism might be established by treaty did not reflect any strong belief in religious freedom. It was nothing more than simple anti-Catholicism, as the remarks about the lack of religious qualification for office-holding clearly indicate. On the other hand, there was some concern expressed in Pennsylvania over the rights of conscientious objectors to military service. See McMaster and Stone, *Pennsylvania and the Constitution*, pp. 480–481.

51 Article III, Section 2. The Constitution made no provision for jury trial in civil cases, because different procedures in the several states had made the formulation of a general method difficult. The Anti-Federalists leaped to the conclusion that the lack of a written guarantee of this right meant certain deprivation of it, and they professed to be thoroughly alarmed. But their primary fear centered around what they regarded as the inadequate guarantees of the right of trial by jury in criminal cases.

52 If George Washington's word is to be trusted, the actions of the Founding Fathers with respect to trial by jury and a bill of rights did not stem from any sinister motives. In a letter to Lafayette on April 28, 1788, he gave this explanation: ". . . There was not a member of the convention, I believe, who had the least objection to what is contended for

by the Advocates for a *Bill of Rights* and *Tryal by Jury*. The first, where the people evidently retained everything which they did not in express terms give up, was considered nugatory. . . . And as to the second, it was only the difficulty of establishing a mode which should not interfere with the fixed modes of any of the States, that induced the Convention to leave it, as a matter of future adjustment." *Documentary History of the Constitution,* Vol. IV, pp. 601–602.

53 In New York, see Elliot, II, p. 400; Virginia, III, pp. 523 ff., North Carolina, IV, pp. 143, 150, 154–155.

54 Elliot, II, pp. 109–111.

55 This method of arguing drove the Federalists to exasperation more than once, as when one delegate in the Virginia Convention, an infrequent speaker, lost patience with Patrick Henry's "bugbears of hobgoblins" and suggested that "If the gentleman does not like this government, let him go and live among the Indians." Elliot, III, p. 580; cf. pp. 632, 644. Also note the reporter's tongue-in-cheek note on Henry's opposition to the President's power of Commander-in-Chief: "Here Mr. Henry strongly and pathetically expatiated on the probability of the President's enslaving America, and the horrid consequences that must result." *Ibid.,* p. 60. But Henry, who was so good at this technique himself, attacked it in his opponents. See *ibid.,* p. 140.

56 See above, pp. 13–15.

57 Elliot, III, p. 167; cf. p. 327.

58 Elliot, IV, pp. 32–34.

59 Thomas B. Wait to George Thatcher, January 8, 1788, in "The Thatcher Papers," selected from the papers of Hon. George Thatcher, and communicated by Captain Goodwin, U.S.A., *The Historical Magazine,* November and December, 1869 (Second Series, Vols. 15–16), No. V, p. 262.

60 Elliot, III, p. 583.

61 Elliot, IV, p. 68; cf. pp. 70, 153, 154–155, 168.

62 *Ibid.,* p. 167.

63 Elliot, II, p. 339.

64 Thus in *The Federalist* 47, Madison felt obliged to defend the Constitution against this charge. This was first pointed out to me by B. F. Wright and was the origin of the present essay. See the discussion in his article *"The Federalist* on the Nature of Political Man," *Ethics* (January, 1949), especially pp. 7 ff.

65 "Objections of the Hon. George Mason, to the proposed Federal Constitution. Addressed to the Citizens of Virginia." Ford, *Pamphlets,* p. 330.

66 "Letters of a Federal Farmer," Ford, *Pamphlets,* p. 299.

67 *Ibid.,* p. 318.

68 Elliot, III, p. 219.

69 *Ibid.,* p. 608.

70 McMaster and Stone, *Pennsylvania and the Constitution,* p. 423. See also pp. 475–477 for discussion back of this.

71 McMaster and Stone, *Pennsylvania and the Constitution,* p. 587.

72 Elliot, III, p. 54.

73 *Ibid.,* p. 164. He then went on to point out that the British House of Lords constituted a check against both the King and the Commons, and that this check was founded on "self-love," i.e., the desire of the Lords to protect their interests against attack from either of the other two branches of the government. This consideration, he said, prevailed upon him "to pronounce the British government superior, in this respect, to any government that ever was in any country. Compare this with your Congressional checks. . . . Have you a resting-place like the British government? Where is the rock of your salvation? . . . Where are your checks? You have no hereditary nobility—an order of men to whom human eyes can be cast up for relief; for, say the Constitution, there is no title of nobility to be granted. . . . In the British government there are real balances and checks: in this system there are only ideal balances." *Ibid.,* p. 164–165.

74 *Ibid.,* pp. 421, 563. Grayson also expressed his preference for a form of government —

if there was to be a national government at all — far less popular than the one proposed. He favored one strikingly similar to the plan Hamilton had suggested in Philadelphia, a president and senate elected for life, and a lower house elected for a three-year term. See Elliot, III, p. 279.

75 Elliot, II, pp. 259, 315.

76 *Agrippa* Letters in Ford, *Essays*, p. 116.

77 Elliot, IV, pp. 308–309.

78 Clinton's *Cato* Letters in Ford, *Essays*, p. 257; *Centinel* in McMaster and Stone, *Pennsylvania and the Constitution*, p. 569. "Centinel" expressed a desire for a unicameral legislature.

79 Clinton in Ford, *Essays*, pp. 261, 266; *Centinel* in McMaster and Stone, *Pennsylvania and the Constitution*, p. 617.

80 McMaster and Stone, *Pennsylvania and the Constitution*, pp. 586–587, 475–477.

81 *The Spirit of American Government* (New York, 1907), p. 9.

82 Elliot, III, p. 353.

83 *Ibid.*, p. 492.

84 *Ibid.*, pp. 493–494.

85 McMaster and Stone, *Pennsylvania and the Constitution*, p. 586.

86 Elliot, IV, pp. 117–118.

87 *Cato* Letters, Ford, *Essays*, pp. 261–262.

88 Elliot, IV, p. 214.

89 Elliot, II, p. 308 (Lansing).

90 *Ibid.*, p. 309 (Smith).

91 Elliot, III, p. 485.

92 Elliot, II, p. 310.

93 Elliot, III, p. 485.

94 Elliot, II, p. 309 (Smith).

95 Elliot, II, p. 295.

96 *Ibid.*, p. 311.

97 *Ibid.*, p. 295. It was in this debate that Lansing made the Madisonian statement quoted above, p. 20.

98 Elliot, II, p. 290.

99 *Ibid.*, p. 299.

100 Elliot, III, p. 325.

101 Elliot, II, p. 406.

102 Elliot, III, p. 471.

103 *Ibid.*, p. 566.

104 J. C. Ballagh, editor, *The Letters of Richard Henry Lee*, 2 vols. (New York, 1911–1914), pp. 421–422.

105 Elliot, III, pp. 318–319; IV, p. 190.

106 Elliot, III, p. 156.

107 *Ibid.*, IV, pp. 88, 169–170.

108 *Ibid.*, pp. 180, 184–185.

109 *Ibid.*, pp. 181–185.

110 *Ibid.*, pp. 289–290.

111 There appears to have been more opposition to the provisions of Article I, Section 10 expressed outside of the Convention than inside. See Trenholme. *Ratification in North Carolina*, p. 42, and Clarence E. Miner, *The Ratification of the Federal Constitution in New York*, Studies in History, Economics and Public Law, Vol. XCIV, No. 3, Whole No. 214, Columbia University (New York, 1921), for the extra-Convention debate in New York. It may be that this was one of the subjects the Anti-Federalists preferred not to debate for the official record. See Trenholme, pp. 166–167, for a discussion of the refusal of North Carolina Anti-Federalists to state in the Convention objections to the Constitution being made outside. There was also apparently a similar situation during the Virginia Convention, where the Federalists objected to what was happening "outdoors." See Elliot, III, p.

237. See also the remarks of Alexander C. Hanson, a member of the Maryland Convention. In discussing these provisions, of which he strongly approved, he wrote, "I have here perhaps touched a string, which secretly draws together many of the foes to the plan." In *Aristides*, "Remarks on the Proposed Plan of a Federal Government," Ford, *Pamphlets*, p. 243.

112 Elliot, II, p. 359.

113 Elliot, II, p. 225.

114 McMaster and Stone, *Pennsylvania and the Constitution*, pp. 566–567.

115 *Ibid.*, p. 655. It may be noted that this Burkeian friend of Tom Paine had not undertaken to submit the radical revolutionary Constitution of Pennsylvania to the people of that state for full, free, and deliberate debate, but had rushed its ratification through the legislature with most unseemly haste.

116 *Agrippa* Letters, Ford, *Essays*, p. 117. See also Elliot, III, p. 499, for a similar statement from William Grayson.

117 See above, footnote 111, for discussion of the possibility of more criticism expressed outside of the conventions.

118 Elliot, III, p. 492.

119 *Ibid.*, pp. 152, 221–222.

120 Elliot, IV, p. 185.

121 *Ibid.*, p. 272.

122 I do not mean to suggest that the Anti-Federalist attitude concerning homogeneity and what modern social scientists refer to as *consensus* was hopelessly wrong. A degree of both is necessary for the successful operation of democracy, and the concept itself is an extremely valuable one. I would merely contend that the Federalist estimate of the degree required was both more liberal and more realistic. On the subject of the extent to which the American people were united in tradition, institutions, and ideas in 1787–1788, see Ranney, "Bases of American Federalism."

123 Nor for that matter, has it been the pattern of representation in state legislatures.

124 See, e.g., E. E. Schattschneider, *Party Government* (New York, 1942), pp. 4 ff.

125 It is worth noting again that the abuses of power dwelt upon by the Anti-Federalists were usually extreme ones, almost amounting to a complete subversion of republican government. They did not regard as of any value the Federalists' argument that a desire to be re-elected would serve to keep the representatives in line. The Federalists had no clear idea of politics as a profession, but they were close to such a notion.

The Worthy Against the Licentious, GORDON S. WOOD

1 Otis quoted by John Eliot to Jeremy Belknap, Jan. 12, 1777, *Belknap Papers*, 104; James Bowdoin to Thomas Pownall, Nov. 20, 1783, quoted in Paul Goodman, *The Democratic-Republicans of Massachusetts: Politics in a Young Republic* (Cambridge, Mass., 1964), 8; John Adams, entry, Feb. 4, 1772, Butterfield, ed., *Diary of Adams*, II, 53; William Goddard, *The Prowess of the Whig Club . . .* (Baltimore, 1777), 7, 12.

2 Charleston *Columbian Herald*, Sept. 23, 1785; "Sober Citizen," *To the Inhabitants of the City and County of New York, Apr. 16, 1776* (N.Y., 1776); Baltimore *Md. Journal*, Mar. 30, 1787; Phila. *Pa. Gazette*, Mar. 31, 1779; Jay to Hamilton, May 8, 1778, Syrett and Cooke, eds., *Hamilton Papers*, I, 483.

3 *The Federalist*, No. 62; Samuel Johnston to James Iredell, Dec. 9, 1776, quoted in Jones, *Defense of North Carolina*, 288; Coleman, *Revolution in Georgia*, 85. For the infusion of new men in the Revolutionary legislatures see Main, "Government by the People," *Wm. and Mary Qtly.*, 3d Ser., 23 (1966), 391–407.

4 James Hogg to Iredell, May 17, 1783, McRee, *Life of Iredell*, II, 46; *Providence Gazette*, Mar. 3, 1787. The Tory, Jonathan Boucher, writing in 1797, reflected in an insightful passage on what he thought was happening in both England and America to the political and

social structure. What alarmed Boucher was the growing tendency for "those persons who are probably the least qualified, and certainly (as far as having much at stake in the welfare of a State can make it proper for any persons to take a lead in the direction of its public affairs) the least proper exclusively to become public men. . . . O that the people, seeing their error, and their misfortune in thus submitting to be dupes of those who in general are their superiors only in confidence, would at length have the resolution (the ability they already have) to assert their undoubted right — and no longer bear to be the marketable property of a new species of public men, who study the arts of debate, and pursue politics merely as a gainful occupation!" The emergence of this "new species of public men," and not the extension of the suffrage, was to Boucher the essence of democratic politics. Boucher, *View of the Causes*, lxxvi.

5 Robert Proud, "On the Violation of Established and Lawful Order, Rule or Government — Applied to the Present Times in Penna in 1776" quoted in Selsam, *Pennsylvania Constitution*, 210; Enos Hitchcock, *The Farmer's Friend, or the History of Mr. Charles Worthy, Who, from Being a Poor Orphan, Rose, through Various Scenes of Distress and Misfortune, to Wealth and Eminence, by Industry, Economy and Good Conduct* . . . (Boston, 1793), 40.

6 *Providence Gazette*, Nov. 12, 1785; Samuel Adams to John Adams, July 2, 1785, Cushing, ed., *Writings of Samuel Adams*, IV, 316; Charleston *Columbian Herald*, Oct. 7, 1785; Gardiner, *Oration, Delivered July 4, 1785*, 33.

7 John Adams, entry, Nov. 5, 1760, Butterfield, ed., *Diary of Adams*, I, 167; Ramsay, *Oration on the Advantages of American Independence*, in Niles, ed., *Principles*, 375; Adams, entry, Dec. 24, 1766, Butterfield, ed., *Diary of Adams*, I, 326. For explicit avowals of the compatibility of social distinctions and republicanism see *Observations on "Considerations upon the Cincinnati,"* 21; Elizur Goodrich, *The Principles of Civil Union and Happiness Considered and Recommended* . . . (Hartford, 1787), 20–22. See also John G. Cawelti, *Apostles of the Self-Made Man* (Chicago, 1965), 34.

8 [Austin], *Observations on the Pernicious Practice of the Law*, 44; Baltimore *Md. Journal*, Feb. 20, 1787; Carey, ed., *Debates of the General Assembly of Pennsylvania*, 21.

9 Charleston *Gazette of the St. of S.-C.*, May 13, Apr. 29, 1784.

10 See especially Forrest McDonald, *We the People: The Economic Origins of the Constitution* (Chicago, 1958).

11 On the relative youth of the Federalists see Charles Warren, "Elbridge Gerry, James Warren, Mercy Warren and the Ratification of the Federal Constitution in Massachusetts," *Mass. Hist. Soc., Proceedings*, 64 (1930–32), 146; Stanley Elkins and Eric McKitrick, "The Founding Fathers: Young Men of the Revolution," *Pol. Sci. Qtly.*, 76 (1961), 203; but cf. Main, *Antifederalists*, 259.

12 Boston *Independent Chronicle*, Dec. 6, 1787; R. H. Lee to Francis Lightfoot Lee, July 14, 1787, Ballagh, ed., *Letters of R. H. Lee*, II, 424; [James Winthrop], "Letters of Agrippa, XVIII," Feb. 5, 1788, Ford, ed., *Essays on the Constitution*, 117; Farrand, ed., *Records of the Federal Convention*, I, 48, II, 647.

13 Minot, quoted in Rutland, Ordeal of the Constitution, 13; Lee to Mason, May 15, 1787, Ballagh, ed., *Letters of R. H. Lee*, II, 419.

14 [Richard Henry Lee], *Observations Leading to a Fair Examination of the System of Government, Proposed by the Late Convention . . . in a Number of Letters from the Federal Farmer* . . . ([N. Y.], 1787), in Ford, ed., *Pamphlets*, 285; Main, *Antifederalists*, 172–73, 177.

15 On the political effectiveness of the Federalists in contrast to the ineptness of the Antifederalists see John P. Roche, "The Founding Fathers: A Reform Caucus in Action," *Amer. Pol. Sci. Rev.*, 55 (1961), 799–816; Main, *Antifederalists*, 252–53; and above all, Rutland, *Ordeal of the Constitution*, 66, 76–77, 113, 165, 210, 236, 243–44, 309, 313.

16 [Ellsworth], "The Landholder, VIII," Dec. 24, 1787, Ford, ed., *Essays on the Constitution*, 176; Aedanus Burke to John Lamb, June 23, 1788, quoted in Rutland, *Ordeal of the Constitution*, 165; Madison to Jefferson, Feb. 19, 1788, Hunt, ed., *Writings of Madison*, V,

101–02; Tobias Lear to Washington, June 2, 1788, in *Documentary History of the Constitution* (Washington, 1894–1905), IV, 676.

17 Rogers, *William Loughton Smith*, 150; Rutland, *Ordeal of the Constitution*, 211, 55, 98, 118–19, 212, 253, 85, 211, 165. Rutland's book is particularly important in demonstrating the political and social inferiority of the Antifederalists.

18 Harding, *Ratification in Massachusetts*, 64; Rufus King to James Madison, Jan. 20, 27, 1788, King, *Life of King*, I, 314, 316–17. See also John Brown Cutting to Jefferson, July 11, 1788, Boyd, ed., *Jefferson Papers*, XIII, 331; Welch, *Sedgwick*, 64–65.

19 Amos Singletary (Mass.), in Elliot, ed., *Debates*, II, 102; Staughton Lynd, ed., "Abraham Yates's History of the Movement for the United States Constitution," *Wm. and Mary Qtly.*, 3d Ser., 20 (1963), 232, 231.

20 Samuel Osgood to Stephen Higginson, Feb. 2, 1784, Burnett, ed., *Letters of Congress*, VII, 435; Phila. *Independent Gazetteer*, Feb. 7, 1788, in Kenyon, ed., *Antifederalists*, 71; Farmington Records, May 6, 1783, quoted in Main, *Antifederalists*, 108–09, see also 76–77.

21 Smith (N.Y.), in Elliot, ed., *Debates*, II, 246; *The Government of Nature Delineated; Or an Exact Picture of the New Constitution* (Carlisle, Pa., 1788), 7; [George Clinton], "Cato, VI," Dec. 16, 1787, Ford, ed., *Essays on the Constitution*, 273; Philip Schuyler to John Jay, July 14, 1777, Johnston, ed., *Papers of Jay*, I, 147. De Pauw, *Eleventh Pillar*, 283–92, questions Clinton's authorship of the "Cato" letters and suggests that Abraham Yates may have written them.

22 [Bryan], "Centinel, No. I," Oct. 5, 1787, McMaster and Stone, eds., *Pennsylvania and the Federal Constitution*, 566–67; Smith (N. Y.), in Elliot, ed., *Debates*, II, 246–47; *Rudiments of Law and Government*, 26; Main, *Antifederalists*, 203.

23 *Government of Nature Delineated*, 8; Smith (N. Y.), in Elliot, ed., *Debates*, II, 246; Bernard Steiner, "Connecticut's Ratification of the Federal Constitution," Amer. Antiq. Soc., *Proceedings*, 25 (1915), 77; "Address and Reasons of Dissent of the Minority of the Convention of the State of Pennsylvania," Dec. 18, 1787, McMaster and Stone, eds., *Pennsylvania and the Federal Constitution*, 472; Smith (N. Y.) and Patrick Henry (Va.), in Elliot, ed., *Debates*, II, 260, 247, III, 54; "John De Witt," Nov. 5, 1787, Kenyon, ed., *Antifederalists*, 105; Carey, ed., *Debates of the General Assembly of Pennsylvania*, 66; Robert Lansing and Smith (N. Y.), in Elliot, ed., *Debates*, II, 293, 13, 247, 260.

24 William Heath (Mass.), Lansing (N. Y.), Smith (N. Y.), and Henry (Va.), in Elliot, ed., *Debates*, II, 13, 293, 247, 260.

25 Samuel Chase quoted in Philip A. Crowl, "Anti-Federalism in Maryland, 1787–1788," *Wm. and Mary Qtly.*, 3d Ser., 4 (1947), 464; Walsh, *Charleston's Sons of Liberty*, 131–32; "Dissent of the Minority," McMaster and Stone, eds., *Pennsylvania and the Federal Constitution*, 472.

26 Edmund Pendleton (Va.), in Elliot, ed., *Debates*, III, 205, 206; Wilson, in McMaster and Stone, eds., *Pennsylvania and the Federal Constitution*, 335; Hamilton (N. Y.), in Elliot, ed., *Debates*, II, 256.

27 Livingston (N. Y.), in Elliot, ed., *Debates*, II, 276–78; Robert Livingston, "An Oration Delivered July 4, 1787. . . ," *American Museum*, 3 (1788), 109–10.

28 Sedgwick to King, June 18, 1787, King, *Life of King*, I, 224; Madison to Jefferson, Oct. 17, 1788, Boyd, ed., *Jefferson Papers*, XIV, 18; Washington to Hamilton, July 10, 1787, Syrett and Cooke, eds., *Hamilton Papers*, IV, 225.

29 Washington to Bushrod Washington, Nov. 10, 1787, *Documentary History of the Constitution*, IV, 373–74; Madison to Tench Coxe, July 20, 1788, quoted in Rutland, *Ordeal of the Constitution*, 172; Madison to Jefferson, Oct. 17, 1788, Boyd, ed., *Jefferson Papers*, XIV, 18.

30 *Providence Gazette*, Feb. 26, 1785; Boston *Independent Chronicle*, Aug. 31, 1786; Francis Hopkinson to Jefferson, Apr. 6, 1788, Boyd, ed., *Jefferson Papers*, XIII, 38–39; Hartford *Conn. Courant*, Nov. 20, 1786; [Ellsworth], "A Landholder, II," Nov. 12, 1787, Ford, ed., *Essays on the Constitution*, 144; [Alexander C. Hanson], *Remarks on the Proposed Plan of a Federal Government . . .* (Annapolis, [1788]), in Ford, ed., *Pamphlets*, 232.

31 Jay to Washington, June 27, 1786, Johnston, ed., *Papers of Jay*, III, 204–05; Thomas Dawes, Jr., *Oration, Delivered July 4, 1787*, 10; Otto to Vergennes, Oct. 10, 1786, in Bancroft, *Formation of the Constitution*, II, 399–400; Goodrich, *Principles of Civil Union*, 20–22; Carey, ed., *Debates of the General Assembly of Pennsylvania*, 38.

32 *The Federalist*, No. 35; Phila. *Pa. Gazette*, Mar. 24, 1779.

33 Welch, *Sedgwick*, 56; St. John de Crèvecoeur to Jefferson, Oct. 20, 1788, Boyd, ed., *Jefferson Papers*, XIV, 30; Edward Rutledge to Jay, Nov. 12, 1786, Johnston, ed., *Papers to Jay*, III, 216–19; Edward Carrington to Jefferson, June 9, 1787, Boyd, ed., *Jefferson Papers*, XI, 408–09.

34 Parsons, *Sermon Preached May 28, 1788*, 22–23; Taylor, *Western Massachusetts*, 164; John Brown Cutting to Jefferson, July 11, 1788, Boyd, ed., *Jefferson Papers*, XIII, 332; Rush to Richard Price, Apr. 22, 1786, Butterfield, ed., *Rush Letters*, I, 386; Carrington to Jefferson, June 9, 1787, Boyd, ed., *Jefferson Papers*, XI, 408–09; William Nelson to William Short, July 12, 1788, quoted in Rutland, *Ordeal of the Constitution*, 253.

35 Rutland, *Ordeal of the Constitution*, 39.

36 [Winthrop], "Agrippa, XVII," Jan. 20, 1788, Ford, ed., *Essays on the Constitution*, 113; Madison to Jefferson, Oct. 24, 1787, Boyd, ed., *Jefferson Papers*, XII, 276. See also [Ellsworth], "A Landholder, III," Nov. 19, 1787, Ford, ed., *Essays on the Constitution*, 147.

37 [Dickinson], *Letters of Fabius*, Ford, ed., *Pamphlets*, 188; Hartford *Conn. Courant*, Nov. 27, 1786; Charleston *Gazette of the St. of S.-C.*, Jan. 3, 1785; Josiah Whitney, *A Sermon, Preached in the Audience of His Excellency Samuel Huntington . . .* (Hartford, 1788), 23.

38 Corbin and Henry (Va.), in Elliot, ed., *Debates*, III, 107, 167; [Pelatiah Webster], *The Weakness of Brutus Exposed . . .* (Phila., 1787), in Ford, ed., *Pamphlets*, 131. See also John Francis Mercer's insight into the social basis of government in Farrand, ed., *Records of the Federal Convention*, II, 289.

39 *The Federalist*, No. 71; "To the Freemen of the United States," *American Museum*, 1 (1787), 429; Hartford *Conn. Courant*, Nov. 20, 1786.

40 Benjamin W. Labaree, *Patriots and Partisans: The Merchants of Newburyport, 1764–1815* (Cambridge, Mass., 1962), 87, 96–97.

41 [Jackson], *Thoughts upon the Political Situation*, 54, 55, 56, 57, 58, 59, 61–62, 69, 76–79, 98, 117–18, 57.

42 Review of "Thoughts upon the Political Situation of the United States of America . . .," *American Magazine*, 1, (1787–88), 804.

43 Madison to Jefferson, Oct. 24, 1787, Boyd, ed., *Jefferson Papers*, XII, 275; *The Federalist*, No. 10; Stiles, *United States Elevated*, in Thornton, ed., *Pulpit*, 420; Madison's Observations on Jefferson's Draft of a Constitution for Virginia (1788), Boyd, ed., *Jefferson Papers*, VI, 308–09.

44 [Beers], *Address to Connecticut*, 18–23, 29.

45 *Providence Gazette*, Aug. 12, 1786; Madison, "Vices of the Political System," Hunt, ed., *Writings of Madison*, II, 369; Wilson, in Farrand, ed., *Records of the Federal Convention*, I, 154; Corbin (Va.), in Elliot, ed., *Debates*, III, 107–08; *The Federalist*, No. 3. For De Lolme's expression of the difference between "a *representative*" and "a *popular*" constitution see Jean Louis De Lolme, *The Constitution of England . . .* (London, 1788), 271.

46 [Mercy Warren], *Observations on the New Constitution . . .* ([Boston, 1788]), in Ford, ed., *Pamphlets*, 6; *Providence Gazette*, Jan. 5, 1788; [Bryan], "Centinel, No. IX," Jan. 8, 1788, "Centinel, No. I," Oct. 5, 1787, McMaster and Stone, eds., *Pennsylvania and the Federal Constitution*, 627, 575; William Goudy (N. C.), in Elliot, ed., *Debates*, IV, 56; "John De Witt," Nov. 5, 1787, Kenyon, ed., *Antifederalists*, 104.

47 [Lee], *Letters from the Federal Farmer*, Ford, ed., *Pamphlets*, 285, 295; George Mason, *Objections . . . to the Proposed Federal Constitution* (n.p., n.d.), *ibid.*, 332; Lee to John Adams, Oct. 8, 1779, Ballagh, ed., *Letters of R. H. Lee*, II, 155; Mason, in Farrand, ed., *Records of the Federal Convention*, I, 359, 49, 56; John Quincy Adams, *Life in a New England Town: 1787–1788 . . .* (Boston, 1903), 46.

48 [Clinton], "Cato, VI," Dec. 16, 1787, Ford, ed., *Essays on the Constitution*, 273; Smith

(N. Y.), in Elliot, ed., *Debates*, II, 246, 245; "Philadelphiensis," Feb. 7, 1788, Kenyon, ed., *Antifederalists*, 72; [Lee], *Letters from the Federal Farmer*, Ford, ed., *Pamphlets*, 295; "John De Witt," Nov. 5, 1787, Kenyon, ed., *Antifederalists*, 108.

49 "Dissent of the Minority," McMaster and Stone, eds., *Pennsylvania and the Federal Constitution*, 471; Smith (N. Y.), in Elliot, ed., *Debates*, II, 246: Boston *Independent Chronicle*, Dec. 13, 1787; Samuel Chase, quoted in Crowl, "Anti-Federalism in Maryland," *Wm. and Mary Qtly.*, 3d Ser., 4 (1947), 464.

50 Smith (N. Y.), in Elliot, ed., *Debates*, II, 247; [Lee], *Letters from the Federal Farmer*, Ford, ed., *Pamphlets*, 317.

51 The "Caesar" letters are reprinted in Ford, ed., *Essays on the Constitution*, 283–91. It now appears that Hamilton did not write them. See Jacob E. Cooke, "Alexander Hamilton's Authorship of the 'Caesar' Letters," *Wm. and Mary Qtly.*, 3d Ser., 17 (1960), 78–85.

52 Hartford *Conn. Courant*, Feb. 5, 1787; *The Federalist*, No. 39; Jay to Washington, Jan. 7, 1787, Johnston, ed., *Papers of Jay*, III, 229. See Martin Diamond, "Democracy and *The Federalist*: A Reconsideration of the Framers' Intent," *Amer. Pol. Sci. Rev.*, 53 (1959), 52–68.

The Founding Fathers: A Reform Caucus in Action, JOHN P. ROCHE

1 The view that the right to vote in the states was severely circumscribed by property qualifications has been thoroughly discredited in recent years. See Chilton Williamson, *American Suffrage from Property to Democracy, 1760–1860* (Princeton, 1960). The contemporary position is that John Dickinson actually knew what he was talking about when he argued that there would be little opposition to vesting the right of suffrage in freeholders since "The great mass of our Citizens is composed at this time of freeholders, and will be pleased with it." Max Farrand, *Records of the Federal Convention*, Vol. 2, p. 202 (New Haven, 1911). (Henceforth cited as *Farrand*.)

2 The classic statement of the *coup d'etat* theory is, of course, Charles A. Beard, *An Economic Interpretation of the Constitution of the United States* (New York, 1913), and this theme was echoed by Vernon L. Parrington, Merrill Jensen and others in "populist" historiographical tradition. For a sharp critique of this thesis see Robert E. Brown, *Charles Beard and the Constitution* (Princeton, 1956). See also Forrest McDonald, *We the People* (Chicago, 1958); the trailblazing work in this genre was Douglas Adair, "The Tenth Federalist Revisited," *William and Mary Quarterly*, Third Series, Vol. VIII (1951), pp. 48–67.

3 A basic volume, which, like other works by Warren, provides evidence with which one can evaluate the author's own opinions, is Charles Warren, *The Making of the Constitution* (Boston, 1928). The best brief summary of the forces behind the movement for centralization is Chapter 1 of *Warren* (as it will be cited hereafter).

4 On Pennsylvania see Robert L. Brunhouse, *Counter-Revolution in Pennsylvania* (Harrisburg, 1942) and Charles P. Smith, *James Wilson* (Chapel Hill, 1956), ch. 15; for New York, which needs the same sort of microanalysis Pennsylvania has received, the best study is E. Wilder Spaulding, *New York in the Critical Period, 1783–1789* (New York, 1932).

5 Stanley Elkins and Eric McKitrick, "The Founding Fathers: Young Men of the Revolution," *Political Science Quarterly*, Vol. 76, p. 181 (1961).

6 *Warren*, p. 55.

7 In *La Republique des Camarades* (Paris, 1914).

8 See Frank Monaghan, *John Jay* (New York, 1935), ch. 13.

9 "[T]he situation of the general government, if it can be called a government, is shaken to its foundation, and liable to be overturned by every blast. In a word, it is at an end; and, unless a remedy is soon applied, anarchy and confusion will inevitably ensue." Washington to Jefferson, May 30, 1787, *Farrand*, III, 31. See also Irving Brant, *James Madison, The Nationalist* (New York, 1948), ch. 25.

10 Merrill Jensen, *The New Nation* (New York, 1950). Interestingly enough, Prof. Jensen

virtually ignores international relations in his laudatory treatment of the government under the Articles of Confederation.

11 The story of James Madison's cultivation of Washington is told by Brant, *op. cit.*, pp. 394–97.

12 The "message center" being the Congress; nineteen members of Congress were simultaneously delegates to the Convention. One gets a sense of this coordination of effort from Broadus Mitchell, *Alexander Hamilton, Youth to Maturity* (New York, 1957), ch. 22.

13 See Sir Lewis Namier, *The Structure of Politics at the Accession of George III*, 2d ed. (New York, 1957); *England in the Age of the American Revolution* (London, 1930).

14 The Annapolis Convention, called for the previous year, turned into a shambles: only five states sent commissioners, only three states were legally represented, and the instructions to delegates named varied quite widely from state to state. Clinton and others of his persuasion may have thought this disaster would put an end to the drive for reform. See Mitchell, *op. cit.*, pp. 362–67; Brant, *op. cit.*, pp. 375–87.

15 See Hamilton M. Bishop, *Why Rhode Island Opposed the Federal Constitution* (Providence, 1950) for a careful analysis of the labyrinthine political course of Rhode Island. For background see David S. Lovejoy, *Rhode Island Politics and the American Revolution* (Providence, 1958).

16 The terms "radical" and "conservative" have been bandied about a good deal in connection with the Constitution. This usage is nonsense if it is employed to distinguish between two economic "classes" — *e.g.*, radical debtors versus conservative creditors, radical farmers versus conservative capitalists, etc. — because there was no polarization along this line of division; the same types of people turned up on both sides. And many were hard to place in these terms: does one treat Robert Morris as a debtor or a creditor? or James Wilson? See Brown, *op. cit.*, *passim*. The one line of division that holds up is between those deeply attached to states' rights and those who felt that the Confederation was bankrupt. Thus, curiously, some of the most narrow-minded, parochial spokesmen of the time have earned the designation "radical" while those most willing to experiment and alter the *status quo* have been dubbed "conservative"! See Cecelia Kenyon, "Men of Little Faith," *William and Mary Quarterly*, Vol. 12, p. 3 (1955).

17 Yet, there was little objection to this crucial modification from any quarter — there almost seems to have been a gentlemen's agreement that Rhode Island's *liberum veto* had to be destroyed.

18 See Mason's letter to his son, May 27, 1787, in which he endorsed secrecy as "a proper precaution to prevent mistakes and misrepresentation until the business shall have been completed, when the whole may have a very different complexion from that in which the several crude and indigested parts might in their first shape appear if submitted to the public eye." *Farrand*, III, 28.

19 See Madison to Jefferson, June 6, 1787, *Farrand*, III, 35.

20 Cited in *Warren*, p. 138.

21 See, *e.g.*, Gottfried Dietze, *The Federalist, A Classic on Federalism and Free Government* (Baltimore, 1900); Richard Hofstadter, *The American Political Tradition* (New York, 1948); and John P. Roche, "American Liberty," in M. Konvitz and C. Rossiter, eds., *Aspects of Liberty* (Ithaca, 1958).

22 "I hold it for a fundamental point, that an individual independence of the states is utterly irreconcilable with the idea of an aggregate sovereignty," Madison to Randolph, cited in Brant, *op. cit.*, p. 416.

23 The Randolph Plan was presented on May 29, see *Farrand*, I, 18–23; the state legislatures retained only the power to *nominate* candidates for the upper chamber. Madison's view of the appropriate position of the states emerged even more strikingly in Yates' record of his speech on June 29: "Some contend that states are sovereign when in fact they are only political societies. There is a gradation of power in all societies, from the lowest corporation to the highest sovereign. The states never possessed the essential rights of sovereignty. . . . The states, at present, are only great corporations, having the power of making by-laws, and these are effectual only if they are not contradictory to the general

confederation. The states ought to be placed under the control of the general government — at least as much so as they formerly were under the king and British parliament." *Farrand*, I, 471. Forty-six years later, after Yates' "Notes" had been published, Madison tried to explain this statement away as a misinterpretation: he did not flatly deny the authenticity of Yates' record, but attempted a defense that was half justification and half evasion. Madison to W. C. Rives, Oct. 21, 1833. *Farrand*, III, 521–24.

24 Resolution 6 gave the National Legislature this power subject to review by the Council of Revision proposed in Resolution 8.

25 Resolution 6.

26 *Ibid.*

27 See the discussions on May 30 and 31. "Mr. Charles Pinkney wished to know of Mr. Randolph whether he meant to abolish the State Governts. altogether . . . Mr. Butler said he had not made up his mind on the subject and was open to the light which discussion might throw on it . . . Genl. Pinkney expressed a doubt . . . Mr. Gerry seemed to entertain the same doubt." *Farrand*, I, 33–34. There were no denunciations — though it should perhaps be added that Luther Martin had not yet arrived.

28 *Farrand*, I, 54. (Italics added.)

29 *Ibid.*, p. 242. Delaware's delegates had been instructed by their general assembly to maintain in any new system the voting equality of the states. *Farrand*, III, 574.

30 *Ibid.*, p. 240.

31 *Ibid.*, p. 250.

32 *Ibid.*, p. 258.

33 *Ibid.*, p. 178.

34 *Ibid.*, p. 274.

35 *Ibid.*, pp. 275–76.

36 "But it is said that this national government is to act on individuals and not on states; and cannot a federal government be so framed as to operate in the same way? It surely may." *Ibid.*, pp. 182–83; also *ibid.* at p. 276.

37 *Farrand*, III, 613.

38 *Farrand*, I, 177.

39 *Ibid.*, p. 182.

40 *Ibid.*, p. 255.

41 J. C. Hamilton, cited *ibid.*, p. 293.

42 See, *e.g.*, Mitchell, *op. cit.*, p. 381.

43 Hamilton to Washington, July 3, 1787, *Farrand*, III, 53.

44 A reconstruction of the Hamilton Plan is found in *Farrand*, III. 617–30.

45 Said William Samuel Johnson on June 21: "A gentleman from New-York, with boldness and decision, proposed a system totally different from both [Virginia and New Jersey]; and though he has been praised by every body, he has been supported by none." *Farrand*, I, 363.

46 See his letter to Washington cited *supra* note 43.

47 *Farrand*, III, 338.

48 *Farrand*, I, 321.

49 Maryland's politics in this period were only a bit less intricate than Rhode Island's: the rural gentry, in much the same fashion that Namier described in England, divided up among families — Chases, Carrolls, Pacas, Lloyds, Tilghmans, etc. — and engaged in what seemed, to the outsider, elaborate political Morris dances. See Philip A. Crowl, *Maryland During and After the Revolution* (Baltimore, 1948). The Maryland General Assembly named five delegates to the Convention and provided that "the said Deputies or such of them as shall attend . . . shall have full Power to represent this State." *Farrand*, III, 586. The interesting circumstance was that three of the delegates were Constitutionalists (Carroll, McHenry and Jenifer), while two were opposed (Martin and Mercer); and this led to an *ad hoc* determination of where Maryland would stand when votes were taken. The vote on equality of representation, to be described *infra*, was an important instance of this eccentricity.

50 This formulation was voted into the Randolph Plan on May 30, 1787, by a vote of six states to none, with one divided. *Farrand,* I, 30.

51 *Farrand,* I, 335–36. In agreeing, Randolph stipulated his disagreement with Ellsworth's rationale, but said he did not object to merely changing an "expression." Those who subject the Constitution to minute semantic analysis might do well to keep this instance in mind; if Randolph could so concede the deletion of "national," one may wonder if any word changes can be given much weight.

52 According to Luther Martin, he was alone on the floor and cast Maryland's vote for equality of representation. Shortly thereafter, Jenifer came on the floor and "Mr. King, from Massachusetts, valuing himself on Mr. Jenifer to divide the State of Maryland on this question . . . requested of the President that the question might be put again; however, the motion was too extraordinary in its nature to meet with success." Cited from "The Genuine Information, . . ." *Farrand,* III, 188.

53 Namely Baldwin's vote *for* equality of representation which divided Georgia — with Few absent and Pierce in New York fighting a duel, Houston voted against equality and Baldwin shifted to tie the state. Baldwin was originally from Connecticut and attended and tutored at Yale, facts which have led to much speculation about the pressures the Connecticut delegation may have brought on him to save the day (Georgia was the last state to vote) and open the way to compromise. To employ a good Russian phrase, it was certainly not an accident that Baldwin voted the way he did. See *Warren,* p. 262.

54 For various contemporary comments, see *Warren,* pp. 814–818. On Adams' technique, see Zoltan Haraszti, "The Composition of Adams' *Defense,*" in *John Adams and the Prophets of Progress* (Cambridge, 1952), ch. 9. In this connection it is interesting to check the Convention discussions for references to the authority of Locke, Montesquieu and Harrington, the theorists who have been assigned various degrees of paternal responsibility. There are no explicit references to James Harrington; one to John Locke (Luther Martin cited him on the state of nature, *Farrand,* I, 437); and seven to Montesquieu, only one of which related to the "separation of powers" (Madison in an odd speech, which he explained in a footnote was given to help a friend rather than advance his own views, cited Montesquieu on the separation of the executive and legislative branches, *Farrand,* II, 34). This, of course, does not prove that Locke and Co. were without influence; it shifts the burden of proof, however, to those who assert ideological causality. See Benjamin F. Wright, "The Origins of the Separation of Powers in America," *Economica,* Vol. 13 (1933), p. 184.

55 I share Willmoore Kendall's interpretation of Locke as a supporter of parliamentary supremacy and majoritarianism; see Kendall, *John Locke and the Doctrine of Majority Rule* (Urbana, 1941). Kendall's general position has recently received strong support in the definitive edition and commentary of Peter Laslett, *Locke's Two Treatises of Government* (Cambridge, 1960).

56 The American Locke is best delineated in Carl Becker, *The Declaration of Independence* (New York, 1948).

57 See John P. Roche, "The Electoral College: A Note on American Political Mythology," *Dissent* (Spring, 1961), pp. 197–99. The relevant debates took place July 19–26, 1787, *Farrand,* II, 50–128, and September 5–6, 1787, *ibid.,* pp. 505–31.

58 See the discussion on August 22, 1787, *Farrand,* II, 366–375; King seems to have expressed the sense of the Convention when he said, "the subject should be considered in a political light only." *Ibid.* at 373.

59 *Farrand,* II, 374. Randolph echoed his sentiment in different words.

60 Mason to Jefferson, cited in *Warren,* p. 584.

61 August 29, 1787, *Farrand,* II, 449–50.

62 *Ibid.,* p. 451. The plainest statement of the matter was put by the three North Carolina delegates (Blount, Spaight and Williamson) in their report to Governor Caswell, September 18, 1787. After noting that "no exertions have been wanting on our part to guard and promote the particular interest of North Carolina," they went on to explain the basis of the negotiations in cold-blooded fashion: "While we were taking so much care to guard

ourselves against being over reached and to form rules of Taxation that might operate in our favour, it is not to be supposed that our Northern Brethren were Inattentive to their particular Interest. A navigation Act or the power to regulate Commerce in the Hands of the National Government . . . is what the Southern States have given in Exchange for the advantages we Mentioned." They concluded by explaining that while the Constitution did deal with other matters besides taxes — "there are other Considerations of great Magnitude involved in the system" — they would not take up valuable time with boring details! *Farrand*, III, 83–84.

63 See John C. Calhoun, *A Disquisition on Government* (New York, 1943), pp. 21–25, 38. Calhoun differed from Mason, and others in the Convention who urged the two-thirds requirement, by advocating a functional or interest veto rather than some sort of special majority, *i.e.*, he abandoned the search for quantitative checks in favor of a qualitative solution.

64 The Committee on Detail altered the general grant of legislative power envisioned by the Virginia Plan into a series of specific grants; these were examined closely between August 16 and August 23. One day only was devoted to the Judicial Article, August 27, and since no one raised the question of judicial review of *Federal* statutes, no light was cast on the matter. A number of random comments on the power of the judiciary were scattered throughout the discussions, but there was another variable which deprives them of much probative value: the proposed Council of Revision which would have joined the Executive with the judges in *legislative* review. Madison and Wilson, for example, favored this technique — which had nothing in common with what we think of as judicial review except that judges were involved in the task.

65 For what it may be worth, I think that judicial review of congressional acts was logically on all fours with review of state enactments and that it was certainly consistent with the view that the Constitution could not be amended by the Congress and President, or by a two-thirds vote of Congress (overriding a veto), without the agreement of three-quarters of the states. *External* evidence from that time supports this view, see Charles Warren, *Congress, the Constitution, and the Supreme Court* (Boston, 1925), pp. 41–128, but the debates *in* the Convention prove nothing.

66 Or so Madison stated, *Farrand*, II, 643. Wilson too may have contributed; he was close to Franklin and delivered the frail old gentleman's speeches for him.

67 See a very interesting letter, from an unknown source in Philadelphia, to Jefferson, October 11, 1787: "Randolph wishes it well, & it is thought would have signed it, but he wanted to be on a footing with a popular rival." *Farrand*, III, 104. Madison, writing Jefferson a full account on October 24, 1787, put the matter more delicately — he was working hard on Randolph to win him for ratification: "[Randolph] was not inveterate in his opposition, and grounded his refusal to subscribe pretty much on his unwillingness to commit himself, so as not to be at liberty to be governed by further lights on the subject." *Ibid.*, p. 135.

68 See Edward P. Smith, "The Movement Towards a Second Constitutional Convention in 1788," in J. F. Jameson, ed., *Essays in the Constitutional History of the United States* (Boston, 1889), pp. 46–115.

69 See Bishop, *op. cit., passim.*

70 See *Elliot's Debates on the Federal Constitution* (Washington, 1836), Vol. 3, pp. 436–438.

71 This should be quoted to give the full flavor: "Without vanity, I may say I have had different experiences of [militia] service from that of [Henry]. It was my fortune to be a soldier of my country. . . . I saw what the honorable gentleman did not see — our men fighting. . . ." *Ibid.*, p. 178.

72 *Ibid.*, p. 329.

73 Washington offered him the Chief Justiceship in 1796, but he declined; Charles Warren, *The Supreme Court in United States History* (Boston, 1947), Vol. 1, p. 139.

74 He was a zealous prosecutor of seditions in the period 1798–1800; with Justice Samuel Chase, like himself an alleged "radical" at the time of the Constitutional Convention,

Martin hunted down Jeffersonian heretics. See James M. Smith, *Freedom's Fetters* (Ithaca, 1956), pp. 342–43.

75 Crosskey in his sprawling *Politics and the Constitution* (Chicago, 1953), 2 vols., has developed with almost unbelievable zeal and intricacy the thesis that the Constitution *was* designed to establish a centralized unitary state, but that the political leadership of the Republic in its formative years betrayed this ideal and sold the pass to states'-rights. While he has unearthed some interesting newspaper articles and other material, it is impossible for me to accept his central proposition. Madison and the other delegates, with the exceptions discussed in the text *supra*, did *want* to diminish the power of the states and create a vigorous national government. But they were not fools, and were, I submit, under no illusions when they departed from Philadelphia that this end had been accomplished. The crux of my argument is that *political realities* forced them to water down their objectives and they settled, like the good politicians they were, for half a loaf. The basic difficulty with Crosskey's thesis is that he knows too much — he assumes that the Framers had a perfectly clear idea of the road they were taking; with a semantic machete he cuts blandly through all the confusion on the floor of the meeting to the *real* meanings. Thus, despite all his ornate research apparatus, there is a fundamentally non-empirical quality about Crosskey's work: at crucial points in the argument he falls back on a type of divination which can only be described as Kabbalistic. He may be right, for example, in stating (without any proof) that Richard Henry Lee did *not* write the "Letters from a Federal Farmer," but in this country spectral evidence has not been admissible since the Seventeenth Century.

Democracy and *The Federalist*, MARTIN DIAMOND

1 The authorship of the 85 papers has long been disputed. According to the convincing attribution of Douglass Adair, Hamilton wrote 51 papers (1, 6–9, 11–13, 15–17, 21–36, 59–61, 65–85), Madison 29 (10, 14, 18–20, 37–58, 62–63), and Jay 5 (2–5, 64).

2 See the fine essay by Douglass Adair, "A Note on Certain of Hamilton's Pseudonyms," *William and Mary Quarterly*, third series, XII (April 1955).

3 *The Federalist*, ed. Henry Cabot Lodge, introduction by Edward Mead Earle (New York: Modern Library, 1941) 1, p. 6. Italics original.

4 *Federalist* 15, p. 89.

5 The organization of the essays is perfectly revealed in *Federalist* 39 which defends the Constitution on two grounds, that it is sufficiently republican and sufficiently federal. That is, in this essays, which links the two main divisions of the book and is in a sense the central essay, the issue is stripped to its essentials: union and republicanism.

6 *Federalist* 10, pp. 53–54.

7 *Federalist* 14, p. 84.

8 *Ibid.*, p. 85.

9 *Federalist* 49, p. 327.

10 *Federalist* 10, p. 57. *Federalist* 39, p. 244. See also *Federalist* 52, pp. 341–342: "The definition of the right of suffrage is very justly regarded as a fundamental article of republican government." It is "to be the same with those of the electors of the most numerous branch of the State legislatures." "It cannot be feared that the people of the States will alter this part of their constitutions in such a manner as to abridge the rights secured to them by the federal Constitution." The national suffrage is made as democratic as the very democratic suffrage in the states, and there is no likelihood that the suffrage will become less popular.

11 *Federalist* 39, p. 243.

12 *Federalist* 10, p. 58. Italics supplied.

13 Alexander Hamilton, *Writings*, ed. Henry Cabot Lodge (12 vols.; New York: Putnam, 1904), II, 92. Italics original.

14 *Federalist* 10, p. 58.

15 *Ibid.*, p. 59.

16 *Federalist* 14, p. 80.

17 *Ibid.*, p. 81. Italics supplied.

18 *Federalist* 10, p. 54.

19 *Federalist* 63, p. 412.

20 *Ibid.*, p. 413.

21 *Federalist* 9, pp. 48–49.

22 *Federalist* 28, p. 173. Italics supplied.

23 *Federalist* 57, p. 371.

24 *Federalist* 28, p. 173.

25 *Federalist* 55, p. 364.

26 *Federalist* 51, p. 339.

27 *Federalist* 10, p. 57.

28 *Federalist* 51, p. 339.

29 *Federalist* 34, pp. 203–4.

30 *Federalist* 51, p. 339.

31 *Ibid.*, p. 338.

32 *Federalist* 48, p. 322.

33 *Federalist* 51, p. 337.

34 *Federalist* 71, pp, 465–66.

35 *Federalist* 51, p. 337.

36 *Federalist* 10, p. 59.

37 *Federalist* 57, p. 370.

38 *Federalist* 11, p. 62.

39 *Federalist* 47, p. 313.

40 See also *Federalist* 10, p. 59, where Publius notes that the "effect" of representation "may be inverted."

41 *Federalist* 10, p. 58.

42 *Ibid.*, pp. 60–61.

43 *Federalist* 51, pp. 339–40.

44 *Ibid.*, p. 341.

45 *Ibid.*, *p.* 337.

SUGGESTIONS FOR FURTHER READING

Good historiographic surveys can be found in Richard B. Morris, "The Confederation Period and the American Historian," *William and Mary Quarterly*, 3d Ser., 13 (1956), 139–156, which has been essentially incorporated into Richard B. Morris, *The American Revolution Reconsidered** (New York, 1967); and in the introduction to Jack P. Greene, ed., *The Reinterpretation of the American Revolution 1763–1790** (New York, 1968), which includes many of the important articles bearing on the period. The new lines of research and interpretation can be followed in the articles and reviews of the chief periodical in the field of early American history, the *William and Mary Quarterly*, 3d Series, published by the Institute of Early American History and Culture, Williamsburg, Virginia (hereafter cited as *WMQ*).

Modern scholarly interest in the origins and nature of the Constitution dates back to the latter part of the nineteenth century when historians began to approach American political institutions not as strokes of genius or as inheritances from Europe but as products of American experience. For a bibliography of earlier studies of the Constitution see A. P. C. Griffin, *Select List of Books on the Constitution of the United States* (Washington, D.C., 1903). George Bancroft's *History of the Formation of the Constitution of the United States of America,* 2 vols. (New York, 1882), was the first investigation of the Constitution to be based on an extensive use of the records, some of which Bancroft reprinted in his volumes. Although Bancroft assumed the dominant nineteenth-century view that the Constitution was the providential expression of American democracy, his study still bears careful reading. J. H. Robinson's "The Original and Derived Features of the Constitution," American Academy of Political and Social Science, *Annals,* 1 (1890), 203–243, was an important article in the shift to a new appreciation of American experience in explaining the Constitution, a shift that was made explicit in Sidney G. Fisher, *The Evolution of the Constitution of the United States, Showing That It Is a Development of Progressive History and Not an Isolated Document Struck Off at a Given Time or an Imitation of English or Dutch Forms of Government* (Philadelphia, 1897). This experiential approach culminated in the superb work of Max Farrand, *The Framing of the Constitution of the United States** (New Haven, 1913), and was elaborated and refined by Andrew C. McLaughlin, *The Confederation and the Constitution** (New York, 1905) which is still the best short survey of the period.

While John Fiske, *The Critical Period of American History* (New York,

---

* An asterisk following a title indicates that it is available in paperback.

1888), popularized the Federalist view of the Confederation, Henry B. Dawson, "The Motley Letter," *Historical Magazine,* 2d Ser., 9 (1871), kept the Antifederalist perspective alive. By the end of the nineteenth century, historians were beginning to question the relation of democracy to the Constitution. Henry Jones Ford, *The Rise and Growth of American Politics* (New York, 1898), described the movement for a new Constitution as a "conservative reaction" and the Federalist victory as "the restoration," implying a parallel with 1660 in England. A more explicit and effective development of this argument was J. Allen Smith, *The Spirit of American Government, A Study of the Constitution: Its Origin, Influence and Relation to Democracy* (New York, 1907), followed by the even more notable work of Charles A. Beard, *An Economic Interpretation of the Constitution** (New York, 1913). A year earlier, however, Andrew C. McLaughlin, in "Democracy and the Constitution," American Antiquarian Society, *Proceedings,* N.S., 22 (1912), 293–320, had already summed up the doubts of professional historians about the democratic origins and character of the Constitution. The persistent effort of American historians to relate American history and institutions to democracy is dealt with by Irving Kristol, "American History and the Democratic Idea," *American Scholar,* 39 (1969–70), 89–104. Recently historians have attempted to clarify the relationship by setting the concept of democracy in historical context. J. R. Pole cleared the air in "Historians and the Problem of Early American Democracy," *American Historical Review,* 67 (1962), 626–646. Other studies dealing with the meaning of democracy are R. R. Palmer, "Notes on the Use of the Word 'Democracy,' 1789–1799," *Political Science Quarterly,* 68 (1953), 203–226; Richard Buel, Jr. "Democracy and the American Revolution: A Frame of Reference," *WMQ,* 3d Ser., 21 (1964), 165–190; Bernard Bailyn, *The Ideological Origins of the American Revolution** (Cambridge, Mass., 1968); Gordon S. Wood, *The Creation of the American Republic, 1776–1787** (Chapel Hill, 1969); and Robert Shoemaker, " 'Democracy, and Republic' as Understood in Late Eighteenth-Century America," *American Speech,* 41 (1966), 83–95. John P. Roche, "The Founding Fathers: A Reform Caucus in Action," *American Political Science Review,* 55 (1961), 799–816; Martin Diamond, "Democracy and the Federalist: A Reconsideration of the Framers' Intent," *American Political Science Review,* 53 (1959), 52–68; and Diamond, "The Federalist, 1787–1788," in Leo Strauss and Joseph Cropsey, eds., *History of Political Philosophy* (Chicago, 1963), 573–593, sum up the current view of the democratic character of the Constitution.

For all the interest in democracy and the origins of the Constitution displayed by historians, however, very little time was spent on the Antifederalists through much of the first half of the twentieth century. Apart from a few scattered studies like Philip A. Crowl, "Anti-Federalism in Maryland, 1787–1788," *WMQ,* 3d Ser., 4 (1947), 446–469, little scholarly attention was paid to the Antifederalists until the appearance of Cecelia Kenyon's provocative article "Men of Little Faith: The Anti-Federalists on the Nature of Representative Government," *WMQ,* 3d Ser., 12 (1955), 3–43, which was refined and expanded in an introduction to her excellent collection of Antifederalist tracts, *The Antifederalists** (Indianapolis, 1966). Other recent collections of Antifederalist documents are Morton Borden, ed., *The Antifederalist Papers* (East Lansing, 1965), and Alpheus Thomas Mason, *The States Rights Debate: Antifederalism and the Constitution,** 2d ed. (New York, 1964).

Three sympathetic studies of the Antifederalists are Jackson Turner Main, *The Antifederalists: Critics of the Constitution, 1781–1788** (Chapel Hill, 1961); Robert Allen Rutland, *The Ordeal of the Constitution: The Antifederalists and the Ratification Struggle of 1787–1788* (Norman, Okla., 1966); and Forrest McDonald, "The Anti-Federalists, 1781–1789," *The Wisconsin Magazine of History*, 46 (1963), 206–214.

Charles Beard's *An Economic Interpretation of the Constitution* generated considerable literature dealt with in the following: Maurice Blinkhoff, "The Influence of Charles Beard on American Historiography," *University of Buffalo Studies* 12 (1936), 16–36; Howard K. Beale, ed., *Charles A. Beard: An Appraisal* (Lexington, Ky., 1954); Cecelia M. Kenyon, "An Economic Interpretation of the Constitution After Fifty Years," *Centennial Review*, 7 (1963), 327–352, and Richard Hofstadter, *The Progressive Historians: Turner, Beard, Parrington** (New York, 1968), which also includes an extensive bibliography. Critical studies of Beard's assumptions and findings include Robert E. Thomas, "The Virginia Convention of 1788," *Journal of Southern History*, 19 (1953), 63–72; Thomas, "A Reappraisal of Charles A. Beard's *An Economic Interpretation of the Constitution of the United States*," *American Historical Review*, 57 (1951–1952), 370–375; William C. Pool, "An Economic Interpretation of the Ratification of the Federal Constitution in North Carolina," *North Carolina Historical Review*, 27 (1950), 119–141, 289–313, 437–461; Oscar and Mary Handlin, "Radicals and Conservatives in Massachusetts after Independence," *New England Quarterly*, 17 (1944), 345–355; and more generally Robert E. Brown, *Charles Beard and the Constitution** (Princeton, 1956); Lee Benson, *Turner and Beard: American Historical Writing Reconsidered** (New York, 1960); and Forrest McDonald, *We the People: The Economic Origins of the Constitution** (Chicago, 1958). For examples of the polemics generated by the criticism of Beard see Jackson Turner Main, "Charles A. Beard and the Constitution: A Critical Review of Forrest McDonald's *We the People,*" *WMQ*, 3d Ser., 17 (1960), 86–102, and McDonald's reply, *ibid.*, 102–110; Robert L. Schuyler, "Forrest McDonald's Critique of the Beard Thesis," *Journal of Southern History*, 28 (1961), 73–80.

The principal historian carrying the Beardian or Progressive tradition into the present is Merrill Jensen, whose work on the Revolutionary era is summed up in three books: *The Founding of a Nation: A History of the American Revolution, 1763–1776* (New York 1968); *The Articles of Confederation: The Interpretation of the Social-Constitutional History of the American Revolution, 1774–1781**, 3d ed. (Madison, Wisc., 1959); *The New Nation: A History of the United States, 1781–1789** (New York, 1950). The neo-Progressive emphasis on social cleavage in the period is refined and reinforced in E. James Ferguson, *The Power of the Purse: A History of American Public Finance, 1776–1790** (Chapel Hill, 1961), and in the works of Jackson Turner Main. In addition to Main's study of the Antifederalists cited earlier, compare his *The Social Structure of Revolutionary America* (Princeton, 1965), which is too static and too rigid in its categories to trace any change in the Revolutionary era, with his "Government by the People: The American Revolution and the Democratization of the Legislatures," *WMQ*, 3d Ser., 28 (1966), 391–407, and his *The Upper House in Revolutionary America, 1763–1788* (Madison, Wisc., 1967), both of which document the displacement of elites in politics during the Revolution. In his most recent study, *Political Parties Before the Constitution*

184 SUGGESTIONS FOR FURTHER READING

(Chapel Hill, 1973), Main found the existence of fairly cohesive parties in the states dividing along social, economic, and geographical lines. See also his, "The Results of the American Revolution Reconsidered," *The Historian*, 31 (1969), 539–554.

For an older suggestion of the revolutionary character of the Revolution consult James Franklin Jamison, *The American Revolution as a Social Movement** (Princeton, 1926) together with an extended critique by Frederick B. Tolles, "The American Revolution as a Social Movement: a Re-evaluation," *American Historical Review*, 59 (1954), 1–12. See also Clarence Ver Steeg, "The American Revolution Considered as an Economic Movement," *Huntington Library Quarterly*, 20 (1957), 361–372. Elisha P. Douglass, *Rebels and Democrats: The Struggle for Equal Political Rights and Majority Rule During the American Revolution** (Chapel Hill, 1955), also stressed the transforming character of the Revolution in the states and is a good antidote to Allen Nevins' older but still valuable, *The American States During and After the Revolution, 1775–1789* (New York, 1924). The articles of Staughton Lynd, conveniently brought together in his *Class Conflict, Slavery, and the United States Constitution* (Indianapolis, 1968); George Dangerfield, *Chancellor Robert R. Livingston of New York, 1746–1813* (New York, 1960); and Alfred F. Young, The *Democratic Republicans of New York: The Origins, 1763–1797* (Chapel Hill, 1967) all in various ways focusing on New York updated and strengthened a social interpretation of the struggle over the Constitution. Wood, *The Creation of the American Republic, 1776–1787,** cited earlier, also found working through the ideas a social, but not strictly speaking a class, division over the Constitution. Forrest McDonald, *E Pluribus Unum: The Formation of the American Republic, 1776–1790** (Boston, 1965), relying on Beard's assumption about the nature of politics, presented his own economic interpretation of the origins of the Constitution.

The nationalists of the early 1780's, as distinct from the Federalists of 1787–88, have been the subject of study in Merrill Jensen, "The Idea of a National Government During the American Revolution," *Political Science Quarterly*, 58 (1943), 356–379; and E. James Ferguson, "The Nationalists of 1781–1783 and the Economic Interpretation of the Constitution," *Journal of American History*, 56 (1969), 241–261. For an exchange between Stuart Bruchey and Ferguson see "The Forces Behind the Constitution: a Critical Review of the Framework of E. James Ferguson's *The Power of the Purse*," *WMQ*, 3d Ser. 19 (1962), 429–438. Curtis P. Nettels, *The Emergence of a National Economy, 1775–1815* (New York, 1961), is a survey of economic developments in the period. Clarence L. Ver Steeg, *Robert Morris, Revolutionary Financier* (Philadelphia, 1954) is an important study of the economic politics of the 1780's. In "Toward a Reappraisal of the 'Federal' Government: 1783–1789," *Journal of Legal History*, 8 (1964), 314–325, Herbert A. Johnson calls for new investigation of the administrative and constitutional history of the Confederation government, filling out what Jensen in his *New Nation* could only touch upon.

The consensus approach which viewed the Constitution as a fulfillment and consummation of the Constitution rather than as a reaction to it was synthesized by Edmund S. Morgan, *The Birth of the Republic, 1763–1789** (Chicago, 1956). Daniel Boorstin's interpretation of the Revolution can be found in his *The Genius of American Politics** (Chicago, 1953) and Louis Hartz's in his *The Liberal Tradition*

in America: An Interpretation of American Political Thought Since the Revolution*
(New York, 1955). Robert E. Brown attempted to slay the principal proponents of
the Progressive interpretation in *Charles Beard and the Constitution** (Princeton,
1956) and *Carl Becker on History and the American Revolution* (East Lansing,
1970). For Brown's interpretation of the colonial period and the Revolutionary era
see *Middle-Class Democracy and the Revolution in Massachusetts, 1691-1780**
(Ithaca, 1955); with his wife, Katherine B., *Virginia, 1705-1786: Democracy or
Aristocracy?* (East Lansing, 1964); and *Reinterpretation of the Formation of the
American Constitution* (Boston, 1963). Benjamin F. Wright, Jr., attacked the Progressive duality in *Consensus and Continuity, 1776-1787** (Boston, 1958). Stanley M.
Elkins and Eric McKitrick, "The Founding Fathers: Young Men of the Revolution,"
Political Science Quarterly, 76 (1961), 181-216, also see the Constitution as a fulfill-
ment of the Revolution.

   One significant development of the consensual approach to the Revolutionary era was a renewed interest in the ideas of the period. Of course, many
nonbehaviorists in government departments and law schools had kept alive a traditional interest in political theory throughout the first half of the twentieth century.
For their works see especially: Andrew C. McLaughlin, "Social Compact and Con-
stitutional Construction," *American Historical Review*, 5 (1900), 467-490; *The
Courts, The Constitution and Parties* (Chicago, 1912); *The Confederation and the
Constitution** (New York, 1905); *A Constitutional History of the United States* (New
York, 1935); and *The Foundations of American Constitutionalism** (New York,
1932); Edwin S. Corwin, "The Progress of Constitutional Theory Between the
Declaration of Independence and the Meeting of the Philadelphia Convention,"
American Historical Review, 30 (1925), 511-536; *The "Higher Law" Background of
American Constitutional Law** (Ithaca, 1955); and "The Establishment of Judicial
Review," *Michigan Law Review*, 9 (1910-1911), 102-125, 283-316; Charles G.
Haines, *The American Doctrine of Judicial Supremacy* (Berkeley, 1932); William S.
Carpenter, *The Development of American Political Thought* (Princeton, 1930);
Charles Warren, *The Making of the Constitution* (Boston, 1928); and Benjamin F.
Wright, Jr., *American Interpretations of National Law* (Cambridge, Mass., 1931).
All of these writers were interested in the origins of the rule of law and the way
in which the Constitution became a means of restraining legislative will. Beard
made his own contribution to this development in *The Supreme Court and the
Constitution** (New York, 1912). The 1962 paperback edition edited by Alan F.
Westin has a full bibliography on the problem of judicial review. The interpretation
of these constitutional historians was summed up in Robert L. Schuyler, *The Constitution of the United States: An Historical Survey of its Formation* (New York,
1923).

   It was not until the 1950's, however, that ordinary historians, as distinct
from constitutional historians and theorists, began devoting serious attention to the
ideology of the period. Although Douglass Adair, in his doctoral dissertation, "The
Intellectual Origins of Jeffersonian Democracy," Yale, 1943, and Clinton Rossiter,
*Seedtime of the Republic: The Origin of the American Tradition of Political
Liberty* (New York, 1953), had minimized the importance of Locke in American
political thinking, it was not until the work of Caroline Robbins, *The Eighteenth-*

*Century Commonwealthmen: Studies in the Transmission, Development, and Circumstances of English Liberal Thought from the Restoration of Charles II until the War with the Thirteen Colonies** (Cambridge, Mass., 1959); J. G. A. Pocock, "Machiavelli, Harrington, and English Political Ideologies in the Eighteenth Century," *WMQ*, 3d Ser., 22 (1965), 549–583; Pocock, "Civic Humanism and Its Role in Anglo-American Thought," *Il Pensiero Politico*, 1 (1968), 172–189; Isaac Kramnick, *Bolingbroke and His Circle: The Politics of Nostalgia in the Age of Walpole* (Cambridge, Mass., 1968); J. R. Pole, *Political Representation in England and the Origins of the American Republic** (London, 1966); and Bernard Bailyn, *The Ideological Origins of the American Revolution** (Cambridge, Mass., 1967), that historians began to realize just how complex and peculiar was the intellectual world the American Revolutionaries were operating in. With works like H. Trevor Colbourn, *The Lamp of Experience: Whig History and the Intellectual Origins of the American Revolution* (Chapel Hill, 1965); and Richard Gummere, *The American Colonial Mind and the Classical Tradition* (Cambridge, Mass., 1963), Revolutionary scholarship seemed to be returning to a renewed interest in America's intellectual inheritance from Europe. For a denigration of Locke's influence on eighteenth-century American political thinking see John Dunn, "The Politics of Locke in England and America in the Eighteenth Century," in John W. Yolton, ed., *John Locke: Problems and Perspectives* (Cambridge, England, 1969). Wood, *The Creation of the American Republic,** cited earlier, tried to set the formation of the Constitution within a continuing debate over republicanism. John R. Howe, *The Changing Political Thought of John Adams* (Princeton, 1966); W. Paul Adams, "Republicanism in Political Rhetoric Before 1776," *Political Science Quarterly*, 85 (1970), 397–421; and Gerald Stourzh, *Alexander Hamilton and the Idea of Republican Government* (Stanford, 1970) all write with a new appreciation of the peculiar tradition of eighteenth-century republicanism. For a historiographic summary of the recovery of this tradition see Robert E. Shalhope, "Toward a Republican Synthesis: The Emergence of an Understanding of Republicanism in American Historiography," *WMQ*, 3d Ser., 29 (1972), 49–80. Other discussions of the ideas of the Founding Fathers include Douglass Adair, " 'That Politics May Be Reduced to a Science': David Hume, James Madison, and the Tenth Federalist," *Huntington Library Quarterly*, 20 (1957), 343–360; Adair, " 'Experience Must Be Our Only Guide': History, Democratic Theory, and the United States Constitution," in Ray A. Billington, ed., *The Reinterpretation of Early American History: Essays in Honor of John Edwin Pomfret** (San Marino, Calif., 1966); David G. Smith, *The Convention and the Constitution: The Political Ideas of the Founding Fathers* (New York, 1965); Edward Dumbauld, *The Constitution of the United States* (Norman, Okla., 1964); Paul Eidelberg, *The Philosophy of the American Constitution: A Reinterpretation of the Intentions of the Founding Fathers** (New York, 1968); Adrienne Koch, *Jefferson and Madison: The Great Collaboration** (New York, 1950); Koch, *Power, Morals, and the Founding Fathers** (Ithaca, 1961); William P. Murphy, *The Triumph of Nationalism: State Sovereignty, the Founding Fathers and the Making of the Constitution* (Chicago, 1967). Hannah Arendt, *On Revolution** (New York, 1963), and Robert R. Palmer, *The Age of the Democratic Revolution: A Political History of Europe and America, 1760–1800,** 2 vols. (Princeton, 1959, 1964), placed the American Revolutionary experience in comparative perspective. Peter Gay, *The Enlightenment: The Science of Freedom* (New York, 1969), depicted the Constitution as the Enlightenment put into practice. For an antidote to Gay's liberal and humanist interpretation of the Enlightenment see Franco Venturi, *Utopia and Reform in the Enlightenment* (Cambridge, England, 1971), which stresses the importance of republicanism in eighteenth-century European thinking.

The literature on the making of the Constitution is enormous. The most recent studies are Clinton Rossiter, *1787: The Grand Convention** (New York, 1966), and Catherine D. Bowen, *Miracle at Philadelphia: the Story of the Constitutional Convention, May to September, 1787* (Boston, 1966). These have not supplanted Farrand, *Framing of the Constitution,** and Warren, *Making of the Constitution,* cited earlier. Other studies of the formation of the Constitution include William M. Meigs, *The Growth of the Constitution* (Philadelphia, 1900); Robert L. Schuyler, *The Constitution of the United States* (New York, 1923); Carl Van Doren, *The Great Rehearsal* (New York, 1948); Broadus and Louise P. Mitchell, *A Biography of the Constitution of the United States: Its Origins, Formation, Adoption, Interpretation* (New York, 1964). A sure-footed description of the Convention can be found in vol. 3 of Irving Brant's biography of *James Madison,* 6 vols. (Indianapolis, 1948–1956). William W. Crosskey, *Politics and the Constitution,* 2 vols. (Chicago, 1953), argued that the framers in 1787 intended to establish a centralized unitary state. See also Edward P. Smith, "The Movement Towards a Second Convention," in James F. Jameson, ed., *Essays on the Constitutional History of the United States, 1775–1789* (Boston, 1899). On the bill of rights see Robert A. Rutland, *The Birth of the Bill of Rights** (Chapel Hill, 1955); and Irving Brant, *The Bill of Rights: Its Origin and Meaning* (Indianapolis, 1965).

There have been numerous studies of *The Federalist* papers, including: the pieces by Diamond cited earlier; Benjamin F. Wright, "*The Federalist* on the Nature of Political Man," *Ethics,* 59 (1945), No. 2, Pt. 2, 1–31; Douglass Adair, "The Tenth *Federalist* Revisited," *WMQ,* 3d Ser., 8 (1951), 48–67; Adair, "*The Federalist* Papers: A Review Article," *WMQ,* 3d Ser., 22 (1965), 131–139; Alpheus T. Mason, "*The Federalist* — A Split Personality," *American Historical Review,* 57 (1952), 625–643. James B. Scanlon, "*The Federalist* and Human Nature," *Review of Politics,* 21 (1959), 657–677; and Gottfried Dietze, *The Federalist* (Baltimore, 1960). The best editions of *The Federalist* are Benjamin F. Wright, ed., *The Federalist* (Cambridge, Mass., 1961); and Jacob E. Cooke, ed., *The Federalist* (Middletown, Conn., 1961). On the disputed authorship of the Federalist papers see Douglass Adair, "The Authorship of the Disputed *Federalist* Papers," *WMQ,* 3d Ser., 1 (1944), 92–122, 235–264; and Frederick Mosteller and David L. Wallace, *Inference and Disputed Authorship: The Federalist* (Reading, Mass., 1964).

Serious study of the ratification of the Constitution began in the late nineteenth century with the most important work being that of O. G. Libby, *The Geographical Distribution of the Vote of the Thirteen States on the Federal Constitution* (Madison, Wisconsin, 1894). Working in the same quantitative tradition pioneered by Libby is Charles W. Roll, Jr., "We, Some of the People: Apportionment in the Thirteen State Conventions Ratifying the Constitution," *Journal of American History,* 5 (1969), 21–40.

For studies of the various states during the Confederation period and ratifi-
cation see: on New Hampshire: Joseph P. Walker, *A History of the New Hampshire
Convention* (Boston, 1888); Richard F. Upton, *Revolutionary New Hampshire*
(Hanover, N.H., 1936); Jere Daniell, *Experiment in Republicanism: New Hamp-
shire Politics and the American Revolution 1741–1794* (Cambridge, Mass., 1970);
on Massachusetts: Samuel B. Harding, *The Contest Over Ratification of the Federal
Constitution in the State of Massachusetts* (New York, 1896); Robert A. East, "The
Massachusetts Conservatives in the Critical Period," in Richard B. Morris, ed., *The
Era of the American Revolution** (New York, 1939); on Rhode Island: Frank G.
Bates, *Rhode Island and the Formation of the Union* (New York, 1898); Hillman M.
Bishop, "Why Rhode Island Opposed the Federal Constitution," *Rhode Island
History*, 8 (1949), 1–10, 33–44, 85–95, 115–126; Irwin H. Polishook, *Rhode Island
and the Union, 1774–1795* (Evanston, Ill., 1969); on Connecticut: Bernard C. Steiner,
"Connecticut's Ratification of the Federal Constitution," American Antiquarian
Society, *Proceedings*, 25 (1915), 70–127; on New York: in addition to the works by
Dangerfield, Lynd, and Young, cited earlier, C. E. Miner, *The Ratification of the
Federal Constitution by the State of New York*. (New York, 1921); E. Wilder Spauld-
ing, *New York in the Critical Period, 1783–1789* (New York, 1932); Thomas C.
Cochran, *New York in the Confederation: An Economic Study* (Philadelphia, 1932);
Linda Grant DePauw, *The Eleventh Pillar: New York State and the Federal Con-
stitution* (Ithaca, New York, 1966); and Robin Brooks, "Alexander Hamilton,
Melancton Smith, and the Ratification of the Constitution in New York," *WMQ*,
3d Ser., 24 (1967), 339–358; on New Jersey: Richard P. McCormick, *Experiment in
Independence: New Jersey in the Critical Period, 1781–1789* (New Brunswick, 1950);
on Pennsylvania: John B. McMaster and F. D. Stone, eds., *Pennsylvania and the
Federal Constitution, 1787–1788* (Lancaster, Pa., 1888); Robert L. Brunhouse, *The
Counter-Revolution in Pennsylvania, 1776–1790* (Harrisburg, 1942); on Delaware:
John A. Munroe, *Federalist Delaware, 1775–1815* (New Brunswick, 1954); on Mary-
land: Bernard C. Steiner, "Maryland's Adoption of the Federal Constitution,"
American Historical Review 5 (1900), 22–44, 207–223; Philip A. Crowl, *Maryland
During and After the Revolution* (Baltimore, 1943); on Virginia: H. B. Grigsby,
History of the Virginia Federal Convention of 1788, 2 vols. (Richmond, Va., 1890–
1891); on North Carolina: Louise Trenholme, *The Ratification of the Federal Con-
stitution in North Carolina* (New York, 1932); A. R. Newsome, "North Carolina's
Ratification of the Federal Constitution," *North Carolina Historical Review*, 17
(1940), 287–301; William C. Pool, "An Economic Interpretation of the Ratification
of the Federal Constitution in North Carolina," *North Carolina Historical Review*,
27 (1950), 119–141, 289–313, 437–461; on South Carolina: Charles G. Singer, *South
Carolina in the Confederation* (Philadelphia, 1941); on Georgia: Kenneth Coleman,
The American Revolution in Georgia, 1763–1789 (Athens, Ga., 1958); William W.
Abbot, "The Structure of Politics in Georgia: 1782–1789," *WMQ*, 3d Ser., 14 (1957),
47–65.

Since Shays's Rebellion has long been regarded as an important precipitant
in the formation of the Constitution, it has been the subject of numerous studies
beginning with the contemporaneous account by George R. Minot, *History of the
Insurrections in Massachusetts* (Boston, 1788). Others include Joseph P. Warren,

"The Confederation and Shays's Rebellion," *American Historical Review*, 11 (1905), 42–67; Richard B. Morris, "Insurrection in Massachusetts," in Daniel Aaron, ed., *America in Crisis* (New York, 1952); and Robert J. Taylor, *Western Massachusetts in the Revolution* (Providence, 1954); Robert A. Freer, "Shays's Rebellion and the Constitution: a Study in Causation," *New England Quarterly*, 42 (1969), 388–410; and the superb but brief section in J. R. Pole, *Political Representation in England and the Origins of the American Republic** (London, 1966), 226–244.

For documentary collections of the convention debates see Max Farrand, ed., *The Records of the Federal Convention of 1787,** 4 vols. (New Haven, 1911, 1937); Jonathan Elliot, ed., *The Debates in the Several State Conventions on the Adoption of the Federal Constitution,* 5 vols. (Philadelphia, 1876). *Documentary History of the Constitution of the United States of America,* 5 vols. (Washington, 1894–1905) contains important letters of the period, as does E. C. Burnett, ed., *Letters of the Members of the Continental Congress,* 8 vols. (Washington 1921–1936). Collections of writings on the Constitution can be found in Paul L. Ford, ed., *Essays on the Constitution of the United States* (Brooklyn, 1892), and Ford, *Pamphlets on the Constitution of the United States* (Brooklyn, 1888). The writings of the notable Founding Fathers have been published at one time or another and many of them are receiving fuller treatment in the mammouth publication programs of their papers undertaken in the past two decades or so. The numerous biographies are useful particularly those of Irving Brant on Madison, cited earlier, and John C. Miller, *Alexander Hamilton: Portrait in Paradox** (New York, 1959).